White Face
Black Mask

White Face

AFRICANEITY AND THE EARLY SOCIAL HISTORY OF POPULAR MUSIC IN BRAZIL

Black Mask

Darién J. Davis

Michigan State University Press • *East Lansing*

⊖ The paper used in this publication meets the minimum requirements
of ANSI/NISO Z39.48-1992 (R 1997) (Permanence of Paper).

 Michigan State University Press
East Lansing, Michigan 48823-5245

Printed and bound in the United States of America.

18 17 16 15 14 13 12 11 10 09   1 2 3 4 5 6 7 8 9 10

LIBRARY OF CONGRESS CATALOGING- IN- PUBLICATION DATA
Davis, Darién J., 1964–
White face, black mask : Africaneity and the early social history of popular music in
Brazil / Darién J. Davis.
p. cm.
Includes bibliographical references and index.
ISBN 978-0-87013-834-8 (pbk. : alk. paper) 1. Popular music—Brazil—20th century—
African influences. 2. Ethnicity—Brazil—History—20th century. 3. Brazil—Social life and
customs—20th century. 4. Brazil—Race relations—History—20th century. I. Title.
ML3487.B7D38 2008
781.64089-96081-dc22
2008015193

BLACK AMERICAN AND DIASPORIC STUDIES SERIES
Curtis Stokes, *Series Editor*

Book design by Sharp Des!gns, Lansing, MI
Cover design by Erin Kirk New
Cover art is from the caricature "Reveillon dos artistas" by Mendez courtesy of Museu da
Imagem e do Som.

green Michigan State University Press is a member of the Green Press Initiative
press and is committed to developing and encouraging ecologically responsible
INITIATIVE
publishing practices. For more information about the Green Press Initiative and the use of
recycled paper in book publishing, please visit *www.greenpressinitiative.org.*

Visit Michigan State University Press on the World Wide Web at *www.msupress.msu.edu.*

Contents

Preface

A Note on Race and Popular Music

Any work on race in Brazil in English must necessarily comment on the complications of cross-national studies and translation of racial terminologies. As in other countries, official and unofficial Brazilian racial and ethnic terminologies continue to evolve, and popular music continues to serve as a vehicle for the expression of slang and the popular argot. Racial terminologies in the United States, Great Britain, and other English-speaking areas have also evolved over time. Some terms are clearly associated with given historical eras, while others have emerged as a result of the struggles of people insisting that they be called or referred to by names of their own choosing and not by names chosen by the dominant society. Terms such as African American, Roma, and Inuit are three examples. "Political correctness" has also played a role in shaping racial and ethnic terminologies in English. Applying English-speaking cultural sensitivities to other cultures does not necessarily help scholars, particularly when trying to describe the internal dynamics of a given culture. This is particularly true when translating Brazilian racial terminologies related to blackness. Unlike mainstream U.S. culture today, Brazilians utilize several different terms to refer to blackness, most of them relating to skin color, to hair, and, to a lesser extent, to somatic features, or a combination of factors, including economic class considerations. In some ways this phenomenon, which is prevalent throughout the Caribbean and in black communities in the United States, indicates how central blackness is to Brazil.

Terms such as "Negro," "black," or "African American" in the United States may not necessarily mean *negro* in Portuguese. While the term "African American" is ubiquitous in the United States, Brazilians do not use the term "African Brazilian" (*Africano brasileiro*). In fact, most Brazilians find it strange. The term "*Afro-brasileiro*," however, has gained some currency in recent decades as a term to describe one's identity, although some have argued that even this term is inadequate and has been influenced by the "political correctness" movement in the United States. The term "Afro-Brazilian," nonetheless, provides scholars writing in English with a helpful umbrella term to denote groups of people (black and brown) who identify themselves with Afro-Brazilian or black culture.

Thus, in this work I employ the term "Afro-Brazilian/s" to include *mulato/a(s)* and *negro/a(s)*, *preto/a(s)* and some *mestiço/a(s)*, or on a few occasions when using the Brazilian census term "*pardo/a(s)*" (brown). The term *mestiço* may also be used for the progeny of Native Americans and Europeans. At the same time, many Brazilians who are biologically *mestiços* may refer to themselves as white because they "look white," and thus the racial designation may change based on who is doing the looking and who is doing the defining. Because of these subtleties, however, I have chosen to use the italicized Brazilian terms "*mulatos*," "*mestiço*," "*parda*," and so forth rather than the translated English terms. The term "mulatto" has fallen out of use in the United States, and "*mulato*" is fast becoming obsolete in Brazil. Because racial identities in Brazil are often contextual in all cases and whites often use black racial identities to refer to one another, I have elected to describe Brazilians as Afro-Brazilians only in cases where official documents or scholars describe people as *mulato, negro, preto, pardo,* or *mestiço,* or where Brazilians describe themselves in such terms.

When I refer to Africaneity, I am not insisting on any direct transfer of African culture to Brazil. Rather, I use Africaneity and blackness synonymously in a sociological sense to refer to a group of cultural practices, ideas, or sensitivities understood by Brazilians as pertaining to Afro-Brazilian culture, associated with or representing blackness.

Studying popular music can be equally as contentious as studying race. Many scholars have debated the definition and nature of popular music. This work cites many of these works but does not engage in the debates of what may be considered popular Brazilian music or the difference between folk and popular musical traditions. The focus of this work is the mainstream popular music, propagated through mass media and emerging mostly out of Rio de Janeiro in the 1930s and 1940s. Brazil has inherited a host of musical traditions, forms, and genres that constituted part of the popular musical tradition. Many of them are not mentioned in this book. Throughout the text, however, I have italicized the major Brazilian music genres and define them briefly in the glossary.

I have also chosen to use the word "musician" and "performer" as synonyms, as well as broadly to refer to those individuals engaged in the active production of music, including composers, instrumentalists, and singers. This work is a tribute to all those musicians who have inspired me in my twenty years as a student of Brazil.

Finally, I would like to offer a brief comment on Brazilian spelling and translation of songs. All the translations from Portuguese are my own and are provided to help readers understand the general meaning. The spelling of proper names of individuals is standardized throughout the text except in cases of official documents or in quotes. "Mário," for example, is spelled with an accent, but not in the book title *Mario Reis: O fino do samba,* because the author of this book does not use the accent. Many Brazilian names have diverse spellings: Ari and Ary, Araci and Aracy, and Bahiana and Baiana. Here too I have attempted to standardize the spellings although I maintain the spellings used in original titles of books or songs and in direct quotes.

Acknowledgments

Many individuals and institutions have assisted me in bringing this book to fruition. I would like to thank the many Brazilians who have helped me understand the importance of popular music to Brazil's history. Countless librarians and archivists assisted me in Rio de Janeiro and São Paulo. Special thanks go to Sátiro Nunes at the National Archives, Márcia Claudia Figueredo at Funarte, and the staff at the Museum of Image and Sound (MIS) for putting up with all of my questions and helping me to find many documents and photographs. I am also indebted to the librarians at the National Library, Division of Music, and at the Funarte library for also helping me uncover documents.

A number of individuals deserve special mention. Ashley Kerr, my research assistant during 2005 and 2006, helped me organize many of the archival documents and information. Conversations with and comments from other individuals in Rio helped me to develop and change my focus several times along this journey. My sincere thanks to Ricardo Cravo Albin, who welcomed me into his new museum, and to Jorge Rodrigues, a friend, Brazilian scholar, and passionate aficionado of *música popular brasileira*. Conversations with Jorge and John McCarthy, both residents of Rio, have helped me to fine tune my understanding of life in Brazil. The late Abel Cardoso was a teacher in many respects. He shared his passion for popular music with me and sent me various documents through the mail from his home in Sorocaba while I was living in Rio. He also helped me contextualize various aspects of Brazil's musical history in the 1930s. Peggy Donnaruma furnished a number of old albums and information about the "Old Guard" of Brazilian popular music. Carmen Miranda's family, and in particular Carmen Carvalho and Gabriel Richard, opened up their doors to me and shared many important aspects of their family's history. Senhora da Silva, wife of Sinval Silva, composer of the popular classic "Adeus Batucada," and Norma Tapajós did likewise. I am humbled by how much Brazilians continue to share with the world. These chapters have gone through many versions as a result of conversations with and comments from individuals both in Brazil and in the United States. Miguel Pérez gave me a quiet apartment in Montreal to begin the original draft of this work when I returned to North America from Brazil. Johann and Cristine Hanta provided me with research access and a place to stay and work when I was away from home. Keith Conkin, Bond Dandoe and David Donaldson Santos read early versions of two of the chapters. Their comments gave me a great deal of encouragement. Dialogue with John Klein in California was fruitful as I worked through the intricacies of cross-national performance. Graça Salgado assisted me with in correcting the Portuguese text. I would also like to thank Curtis Stokes and Julie Loehr at Michigan State University (MSU) Press for their insights. The comments from anonymous readers helped me to make my prose clearer. This work would not be what it is without the guidance and copyediting of Kristine Blakeslee at MSU Press and Robert Burchfield.

Their comments helped me clarify my ideas and my writing and kept me from falling into academic jargon.

I am indebted to Middlebury College for its generous financial support in helping me travel to Brazil for four summers. Thanks also go to the Fulbright Hays Faculty Research Abroad Fellowship Program and its support while I lived in Brazil. Finally, I would be remiss if I did not thank my family for the multiple levels of support and patience over the last five years. I dedicate this book to my wife, Karin Hanta, and to my children, Caetano Hanta-Davis and Marcelo Hanta-Davis.

Setting the Stage

Actors, taught not to let any embarrassment show on their
faces, put on a mask. I will do the same. So far, I have been
a spectator in this theatre, which is the world, but I am now
about to mount the stage, and I come forward masked.

——————————— René Descartes, *Praeambula*

"**M**usically, we have progressed more than the United States," declared
Elsie Houston, the Brazilian performer and European-trained
singer. "Who here besides George Gershwin has shown in his scores a
feeling of the real Negro music? It is the primitive quality of the native
melodies that made Brazil so modern."[1] Houston's 1940 remarks to an
American journalist illustrate that putting on a mask is more about
discourse than deception, particularly when expressing national pride.
Ironically, the positive inclusion of blacks into Houston's discourse
on cultural production did not translate, at least in this instance, into
a reevaluation of black culture, and by extension "blackness" as primitive. On the contrary, prejudice was inherent to the Brazilian brand
of inclusion and celebration of blackness in the emerging mass media,

which, as in the United States, represented what bell hooks has called "a system of knowledge and power reproducing and maintaining white supremacy."[2]

The Brazilian context requires further explanation. One generation after the abolition of slavery in 1888, Brazil's focus on cultural inclusion and mixture as a means to celebrate its national culture, led by patriotic writers such as Gilberto Freyre, masked, or covered up, the endemic social displacement of blacks in Brazil. Nonetheless, Brazilians such as Freyre and Houston were members of a generation that embraced and promoted the centrality of Africa to Brazilian culture and incorporated black rhythms, idioms, symbols, and styles into their musical performances. Yet paradoxically, they did not insist that blacks be given equal footing on Brazilian stages.

The imprint and influence of Afro-Brazilians—that is to say, Brazilian blacks and *mulatos*—are, nonetheless, almost everywhere in Brazil. Afro-Brazilians such as Manoel da Cunha and Leonardo Joaquim were responsible for much of the cultural production of the colonial era, both sacred and profane. Afro-Brazilian lay brotherhoods created images, statutes, architectural designs, and musical compositions for many of the Catholic religious establishments, but popular Brazilian music represents one of the richest manifestations of that contribution. Indeed, the African influence on Brazilian popular music is so ubiquitous that it is difficult to treat "Afro-Brazilian popular music" and "Brazilian popular music" as two distinct categories.

Freyre's and Houston's patriotism only makes sense in the context of a syncretic Brazilian culture that has resulted from cultural intermingling. The political, social, and economic exclusion of Afro-Brazilians undermines the celebratory premise of this mode of patriotism, however, and reveals a complex mode of race relations within Brazil as well as a multilayered dialogue and relationship with the African diaspora, particularly in the postabolition era. An examination of popular music performance from the 1920s to the 1950s provides us with an opportunity to understand these relationships.

At the turn of the twentieth century, Afro-Brazilian musicians such as Irineu de Almeida, Patricio Teixeira, Pattápio Silva, and Anacleto de

Medeiros joined others who would come to be known affectionately simply by nicknames such as Baiano, Sinhô, Pixinguinha, Caninha, Bide, Cartola, and João da Bahiana in laying the foundations for Brazil's modern popular music industry. These contributions notwithstanding, white popular singers with strong, legitimate, and intimate connections to Afro-Brazilian cultural roots would become the most important national icons. Indeed, understanding these legitimate linkages and the Afro-diasporic influences on most Brazilians is indispensable to any discussion of race and Brazilian popular performance.

White or at least nonblack performers, literally and figuratively, utilized black masks as a way to demonstrate that they were authentically Brazilian. Important popular musical icons of the 1930s and 1940s in Brazil such as Carmen Miranda, Aurora Miranda, Francisco Alves, and Mário Reis, all of whom were white, celebrated the Afro-Brazilian popular idioms in their repertoires. In their performances, on and off the radio, and in their recordings, white performers unapologetically sang about black characters and took on black personalities, including the *mulata* or *mulato*, the *malandro*, the street smart trickster, or the Bahiana, the street vendor from the northeastern city of Salvador. They sang about black social issues such as living in the favela, the Brazilian slum, making ends meet, and personal problems from beauty to finding a mate. Many also popularized the slang of the popular black classes and performed dances associated with Afro-Brazilians. Indeed, many white performers grew up in multicultural, multiracial neighborhoods, and viewed these cultural manifestations not simply as black idioms but also as popular Brazilian cultural customs that had influenced their worldview, and thus they claimed them as their own.

Mulato performers, or performers who appeared to be "neither black nor white," to use Carl Degler's phrase, add another layer of complication. Many *mulatos* and *mulatas* such as Orlando Silva, Sílvio Caldas, Dorival Caymmi, Assis Valente, Aracy Cortes, Araci de Almeida, and Angela Maria attained national recognition and became national icons by the early 1940s, although (with the exception of Orlando Silva) none matched the extended popularity or benefited from the opportunities available to Reis, Alves, or the Miranda sisters. *Mulato* performers, nonetheless, paved the way for the acceptance of black performers. Although *mulatos* often faced discrimination and marginalization, political solidarity with blacks was not necessarily a given. Nor did all *mulatos* necessarily view blacks as equals. Indeed, Abdias do Nascimento, black activist and founder of the Black Experimental Theater inaugurated in 1944, believed that the greatest challenge to *mulatos* was learning that they were black.[3]

That lesson would be a difficult one in a society where racial identities have been historically shaped by both class and color, and where miscegenation and cultural intermingling meant that people who defined themselves as black (*negro* in Portuguese) constituted an absolute minority. Yet blackness or Africaneity became the focal point against or through which many Brazilians defined themselves. At the same time, many others who defined themselves as *mulato, mestiço,* or *branco* (white) often recognized or claimed their African ancestry depending on the context. Houston, after all, may not have been white, although her upper-class background meant that in Brazil, she clearly did not consider herself black or even *mulata.* This situational or structural identity, which "achieves its positive through the narrow eye of the negative," according to Stuart Hall, also mutates depending on the circumstances, as Caetano Veloso and Gilberto Gil's 1993 song "Haiti" explains.[4] Veloso and Gil's descriptions of Brazilians as "*mulatos*" (mulatos), "*quase pretos*" (almost black), "*brancos pobres como pretos*" (whites poor like blacks), and "*quase brancos*" (almost white) evoke the ambiguities of racial identities in Brazil, while highlighting the centrality of blackness in the song's title, which refers to the first black republic in the Americas.[5]

In the realm of cultural production in general, and Brazilian popular music in the 1930s and 1940s in particular, most Brazilians, like Houston, understood the significance of the black musical forms to the Brazilian musical stage. In *Música popular brasileña,* Oneyda Alvarenga outlines thirteen major influences of African forms and practices on Brazilian music. These influences, which are often called Africanisms, have helped shaped a host of Brazilian performance practices and styles, from rhythm and syncopation, melody, and improvisation, to postures and the role of dance in musical performance. Africans and Afro-Brazilians also shaped the development and performance of European music in Brazil. As Mariza Lira reminds us, to play an instrument, sing, or perform any artistic work was the purview of slaves or of freed blacks and mulatos. Thus, over centuries, the Brazilian elite believed that artists were inferior. This did not change the fact that by the time of the abolition of slavery in 1888 and the creation of the republic one year later, African musical and cultural influences were ubiquitous throughout Brazil.[6]

While this work aims to highlight the national and individual recognition of black musical influences, it asks the broader questions: Who owns and defines "blackness" in Brazil? And who benefited from performing blackness for national and international consumption? The answers to these questions may seem apparent when one considers that pervading social practices before the 1950s often prohibited blacks from performing on the most important national stages and representing Brazil abroad. Yet many white performers did not simply co-opt or appropriate African forms. They employed, consulted, and validated black musicians and composers and helped pave the way to increased demand and opportunities for blacks to perform in Brazil.

Brazilian performers of all backgrounds also exported Afro-Brazilian rhythms to other Latin American countries, to Europe, and to the United States. Performing Brazilian music abroad, and especially in the United States, as Houston intimates, required adjustments to a different national or intercultural gaze. In her assessment of the representation of foreign cultures in the theater, which can be used to explain all forms of performance, Patrice Pavis observes that foreign cultures can be represented through imitation of reality or as a substitute for a given ritual or practice. Both types of performances involve convincing audiences that they are participating in what she calls a "sacred ceremony," in which music and dance play crucial roles in projecting authenticity. Brazilian performers in the United States such as Elsie Houston, Aurora Miranda, and Carmen Miranda, who were not coincidently all female, were involved in complex intercultural and multilayered levels of transmitting Brazilian culture through imitation and re-creation of Afro-Brazilian codes and practices.[7]

A host of scholars have written comparative studies of race and race relations in the United States and Brazil from slavery to the modern era.[8] Yet few scholars have emphasized the cultural legacies of racially mixed black peoples in either country or the different ways in which Afro-Brazilians and African Americans have incorporated African remnants into their own racial identities and into their heterogeneous regional or national cultures. F. James Davis has argued for the importance of keeping the racial and cultural processes separate in our thinking. He contends that "races are groupings of human beings based on average differences in biological characteristics, while cultures are group patterns of behavior and beliefs. Racial traits are transmitted from generation to generation by genes, while culture is transmitted in the process of socialization, by social communication."[9] In Brazil, the process of socialization, particularly among the popular classes, brought whites and blacks into close proximity with one another. Interracial unions were only one product of that socialization. Shared cultural traits and practices independent of race was another. Thus, race played paradoxical roles in the forging of the Brazilian popular music tradition in Brazil and abroad.

This work examines the role of race in the quest of authentic sounds of Brazilian nationhood from 1930 to 1954, a period that scholars call the "Vargas era," in honor of President Getúlio Vargas, who governed Brazil from 1930 to 1944 and again from 1950 to 1954. This era also coincided with the "Golden Age of Radio" in Brazil and saw the emergence of a national Brazilian cinema. I do not intend to provide an exhaustive analysis of the history of Brazilian popular music in the first half of the twentieth century. Many Brazilian scholars have already produced important contributions to that literature. The most interesting in the past decade include Ricardo Cravo Albin's *O livro de ouro de MPB* (2004), the Museum of Image and Sound's *500 anos da música popular brasiliera* (2001), and José Ramos Tinhorão's *História social da música popular brasileira* (1998).

Only recently has the history of Brazilian popular music been treated by scholars in English: Brian McCann's *Hello, Hello Brazil: Popular Music in the Making of Modern Brazil* (2004), Lisa Shaw's *The Social History of the Brazilian Samba* (1999) and Tamara Elena Livingston-Isenhou and Thomas García's *Choro: A Social History of a Brazilian Popular Music* (2005) all explore various aspects of Brazilian popular music. While McCann focuses on re-creating the musical milieu and the complex development of the radio industry, Shaw emphasizes the lyrics and music of the early period, and Livingston-Isenhou and García focus on the history of the *choro*, an important Brazilin musical genre. Several works by Christopher Dunn and Charles A. Perrone, including the edited volume *Brazilian Popular Music and Globalization* (2001), provide important information and insights on the historical roots of contemporary musical production.

Few works have explicitly examined the role of blackness to the historical creation of the Brazilian popular musical tradition and connected that tradition to Brazilian performance abroad. Two important exceptions are José Ligeiro Coelho's 1998 dissertation, "Carmen Miranda: An Afro-Brazilian Paradox," which focuses on the singular importance of Miranda as an ambassador of Afro-Brazilian musical rhythms, and Samuel Araújo's study of early samba in Rio de Janeiro. Coelho's work, in particular, dialogues with my previous work on Brazilian patriotism and on Carmen Miranda's performance in the United States.[10] Micol Seigel and Judith Williams have written on a number of important ideas related to Afro-diasporic performance in the early twentieth century. Seigel's 2001 dissertation provides insights on Afro-diasporic exchange and cultural production, while Williams has focused on race and performance of two important women of the theater, Josephine Baker and Aracy Cortes.[11]

Scholars of race and performance in the United States have also provided critical insights to this work, particularly in my attempt to reread the archival sources on music through the lens of race and transnationality. Susan Gubar's *Racechanges: White Skin, Black Face in American Culture* and Eric Lott's *Love and Theft: Blackface Minstrelsy and the American Working Class* offer theoretical approaches to masquerading, masking, and appropriation in the United States that provide counterpoints to the Brazilian case. Alicia Arrizón's *Latina Performances: Traversing the Stage*, together with works by various authors in *A Companion to Latino Literatures*, highlights the ways in which Latinos have navigated the complex racialized, gendered, and class-determined spaces of performance in the United States. John Storm Roberts's pioneering work on Latino music in the United States and black music in the Atlantic world is fundamental to any study of Afro-diasporic traditions in the modern world.[12]

In analyzing the role of race in general and blackness in particular to the development of the "Golden Age" of Brazilian popular music, I hope to highlight the contributions of the major Brazilian black performers, musicians, and composers in the first half of the twentieth century. Given my interest and commitment to the study of the African diaspora, it would have been tempting to focus exclusively on black artists who have been marginalized in order to "give voice" to those often neglected in official histories. This, however, would not have been a wise decision, and perhaps would have fallen into the all too frequent practice of assuming that the history of racial oppression in Latin America mirrored the modes and practices prevalent in the United States, in which segregation and Jim Crow made it more or less possible to discuss "black music" and "white music" as if they were mutually exclusive.

The profound and lengthy impact of the African diaspora throughout Brazil meant that despite black marginalization and racial oppression, Africans and their progeny played pivotal roles in the lives of most Brazilians. Thus, this work also underscores the Africaneity in the performances of white Brazilians. The celebration of blackness by whites, however, must be carefully analyzed in the context of Brazilian national and racial discourses that encouraged, if not mandated, that Brazilians view themselves as modern, and therefore more white than black. It was not without reason that Thomas Skidmore's classic work on race in Brazilian society was titled *Black into White: Race and Nationality in Brazilian Thought*. As elsewhere, whites, the descendants of European colonizers, have controlled the shaping of Brazilian nationality for most of Brazil's history, although in Brazil, many whites are also the descendants of African slaves. Indeed, the history and role of miscegenation complicate the ways in which Brazilians discuss blackness, which carries both racial and class connotations, and in many respects is closely related to gender.

Many instrumentalists, producers, composers, intellectuals, and political actors contributed to popular music in the Vargas era, but singers became the most important icons of the era and the repositories of the nation's dreams and desires and its contradictions. The most important singers were white and male, at least initially. During the development of the "Golden Age of Radio" in the 1930s, four white performers came to represent Brazilian music nationally and internationally: Francisco Alves, Mário Reis, Carmen Miranda, and Aurora Miranda. They quickly became part of a most sought-after circle of performers, although they relied almost exclusively on Afro-Brazilian idioms to help revolutionize Brazil's national music tastes. Their lives, activities, and ideas are well documented in a host of archives, while firsthand information on the thousands of poor and black Brazilians has been lost forever. Yet Afro-Brazilian memories and contributions have survived in the recorded performances of many radio programs, in records, and in films.

The four top performers were joined by many others, some of them *mulato*. By the late 1940s, black Brazilians had broken into the coveted circle of singers. Regardless of their opportunities and position in the popular music industry, most major Brazilian performers worked closely with composers from all walks of life, including professionally trained musicians, *bambas* from the samba school, *malandros* from the vibrant neighborhood of Lapa, and other nonprofessionals from around the city of Rio. They brought the compositions of known and unknown musicians to life on stage. They dialogued with audiences in the theaters and casinos. Their voices graced the radio waves and were immortalized on records. Their images appeared on the country's silver screen, and they became larger than life. In a new political era in a country in the process of securing national consolidation, the development of mass media meant that many performers would become the country's first national icons, and black life, particularly in the city of Rio de Janeiro, provided much of the inspiration to make that happen.

Power and Social History

Brazil's "Golden Age of Radio" emerged under the political watch of President Getúlio Vargas, who rose to power in 1930. It ended in the 1950s, a decade that witnessed the deaths of Vargas, Carmen Miranda, and Francisco Alves. Eras rarely end abruptly, however, since members from different generation continually dialogue with one another. If Juscelino Kubitschek de Oliveira, or JK, the energetic president elected to office in 1955, represented the new Brazilian family, Getúlio Vargas symbolized the old. Brazil mourned his death in 1954 like a family mourns the death of a parent. His funeral was also a moment of national celebration of his legacy. This event was equaled by the funerals of two of the generation's greatest singers. The two popular performers had enjoyed a rapport with the masses that paralleled Vargas's dynamics in the world of politics. Urbanization, immigration, and economic development from the turn of the century to the late 1920s ensured the transformation of race and class dynamics inherent to the new Brazilian worldview. The new Brazilian constitution of 1934 that gave women the right to vote and ensured black citizens a theoretical equality articulated the new vision.[13] The 1934 Brazilian constitution, for example, ensured that, "there will be no privileges, nor distinctions because of birth, sex, race, personal professions or professions of parents, social class, wealth, religious beliefs or political ideas."[14] But nationalism, patriotism, and economic opportunity would define the limits of democratic participation for the overwhelming majority of the Brazilian population that was economically deprived and lacked formal educational instruction.[15]

Writers such as Gilberto Freyre examined the positive contributions of Africans to Brazilian society and for the first time began to encourage Brazilians to celebrate their African heritage. But Freyre was not alone. The modernist intellectuals of the 1920s had played a critical role in encouraging Brazilians to seek national rejuvenation and to promote Brazilian cultural symbols, icons, and practices, including popular music performance in which African descendants played a decisive role.[16] For many, Brazil could now project itself as a nation that had successfully blended elements of "primitive cultures" with European elements, producing a magical union like no other place on earth, a view that remains strong among some Brazilian intellectuals even today. In the introduction to his book on Brazilian popular music, for example, Ricardo Cravo Albin, founder of the Museum of Image and Sound in Rio de Janeiro, claims that "the history of Brazilian popular music was born at the exact moment when in any given slave quarters, Indians began to accompany the clapping of enslaved blacks, while white colonizers allowed themselves to be touched by the movements and by the celebrations."[17] It is also clear, however, as Elsie Houston claimed, that "the most rich musical influence was without doubt the black. Our marvelous variety of syncopated, nervous, sensual, spirited and sensual rhythms, we owe to blacks, as well as its free quality and its sense of invention."[18]

• • •

The Vargas administration's reliance on political repression and its promotion of nationalism impeded the emergence of authentic black voices, particularly those of protest that would represent black communities. Yet to speak of black communities in Brazil in the first half of the twentieth century brings its own challenges in a country that was becoming urban and multicultural, where the government stymied black and other political organizations until 1944, and where miscegenation had blurred the racial lines within families and communities. If there were no "black communities" or "white communities," there certainly were people with power, who were mostly white, and the people without power, the majority of whom were not white.

Class considerations from the 1920s to the 1950s add further complications, although Afro-Brazilians of all colors then and now are disproportionately represented in the lower income classes. At the same time, as many scholars have convincingly shown, the Brazilian class system allowed for the inclusion of what Michael Hanchard has called "exceptional blacks."[19] This seems also true of other immigrant groups, although ironically many groups such as the Japanese, Jews, Turks, and others remained outside the discourse of the national family for decades, as Jeffrey Lesser studies in *Negotiating National Identity: Immigrants, Minorities, and the Struggle for Ethnicity in Brazil* (1999).

It is also important to document what I call the "provisional middle class," to denote the temporary social spaces that allowed people from different classes and social backgrounds to fraternize and celebrate in an environment created by the elite or the government. Moreover, these spaces allowed individuals from the lower classes to appear middle class as long as they were able to adhere to proper social codes, particularly in regard to attire, social interactions, and behavior. These "temporary" middle-class spaces included radio auditoriums, certain concert halls, cinemas, casinos, and certain private and public spaces almost always predominantly white.

Gender also played an important role in the articulation of Brazilian popular music. Throughout the history of most industries in Latin America, national production has been dominated by the interest of elite men. The popular music industry is no exception. Therefore, it comes as no surprise that the owners of the major industries that produced Brazilian popular music for the mass market in the first half of the twentieth century were wealthy white men, often with transnational economic interests. All three major technological means of production—the radio, the recording studios, and the cinema—were controlled and directed by men. Likewise, pioneering directors and organizers from the samba schools, the *teatro de revista* (revue theater), and the casinos, the three major forums that showcased popular music for a distinct clientele, were overwhelming male.

Similar gender dynamics also emerge among the performers who grappled with new compositions and performed in major and minor forums for an emerging national market. Most instrumentalists were male. Indeed, a woman who played a wind or percussion instrument in public was a rarity, although many middle- and upper-class women learned how to play the piano. Surprisingly, women were also under-represented among the vocalists and singers. At the beginning of the 1930s, males dominated all of the forums where popular music was performed, although this would begin to change in the 1930s, reaching a critical stage in the 1940s and 1950s during the enormously popular female radio competitions.

Exceptional women, nonetheless, left their mark on the musical landscape. At the turn of the century, composer Chiquinha Gonzaga created "O Abre Alas," one of the most enduring *marchas* in Brazilian history. Carmen Miranda was a pioneer in the musical cinema and in the casinos, and she, along with her sister Aurora, helped to globalize Brazilian popular music throughout the Atlantic world. The scandalous Aracy Cortes, who owned her own theatrical company, challenged bourgeois values and reigned in the *teatro de revista*, and claimed with pride her *mulata* identity. Angela Maria was one of the first Afro-Brazilians to attain national prominence on the radio in the 1940s. Many others formed partnerships and collaborated in the promotion and celebration of Brazilian popular music.

The representation of Brazilian music abroad was gendered, particularly, although not exclusively, in the United States, where Brazilian popular music and culture became synonymous with exoticism and sensuality during World War II. By the mid 1940s, the top male personalities such as Francisco Alves, Mário Reis, Orlando Silva, and Sílvio Caldas, who wooed Brazilian audiences, had crossed over into the Argentine market, but none would have the international success of Carmen Miranda. This success would cause many Brazilians to reflect on the country's image abroad. Thus the challenge of this work is to unpack and analyze the interrelated issues of race, gender, class, and nationality during the consolidation and globalization of the Brazilian popular music industry from the 1920s to the 1950s. Technologies such as records, cinema, and the radio were critical to these processes.

From Radio-Nation to the World

The radio performances of interpreters were particularly important as radio technology developed and the radio became ubiquitous, although the cinema would play no small role. The new voices struck a chord with audiences all over Brazil as they forged a new modern Brazilian aesthetic while giving audiences a piece of themselves. An entire section of the print media emerged to focus exclusively on the lives and performances of these new national icons. Popular performers came from all over Brazil, but most of the well-revered popular interpreters resided in Rio de Janeiro, the country's political and cultural capital and home to the major radio, cinema, and print media, all of which became reference points for those who would follow.

These pioneering performers, some of them migrants from Minas, Bahia, São Paulo, and other states, played an important role in creating reference points for the national community since they occupied unique positions in the community's collective psyche. As artists, they reflected the cultural aesthetics of communities while becoming the depositories of a nation's desires, hopes, and dreams. This is particularly true of Francisco Alves, Carmen Miranda, Aurora Miranda, and Mário Reis. The entrance of each of these performers into the musical milieu constituted a major watershed for the history of popular music. The same is true for each one's exit, especially in the case of Alves and Carmen Miranda. Indeed, it is no exaggeration to say that the death of both idols in the 1950s changed Brazilian popular music history. Thus, in addition to being times for mourning, the 1950s funerals of Carmen Miranda and Francisco Alves became opportunities for reflection and celebration for a generation that was passing away and for a nation in flux.

Organization and Methodology

This work is divided into six chapters. Chapter 1 highlights the work and importance of Afro-Brazilian instrumentalists and composers from the turn of the twentieth century to the end of the Vargas era, including Sinhô, Ismael Silva, and Pixinguinha. In this chapter, I also explore the importance of French intellectuals in signaling the importance of popular black traditions to Brazilian music and the early experiences of Afro-Brazilian performers in Paris. Important contributions of famous *mulato* singers such as Orlando Silva and Sílvio Caldas will also be examined.

Chapter 2 explores the legacy of President Getúlio Vargas, one of Brazil's greatest statesman, and the musical forums that emerged under his watch beginning in 1930. Although Brazil did not institutionalize segregation similar to the United States, race and class determined where one lived in cities like Rio de Janeiro. Race and class also shaped the major social forums were music was created and performed.

Chapter 3 examines the technological advances that shaped the Brazilian popular music industry and analyzes the role of race in its development. The development of the radio, recording, and film industries made mass consumption of Brazilian popular music possible. Race played an important role in all three. One generation after abolition, Afro-Brazilians played key roles in all three industries, although they were not necessarily in positions of economic power.

Chapters 4 and 5 utilize the lives of two of the most important national icons to allow us to explore the interconnections of class, race, gender, and nation in the articulation and presentation of Brazilian popular music. Understanding the contributions of Francisco Alves and Carmen Miranda to the Brazilian musical tradition will become crucial to our understanding of the era. Alves and Miranda came from poor Portuguese immigrant backgrounds, and grew up around musicians and performers in downtown Rio. By the 1930s, however, they had emerged as the preeminent performers of their time. Their lives not only served as a source of inspiration to the popular classes, but also gave them a level of legitimacy as popular singers even as they left their neighborhoods and secured their position in the upper middle class. Throughout the 1930s and 1940s, these two performers maintained their links with popular music through collaborations with talented musicians from the popular classes and through extolling the virtues and aesthetics of popular revelry, including samba, carnival, and the social reality of the common folk.

Chapter 4 focuses on the so-called King of the Voice and the radio pioneer of samba, Francisco Alves. It was no coincidence that the major male singers and promoters of Brazilian popular music on the radio, the most important media of the 1930s, were white. Alves represented the dreams and aspirations of an entire generation, and he surrounded himself with other talented performers. His partnership with Mário Reis allowed him to project a gentrified image to the elite and the emerging middle classes, but he continued to rely on the largely Afro-Brazilian popular musicians for inspiration and for compositions.

Chapter 5 turns more specifically to the roles and contributions of female performers prior to the 1950s. Carmen Miranda was the most important female performer and would become Brazil's most important popular music ambassador. Although she was white, I argue that her performances relied on Africanisms, particularly from black people in Rio de Janeiro. The chapter begins with Miranda's death and funeral as a springboard into understanding the singular impact that she made on Brazilian popular music. Her move abroad made her the most visible Brazilian popular performer of her time. Carmen Miranda's life and performances are contrasted to those of her sister Aurora, and to Afro-Brazilian women who followed them.

Chapter 6 explores the pioneers and places of the early globalization of Brazilian popular music and provides commentary about race and transnational performance. This chapter highlights the international experiences of Brazilian artists in the United States from the 1930s to the 1950s. The conclusion looks back at the social history of Brazilian popular music and makes several observations about the growth and development of popular music in Brazil since the 1950s.

Afro-Brazilian Pioneers, Blackness, and the Roots of Brazilian Popular Music

. . . They were obliged to enter the Copacabana Hotel through the back entrance because they were musicians, and on top of that they were black.

———————————— Ricardo Cravo Albin, *O livro de ouro da MPB: A história de nossa música popular de sua origem até hoje*

The Brazilian use of racial terms, including all the Portuguese equivalents for the English term "black"—(*negro/a, preto/a, mulato/a, pardo/a, neguinho/a, negão*)—is often contextual. Indeed, white Brazilians may often use black racial terms such as "*neguinho*" and "*nêga*," short for *negra*, for example, to refer to themselves, mostly as terms of affection. Black Brazilians do not employ white racial terms in similar ways. The use of black racial terms by whites is, nonetheless, indicative of the ubiquity of African and black cultural influences throughout Brazil, and presents a number of challenges for students of Brazilian race relations. In a country where miscegenation played a significant role in most family histories, who qualifies as Afro-Brazilian and what constitutes "Afro-Brazilian contribution" to popular music?

Relying on the pioneering work of Anani Dzidzienyo and Pierre-Michel Fontain, George Reid Andrews provides an answer to the first question: "Any individual described by themselves or by others as black or brown."[1] Therefore "Afro-Brazilian" implies an exclusive category of color related to, but not equivalent to, African ancestry and thus connected to diasporic identity of blackness throughout the Americas. Black Brazilians, like blacks throughout the Americas, were systematically marginalized from positions of political and economic power, and despite miscegenation, were considered a separate category from whites. Furthermore, throughout Brazilian history, "whiteness" constituted privilege, while "blackness" did not.

The answer to the second question necessarily requires a revision of the answer to the first, and more attention to the use of the word "privilege." The term "popular music" often carries distinct and conflicting meanings. It can be used to refer to the production of the common people or specific underprivileged groups in society, or it can be used to denote a given type of music or musical form that is both ubiquitous and enjoyed by a large cross section of a given society. In either case, given the history of colonization and the Portuguese and Brazilian reliance on Africans at all levels of Brazilian society, Afro-Brazilians played significant, if not determining, roles in the foundation and elaboration of Brazilian popular music. Although authorities in Brazil erected a political economy based on forced African labor that denigrated blackness, in many areas of cultural performance and production, Africans and Afro-Brazilians exercised limited autonomy throughout Brazilian history, a fact that Gilberto Freyre recognized in his 1933 classic *The Masters and the Slaves*.

That the underprivileged and politically and economically powerless affected and at times occupied a "privileged" position in the articulation of popular musical tastes and customs is a testament to the resilience of African diasporic cultures. In order to understand the magnitude and context of the Afro-Brazilian influence on and contribution to the Brazilian popular music tradition, it is important to underscore the fact that popular cultural traditions are neither pure nor historically fluid. Nonetheless, in the age in which

Brazil experienced urbanization and mass media, roughly 1918 to 1945, forums where Brazilians performed popular music represented contested sites among varying interest groups, including among different class and racial formations. To understand the dialogue and contestations, we must, as Stuart Hall reminds us, examine "the processes by which these relations of dominance and subordination are articulated."[2]

This chapter examines the influences of Afro-Brazilian pioneers on Brazilian popular music tradition, from the period of abolition in the 1880s to the beginning of the Vargas era and the period of mass propagation of popular music forms. Although "whiteness" and the theories of whitening played fundamental roles in the consolidation of the Brazilian republic, "blackness" also played an important role in the articulation of cultural forms and nationhood. This necessarily meant that in the face of local racism, Afro-Brazilian performers sought out and connected to diasporic trends, particularly with African American musicians and performers. Indeed, black musical forms and Afro-Brazilian pioneers were largely responsible for creating the popular musical foundations that served as springboards for the early globalization of the popular Brazilian music in the 1930s and 1940s. Ironically, Brazilian society in general was often slow to recognize these Afro-Brazilian pioneers, although musicians, singers, and the musical industry long relied on their contributions.

In the 1930s, well-known white singers and performers such as Francisco Alves, Carmen Miranda, Aurora Miranda, and Mário Reis, all of whom served as ambassadors of Brazilian popular music abroad, understood the significance and roles of Afro-Brazilian popular pioneers. Emotions such as esteem and affection have done little to ameliorate the economic and social conditions of black people throughout the Western world. Nor did the Brazilian rhetoric of multiculturalism embodied in "racial democracy" improve the economic possibilities of black musicians. Rio de Janeiro, the center of the Brazilian musical universe, was a racially stratified and class-stratified city. As in the United States, however, these social barriers could not keep "good music" down.

While it is impossible to give voice to all of the black musicians who played foundational roles in the evolution of Brazilian popular music history in the first three decades of the twentieth century, it is possible to examine the ways in which Afro-Brazilians shaped the tone and pitch of the Brazilian sound both in Brazil and abroad, while highlighting their diasporic connections and national significance. The lives and contributions of pioneering Afro-Brazilian musicians help us to understand the Brazilian musical milieu prior to the "Golden Age of Radio" and the development of other mass media. Pixinguinha (Alfredo da Rocha Vianna Filho), Chiquinha Gonzaga, Sinhô (José Barbosa da Silva), Donga (Ernesto Joaquim Maria dos Santos), Cartola (Angenor de Oliveira), and Heitor dos Prazeres provide windows onto the period of time that John Charles Chasteen refers to as the "pre-history of samba," when a number of Afro-Brazilian social dances and music forms, including the *lundu*, the *maxixe*, the *butuque*, and the *choro*, circulated in the neighborhoods of Rio de Janeiro.[3] These individual musicians benefited from the cultural circles and neighborhoods nurtured and guarded by the Afro-Brazilian women known as *tias*, or aunts.

The Bahian Aunts

Although ethnomusicologists have hotly debated whether Rio's popular music has Bahian roots, few deny the role of the *tias bahianas*, who were also *mães de santos*, priestesses of the Afro-Brazilian religion *Candomblé*, and thus respected religious leaders in their communities.[4] Indeed, the names of Tia Bebiana, Tia Presiliana de Santo Amaro, Tia Veridiana, Tia Josefa Rica, Tia Aciata, and Tia Amélia are legendary. Ironically, the *tias* are not remembered as performers, but as typical mother figures who cooked and provided a safe haven for male musicians outside of the watchful eyes of the police. Instrumentalists including Sinhô, Pixinguinha, Donga, Caninha (José Luiz de Morães), and others recall the musical talents of women like Tia

Aciata, whose home became a reference point for the generation prior to the development of radio.[5]

As a *mãe de santo*, Tia Aciata presided over religious music rituals that often lasted for days and which would have a direct impact on popular music performance as the rhythms moved from private to public spaces to mass media. Tia Aciata (or Asseata) lived in a large house with a yard on Rua Visconde de Itauna and brought the community together during the celebration of Afro-Brazilian orishas such as Oxum, the Afro-Brazilian deity of sweetness and beauty. Customarily dressed in the typical attire of the Bahiana, Asseata was a master of religious and profane dance and music. She was also a wise businesswoman responsible for popularizing the Bahiana costume around the city by requiring that the women who sold her food in the streets wear the outfit. She also rented the costumes out to others, thus illustrating that Afro-Brazilian women utilized cultural identities in small-scale capitalist ventures.[6]

Like Tia Aciata, most of the *tías* had stable lives and were not viewed as threats to authorities. This allowed them to provide safe haven to hundreds of musicians and practitioners of capoeira, which was also criminalized.[7] In the tradition of using Catholic images and practices to disguise ceremonies in which they continued to worship African deities, the *tías* also became adept at protecting those who performed popular music. They held parties in their large backyards, for example, away from the gaze of the police. Moreover, the *tías* relied upon their standing in society and their good relations with authorities to protect musicians. At the same time, despite their relative marginalization from mainstream developments, they influenced popular culture tastes and aesthetics on multiple levels and are directly or indirectly connected to all of the major pioneers of Brazilian popular music.

Black Pioneers and the Initial Steps toward Globalization

"Samba" means many things to many people. Across the globe, just as jazz is a symbol of the United States and tango represents a national icon of Argentina, samba signifies Brazil. More specifically, samba is a child of the poor black inhabitants of Rio de Janeiro, as Zé Keti described in his song "A voz do morro" (The voice of the hills) in 1955:

> I am samba
> The voice of the hills I am, yes sir!
> I want to show the world that I have value
> I am the king of the sacred ground
> I am samba
> I am originally from Rio de Janeiro
> I am the one who brings happiness
> To millions of Brazilian hearts.[8]

Zeti is one among many who have penned praises to the samba, which Caetano Veloso and Gilberto Gil called "the father of pleasure" in 1994. At the beginning of the twentieth century, many Brazilians were of a different opinion. Indeed, many were reluctant to associate Brazilianness with pleasure or sensuality. Furthermore, like its older sibling the *maxixe*, samba's association with blackness and sensuality meant that it was not a dance for "decent folk," as Jotâ Efegê aptly conveys in his 1974 book *Maxixe: Dança excomungada* (*Maxixe: The Prohibited Dance*). The registration of the first "official" samba by Ernesto Joaquim Maria dos Santos, known simply as Donga, and his journalist-partner, Mauro de Almeida, at the National Library in Rio de Janeiro in 1918 would change the face of Brazilian popular history.

While earning the distinction of registering the first samba, Donga, a black Brazilian, also brought legitimacy to the community of Afro-Brazilian musicians with whom he performed. Moreover, his act validated the Afro-Brazilian performers before him who had battled against prejudice and marginalization as they created popular Brazilian traditions. Community elders and pioneers, then and now, in Brazil and throughout the diaspora have played critical roles in passing down and adapting Afro-diasporic traditions from one generation to another.

The Pioneers of Rio de Janeiro

Afro-Brazilians claimed ownership of many public spaces to create collective forums for their artistic expression. Daniel Walker has shown that since the era of slavery, subjugated people throughout the African diaspora often utilized restricted public spaces and elite institutionalized festivities to celebrate and support one another. Walker argues, for example, that while participating in the sanctioned festivities and performances of the annual Día de Reyes (Three Kings' Day) festival in Havana and in the weekly activities that took place at New Orleans's Congo Square, people of African descent contested racial oppression and celebrated their cultural heritage in spite of the restrictions that governed their lives. A study of dynamics in Brazil reveals remarkable parallels.[9]

By the time of abolition, Afro-Brazilian cultural influences were everywhere, although class and racial codes ensured that few Afro-Brazilians were visible in elite, private, or foreign musical and artistic organizations. In the first few decades of the twentieth century, blacks were better represented in local conglomerations such as samba schools and neighborhood and municipal bands. Virtuosos such as Pixinguinha were exceptions, but as an instrumentalist and orchestra director, more often than not, he worked behind the scenes.

Pixinguinha's Circle

Pixinguinha, who is often compared to Louis Armstrong because of the enormous influence that each had on his respective country's musical traditions, was a virtuoso with a special ability for improvisation. He spent his early childhood in a musical family between Piedade and Catumbi, two Zona Norte neighborhoods connected to the area known as "Little Africa." His first nickname, "Pizindim," came from his African grandfather and apparently meant "good boy," a moniker included in the 2005 exposition "Pixinguinha: The Good Boy Who Became Immortal," one of countless posthumous dedications to the musician whom the late Tom Jobim has called a "genius of our race" and "the love of his life."[10]

Despite the accolades, like many other Afro-Brazilian musical greats from the turn of the twentieth century, Pixinguinha would die in relative poverty. Other Afro-Brazilians played equally important roles in providing stories for and shaping the musical repertoires of singers on stage. Talented Afro-Brazilian composers such as José Luiz de Morais (1833–1961), João da Baiana (1888–1974), Pattápio Silva (1881–1907), Anacleto de Medeiros (1866–1907), and Irineu de Almeida (1873–1916), Pixinguinha's teacher, emerged around 1900 to become Brazil's most important musicians before the development of mass media, when singers and recording artists would take center stage.

As will be seen throughout this book, Pixinguinha worked with other pioneering performers and with the younger icons of the 1930s. He would also be one of the first popular musicians to take live Brazilian music to Europe. Like Pixinguinha, Chiquinha Gonzaga would leave her influence on Brazilian music for generations, although her entrance into the popular music scene would be different.

The World Around Chiquinha Gonzaga

Chiquinha Gonzaga, who came from a "respectable" family of the empire, could have lived the life of the "white" elite at the beginning of the republic. Her mother, Rosa Maria de Lima, was of mixed racial background, and her father, José Basileu, was a white military officer in the Imperial Army of Pedro II. Because of him, she received a superb classical and musical education. Neither the elite lifestyle nor the mores of her strict upbringing would prevent her introduction to the popular music of the day. Her decision to leave her family and enter the world of popular music would come at a huge price. Gonzaga's "descent" and assimilation into the largely Afro-Brazilian bohemian world also meant that she would suffer poverty and discrimination.

Like Pixinguinha and many of her fellow composers and in-strumentalists, Gonzaga confronted the prevailing social prejudices against black people, against musicians, and against women, although she moved freely and easily within the male musical environment, apparently without being affected by what people said about her.[11] Gonzaga, who is often called "the Godmother of Brazilian Popular Music," wrote Brazilian *polcas*, *choros*, *marchas*, and other composi-tions. In 1899, she changed the face of carnival when she composed her *marcha-rancho* "O abre alas," which became the first official carnival song in Brazilian history.[12]

Oh open up the aisles
I want to come through
Oh open the aisles
I want to come through
I enjoy the good life
This, I cannot deny [13]

Gonzaga's *marcha-rancho* drew upon the prevailing Afro-Brazilian rhythms of her time. Her simple lyrics also dialogued directly with the audience and with society at large following an Afro-diasporic tradi-tion similar to the call-and-response pattern well known throughout the Atlantic world. The social and cultural significance of the first stanza, which speaks directly to a real and imagined audience to "open the aisles"—to make room for new arrivals—was not lost upon the black revelers who for centuries had to claim their own social space in a Eurocentric environment. At the same time, the song's first line calls for the audience to prepare themselves for the beginning of the musi-cal festivities when the black percussionists begin to beat their drums. Gonzaga was not only starting a tradition, she was representing the popular voice in a way that resonated with people at a time when the popular voice was thoroughly discounted.

On her death in early 1935, Benjamin Costallat noted Gonzaga's contribution: "This soft old lady who died yesterday at 88 years of age, and who was called Chiquinha Gonzaga, the *maestra* Francisca

Gonzaga, had one of the greatest attitudes of her time, in the time of her youth, in which women were slaves to all of the prejudices and whose most innocent aspirations were asphyxiated."[14]

Popular sentiments and ideas of nationhood were diverse and varied, as any survey of the black movement attests. Despite Afro-Brazilians' limited political and economic power within the nation, it is helpful to consider what Foucault has described as the netlike organization of power in which socially and politically disenfranchised individuals nonetheless exert influences on and participate in the formation of behavior. While the national elite may have harbored contempt for blackness in general and poor black musicians in particular, the reverse was not true. Moreover, Afro-Brazilian performers welcomed and accommodated outsiders, sympathizers, and especially talented partners, as they had done for centuries. Thus, it is no surprise that Gonzaga benefited from, contributed to, and assimilated into her new predominantly male Afro-Brazilian environment, the creative atmosphere of the musical forums around Rio de Janeiro.

There was no doubt, however, that the musical milieu was a man's world, and the images and bodies of diverse Afro-Brazilian figures, from the down-and-out composer; the *malandro*, the street-smart hipster; and later the *sambista*, the street musician, would come to represent the early era of popular musical development in Rio de Janeiro. These images were not without merit. The Afro-Brazilian musician's body and the music it produced were at the center of Brazil's national discourse and exerted a series of often conflicting influences on the population in general. Elite fear may have been one response, but commercial interests understood the value of black talent to national entertainment, a fact that partly explains the lack of official segregation in the popular music milieu. Ironically, blacks and "people of color" in general continued to be routinely barred from various professions, buildings, theaters, and apartment buildings.

Afro-Brazilian musicians' response to exclusion and marginalization varied. To secure a gig or gain long-term employment, black musicians often relied on personal contacts to *dar un jeitinho*, a cordial, relaxed, and informal phenomenon that presupposed that the social system was flexible and that individuals were willing to break the rules or suspend their prejudices on a case-by-case basis. Indeed, in a labor-intensive market like Brazil's, talent alone was often not enough. Many performers secured employment in the circuses, in popular theaters, in the growing record industry, and in other establishments as a result of the personal relationships they built over time. Still, many Afro-Brazilians joined multiracial organizations such as the Brazilian Society of Theatric Authors (SBAT) and other musicians' organizations.

From the 1920s to the 1940s, other black musicians and performers departed significantly from the multiracial model by creating or joining performing groups that were all black, such as the Companhia Negra de Revistas (Black Revue Company) or the Grupo dos Africanos (African Group), and later through the theater itself, in venues such as the Teatro Experimental do Negro (Black Experimental Theater, or TEN), which promoted blackness as a specific aesthetic or cultural expression or identity. While black groups such as the African Group and the Black Revue Company eventually disintegrated and disappeared from the national memory, individual pioneers continue to serve as reference points—particularly because they left behind rich compositions that are performed and recorded over and over again. One of these pioneers was Sinhô.

The Lord of Sambas

Sinhô, whose name in Portuguese sounds like Senhor—the word for Lord—was not the type of performer who would join social organizations, much less organizations defined by race, although like Gonzaga, Pixinguinha, and others, he was a product of the predominantly Afro-Brazilian environment of the center of Rio de Janeiro. Sinhô was a light-skinned *mestiço*, a term he preferred to *mulato*. This attitude was not uncommon in republican Brazil, when many associated blackness with backwardness and the *mestiço* gained standing as representative of Brazilianness.[15]

Sinhô, who had learned music at an early age and played in public and private forums, would capitalize on the opportunities emerging in the infant recording industry. He began learning how to play a host of instruments, including the flute, the *cavaquinho* (a miniature acoustic guitar), and the piano, and by the early 1920s he had become a part of the vibrating musical world around Praça Onze, an important neighborhood of downtown Rio. The Bahian migrants who had made their way to Rio in the late nineteenth century influenced him, just as the music they sang and danced to in "Little Africa" would influence a host of other musicians. At the same time, Sinhô frequented official music establishments of the growing middle class, such as the Casa Beethoven on the Rua do Ouvidor, a central point where musicians, producers, and others associated with the growing music industry met.[16] In these forums, he would not only inspire and work with emerging singers such as Francisco Alves and Mário Reis, but he would also offer or sell his compositions to them for performances for the radio, for the theater, and for a host of recording companies.

Other Pioneers

Sinhô's style, attitude, and opportunities differed from those of his contemporaries, but he would set an example for other composers who would follow him such as Ismael Silva, Heitor dos Prazeres, and Wilson Batista. Silva was an early Afro-Brazilian pioneer who had founded the samba school Estácio. In 1960, the Museum of Image and Sound would honor him with the official title of "Citizen Samba," in recognition of his role in the propagation of samba. Silva had also left his mark on the radio industry and on a multitude of white and Afro-Brazilian signers.[17] The relationship was hardly one-way, however. Silva found two performers who could popularize and promote his music. In fact, poor performers often benefited from these collaborations, but the system of star performers meant that singers profited exponentially.[18]

The famous case of Donga's registration of the collectively inspired composition "Pelo telefone" in 1917 under his name also merits additional attention because it indicates not only that race and class played fundamental roles in doling out benefits in popular music productions but also that black Brazilians often understood the legal framework under which they created. The place of "Pelo telefone" as the first registered samba has also been contested, however, and many composers claim that it has remnants of other diasporic musical traditions, such as the *batuque* or the *maxixe*. In addition, Donga's registering of the composition illustrates the complexity of property rights in an informal popular culture that thrives on collaboration—but which is governed, nonetheless, by laws and contracts that have the power to determine one's well-being or position in society, if not history. As was common with the oral culture that pervaded the popular musical milieu at the turn of the twentieth century, many versions of one composition could be created in a single night. There were many versions of "Pelo telefone," and even today some musicians argue about whether the composition was a samba, a *maxixe*, or something in between.[19]

Donga's historic move to register the samba would awaken the interest of other *sambistas*, who began to realize the commercial possibilities of music as a product that could be sold, although it would take decades for poor composers to actually benefit from the system. In his interview with the Museum of Image and Sound, for example, Angenor de Oliveira (the legendary Cartola, 1908–1980) recalled how surprised he was that anyone would want to buy one of his songs.[20] Cartola, one of the pioneer black composers of the Mangueira samba school, was another important and talented composer whom many singers sought out. Carmen Miranda, who was called "the Queen of Samba," had recorded one of his songs; Francisco Alves had recorded five; and Mário Reis had recorded three.[21]

Like so many other Afro-Brazilian musicians, Cartola, a native Carioca and a bricklayer, was an autodidact. As in the case of Pixinguinha, music had been a part of Cartola's life since childhood, and he had been nurtured by at least two generations of Afro-Brazilians.

He composed, played various instruments, and could sing, although the world of radio and recording was like a foreign country.[22] Unlike Pixinguinha's and Donga's, Cartola's talent was only recognized in the late 1930s, although he would not be economically compensated until much later when members of the bossa nova generation rediscovered him.[23]

Heitor dos Prazeres had a different story but one that nonetheless provides insight into the complex relationship of musicians with centers of power and prestige in a world that privileged whiteness and all its codes and symbols. João Batista Borges Pereira has shown that the police routinely targeted and harassed black musicians in the suburban neighborhoods around Rio. Like many of the poor black musicians of the city, dos Prazeres had been influenced by the music and environment in the houses of venerated *tias* in "Little Africa" such as Tia Ciata and Tia Hilária, the latter a musician and *mãe de santo* (priestess). Dos Prazeres was also educated on the streets. After losing his father at age six, dos Prazeres enrolled in and then left (or was expelled) from many schools for bad behavior. At age thirteen, dos Prazeres and his family got a wake-up call when he was imprisoned for loafing and taken to the reformatory School Number XV.[24]

Soon thereafter, dos Prazeres's life began to revolve around family, and he took a more concerted interest in music and later in painting. He had also begun to learn the social codes that would keep the police at bay, and one of them was clothing. According to dos Prazeres Filho, his mother had always told him that Black people had the responsibility of proving that they were capable, a reality that was as unfair as it was true. Dos Prazeres took this literally when he began to design and sew his own clothes, including suits, shirts, and ties. In Rio's musical world, he earned a reputation for being an impeccable dresser, and decades later would be honored by the newspaper *O cruziero* as one of the "Ten Most Elegant Men of the City." The *malandro* was also a good dresser, but dos Prazeres's models were members of high society, individuals who earned respect for their vocal talents as well as their image.[25]

In addition to performing, dos Prazeres provided compositions to a host of performers. He contributed to the making of the musical score of *Alô alô carnival*, even though he did not appear in the film. Throughout the 1930s, dos Prazeres celebrated Brazil in his compositions and revolutionized choral singing with the creation of his *pastoras*, choruses of five to seven women who would accompany him in his performances. Pioneers such as Cartola and Heitor dos Prazeres put an interesting twist on the rule that purports that whites only welcome exceptionally talented blacks into their circles. These artists entered the privileged circle, but with certain conditions, and did not reap as many economic benefits as white performers.

Informal urban spaces where creativity blossomed and economic extraction was not at stake engendered multiracial collaborations that celebrated Brazilian culture in the ways Gilberto Freyre might have projected for the entire nation. An assessment of every performer's lineage and racial background would probably reveal more diversity than was often publicly admitted. Still, few racial tensions marked the relationships among performers who intermingled freely in the many social spaces where musicians performed.[26]

The stories of composers and musicians such as Sinhô, Silva, Donga, Pixinguinha, dos Prazeres, and Cartola provide windows onto the history of race and popular music in the first three decades of the twentieth century. They are but a few of the many Afro-Brazilian pioneers. Their stories also illustrate that despite the varied experience and background of Afro-Brazilian musicians, relationships with white performers were all but essential to gain national recognition. This would be particularly true when radio became an instrument for extolling mass consumption. Indeed, Brazilian popular music would begin to lose its stigma and become a national symbol of pride as more whites performed, consumed, and propagated it. This process would also transform the samba school, as Ismael Silva noted in 1975: "The samba school does not only belong to blacks as it used to be. I believe that the infiltration of white people from all social classes gave the schools prestige and proves that samba does not recognize any racial distinctions, but does show that its colors are yellow and green."[27]

Yet Alison Rafael has shown that the later arrival of white Brazilians from middle- and upper-class backgrounds also transformed the samba schools from community organizations to microbusinesses whose profits do not always remain in the community. Today, despite the number of middle-class whites who support the samba schools, the "face" of the samba school continues to be associated with blacks in the poor black neighborhoods where most of the samba schools' headquarters remain. From the 1950s to the present, white and black performers and musicians who participated in a host of movements and genres, including bossa nova, *tropicália*, and contemporary forms of Brazilian popular music, continue to pay homage to the early Afro-Brazilian pioneers and treat the old samba schools like modern-day shrines, directly acknowledging Brazilian music's black heritage and its role in creating an authentic Brazilian sound. Often missing from the patriotic discourse, however, is the cross-national diasporic connections that the early musicians forged.

Pioneers: Afro-Diasporic Connections in North America and Europe

African Americans, Afro-Caribbeans, and Afro-Britons were in the forefront of the Pan-African movement at the beginning of the twentieth century. Early Pan-Africanists began a conversation, particularly among English-speaking black people, to address global issues of racism and marginalization. Henry Sylvester Williams, a Trinidadian-born lawyer based in London, for example, convened the first Pan-African conference in 1900. This conference saw the participation of African Americans such as W. E. B. DuBois, who eventually drafted the most important document to come out of the congress. DuBois's "The Address to the Nations of the World" universalized the plight of people of African descent in the face of Western imperialism.[28] Local, regional, and national politics and economics, not to mention culture and language, nonetheless limited the dialogue among peoples in the diaspora. African American and Afro-British activists and intellectuals often became spokespersons for global injustices and racism and promoted racial solidarity because they were among the few groups of disenfranchised people of African descent who had access to global media in ways that Afro–Latin Americans could not imagine. The fact that English was well on its way to becoming the most important lingua franca also helped.

In 1917, the Jamaican-born Marcus Garvey began to assert his own diasporic vision, and his United Negro Improvement Association (UNIA) would later boast a membership of some four million in the Spanish- and French-speaking world.[29] Two decades later, Aimé Césaire and Léopold Sédar Senghor, two Francophone students living in France, would found the movement dubbed Negritude, which would champion the black race in global terms. The French-speaking black intellectuals of Negritude emphasized the cultural and spiritual contributions of Africans as an antidote to European degeneracy and insisted that the value of black culture be recognized globally.[30]

The emergence of movements for black solidarity from various quarters came in the wake of the European colonization and division of Africa, and precisely when the emerging global print, record, and radio media began to notice and exploit Afro-diasporic cultural products. While Garvey highlighted the performative nature of African practices through the use of symbol colors in his UNIA flag—black for the color of black skin, green for black hopes, and red for black blood and colorful clothing and ornaments—Césaire focused on the soulful nature of Africans and their natural cultural proclivities.[31] These gestures were not unrelated to the fact that black music, mostly from the United States, had also attained a global currency of its own.

During the belle epoque, Afro-diasporic forms such as ragtime, the rumba, the *milonga* tango, and later jazz and jazz derivations such as the charleston could be heard not only in Europe but also throughout Latin America, including Brazil. Ironically, American economic expansion and technological developments, which accompanied U.S. cultural imperialism, were responsible for the importation of a host of African American–inspired sounds from the charleston and the shimmy to the fox-trot. Brazilian musicians performed foreign-derived tunes regularly in clubs and theaters across Brazil. In the 1930s, for example, Rio's dancing club Eldorado hired a pianist responsible for jazz numbers, while relying on other musicians, including Pixinguinha, for playing Brazilian genres such as the *choro*.[32] Two decades earlier, Brazilian musicians had fused European and Afro-Brazilian rhythms with elements of the North American marching band sound to create the *marchina*, a staple of Rio's carnival, a style whose rhythm and pace would accelerate because of the influence of local jazz bands.[33]

Brazilians did not share the same social codes as North Americans. Moreover, social constructions of class, race, and gender remain for the most part national, and rarely travel intact with the cultural products that they have engendered, as the Cuban anthropologist Fernando Ortiz intimated when he coined the term "transculturation" to refer to the holistic way that Africans carried their culture with them to Cuba. Most Brazilians did not necessarily distinguish African Americans' idioms from white Americans' idioms. Although poor and disenfranchised African American musicians had created ragtime in the late nineteenth century, for example, Brazilians, black or white, like most white Americans, would only have learned about ragtime when it had been transformed from an oral tradition to printed music (sheet music) or when it began to be recorded.[34]

Although Afro-diasporic musical forms such as ragtime and jazz from the United Sates and samba and the *marchina* in Brazil emerged from distinct temporal and spatial milieus, their social histories illustrate amazing parallels and confluences. Ragtime, like samba, emerged out of Afro-diasporic oral traditions, although white capitalist interests benefited at the expense of black artists. The music publishing and recording industry in Brazil was centralized in Rio de Janeiro for the first four decades of the twentieth century, while the North American music publishing and recording industry was centralized in New York's Tin Pan Alley from the 1880s to the 1940s. By the 1930s, whites won fame performing black music, while African Americans and Afro-Brazilians remained on the sidelines.[35]

Parallel social inclusion is mirrored in the cultural insertion of African idioms in the two largest countries in the Americas. In 1947, the pioneering Brazilian ethnomusicologist Oneyda Alvarenga reported that Brazilian popular music was saturated with a host of Africanisms, many of which were also present in African American popular music, such as the six-note scale with a flattened seventh note, the call-and-response singing standard, and the importance of drumming to mark the dance patterns.[36] Despite the diasporic commonalities, the hegemony of North America cultural imperialist forces meant that African American forms rather than Brazilian ones would circulate more widely as global commodities, and some American musical forms would have a greater likelihood to have an impact on Brazilian ones than the other way around.

North American cultural imperialism would not reach its peak in Brazil until the destruction of Europe during World War II. Ironically, during this time the U.S. government would directly fund projects that aimed to incorporate many Latin American cultural elements, and later export these same products to Latin America. For much of the nineteenth and early twentieth centuries, however, the Brazilian cultural connection to France was much more important than Brazil's relationship with the United States. Ironically, the Franco-Brazilian cultural alliance was highlighted in the 1920s during the modernist revolution, when intellectuals began to look inward in search of Brazilian roots. After World War I, important French intellectuals established important ties with Brazil, and Brazilian intellectuals, artists, and musicians traveled to Paris in record numbers. To Bernard Gendron, the French interest in Brazil was closely connected to what some critics have called "negrophilia."[37]

The French Connection

Brazilian performers, musicians, and commentators rave about how Brazilian musicians left their mark on France in the pre–World War II era. Brazilian modernist writers such as Oswald de Andrade were un-apologetic Francophiles. Paris was the cultural center of the universe and a mecca for intellectuals, artists, musicians, and performers from all over the world, and Brazil was no exception. After World War I, Brazilian musicians would begin to travel to Paris in record numbers, and among them were pioneering Afro-Brazilians. Donga made his way to Paris during the Roaring Twenties with Pixinguinha and the Brazilian band called the Oite Batutes. Other Afro-Brazilian performers, including the Bahian Antônio Lopes de Amorim Diniz, known simply as Duque; the actor and playwright João Cândido Ferreira, who was known as De Chocolat; and Aracy Cortes would also leave their marks on the Parisian entertainment scene, following the path of other black artists from the Caribbean, Africa, and the United States, including Josephine Baker and Louis Armstrong. De Chocolat, one of the early pioneers of black Brazilian theater, also influenced Brazilian popular music. He created hundreds of compositions for the theater and also collaborated with nationally known composers. In 1934, for example, De Chocolat and Ary Barroso wrote the *marcha* "Nêgo também é gente" (Blacks are people too).[38]

Paris played a critical role in the early globalization of Brazilian popular music prior to the institutionalization of the mass media in the 1930s, but it also served as an international urban space where Afro-Brazilians came into contact with and dialogued with Afro-diasporic musicians, performers, and musical forms, particularly African American musical forms. Few African American performers made their way to Brazil prior to World War II, and few Afro-Brazilians would travel to the United States until the dismantling of segregation in the 1960s. Afro-Brazilian pioneers such as Pixinguinha and De Chocolat who made their way to Paris and performed in cabaret and *cafés-cantantes* continued to face prejudice at home, but "success" in Paris meant international legitimacy and would ultimately lead to increased prestige at home.

Afro-Brazilian Performers in the City of Lights

Brazilian performers, artists, and intellectuals had been traveling to Paris since the early nineteenth century. Brazilians were tied culturally to the French in a number of ways, including the development of the Brazilian educational system. Heitor Villa Lobos, Brazil's most renowned classical composer, first made a name for himself in Paris before he was acclaimed at home.[39] Popular musicians such as Pixinguinha and his Oite Batutes (or the Oito Batutas in Portuguese) are generally heralded as the first popular musical group to export live Brazilian popular music to Paris, although Duque, the Bahian dancer and entertainer, and Arnoldo Guinlé were pioneers in their own right. Neither Guinlé nor Duque called themselves black, like many Brazilians associated with the world of performing artists, they both considered many of the Afro-Brazilian dances and musical forms part of their own histories. Without the two of them—Duque with his entertaining and entrepreneurial skills in the Paris milieu and Guinlé with his funds and contacts—the Oito Batutes would never have set foot in Paris.[40]

A dentist by trade, Duque became one of the masters of the *maxixe* and an ambassador of Brazilian popular dance in Europe. He opened up a dance school in Paris and did sufficiently well to be able to travel back to Brazil regularly. His failed plan to open his own Parisian club, which he was going to call Cabaré Brasil, did not stop him from becoming artistic director of the Sheherazade dance hall and bringing talented musicians from Brazil to perform in Paris. In 1922, he opened his own Chez Duque on the Rue Caumartin and later La Reserve de St. Cloud, where he hosted Brazilian performers and North American jazz performers in what must have been one of the most exciting cross-diaspora fertilizations before World War II. Duque had seen Pixinguinha perform in the Assírio in Rio, and together with Guinlé, he devised a plan to carry the first popular Brazilian live band to Paris.[41]

According to Donga, a member of the Paris group, the band members were fully conscious of their pioneering role. Still, the band's repertoire was comprised mostly, but not solely, of Brazilian standards, mixing in a variety of compositions, including U.S. popular numbers.[42] The Brazilian sambas were, nonetheless, the major attraction, particularly those with lyrics in French, among them a composition by Pixinguinha entitled simply "Les Batutas," with lyrics in French by Duque:

Nous sommes Batutas
Batutas, Batutas
Venus du Brésil
Içi tout droit
Nous sommes Batutas
Nous faisons tout le monde
Danser le samba

Le samba se danse
Toujours en cadence
Petit pas par çi
Il faut de l'essence
Beaucoup d'élégance
Le corps se balance
Dansant le samba[43]

In addition to performing for Parisians, the Oito Batutes attracted Brazilians abroad just as performers today appeal to the growing Brazilian diaspora. The band also performed for the embassy personnel, for the imperial royal family resident in Paris, and for Santos Dumont, who two decades earlier had circled the Eiffel Tower in his airplane.[44]

The Oito Batutes, comprised of Pixinguinha, his brother China, José Alves, Luis Silva, Jacó Palmieri, Raul Palmieri, Nelson Alves, João Pernambuco, Raul, and Donga, would inspire and play with many other performers during the radio era, including the Miranda sisters, Francisco Alves, and Mário Reis, none of whom ever performed in France. Paradoxically, the appearance of the Oito Batutes in Paris in 1922 created an unnecessary uproar in Brazil, and raised questions about race, representation, and the value of popular music to national construction. Comprised of four black, three white, and two *mestiço* instrumentalists, the Oito Batutes had also broken with convention and had become one of the first racially mixed groups to represent Brazil abroad. This was at a time when nonwhites were virtually barred from representing Brazil abroad in official or diplomatic positions. It is worth mentioning that even though the group had performed in Europe, it would not have been able to do so in the segregated United States without considerable difficulties. Moreover, in Paris, the Brazilian musicians and performers came into contact with African Americans and other Latin American musicians, and would return to Brazil to play ragtime, jazz, and other styles of music.[45]

While French producers, artists, and intellectuals helped to create a Pan-African aesthetic based on European desires, a genuine intermingling and exchange among black performers took place. Black performers, especially from the United States, took advantage of the new possibilities in the European capital, having being disregarded by the local cultural elite at home for decades. Like Duque, for example, Josephine Baker opened her own club in the Pigalle in 1926, appropriately called Chez Josephine. During Baker's first trip to Brazil, when she performed at the Casino Theater, she met Rio's local *mulata* star Aracy Cortes. Cortes, in turn, was one of the few Brazilian female performers to perform in Paris in the early 1930s in the midst of the "Golden Age" of Brazilian popular music. When Baker traveled to Brazil in 1939, she performed some of the standards associated with Carmen Miranda at the Cassino da Urca with Grande Otelo, an arrangement that apparently did not sit well with Miranda, who had already left for the United States.[46]

Art and music from the developing world inspired European primitivists such as Pablo Picasso and a host of other intellectuals of the avant-garde. Europeans such as Oswald Spengler bemoaned the decline of Western civilization, while Freyre began to celebrate his *lusotropicalism*, which praised Portuguese colonization in the tropics and celebrated the Brazilian capacity for racial tolerance. Other Brazilian intellectuals were well on their way to incorporating, and studying, their own roots thanks in part to the French "negrophilia" and interest in popular musicians such as Pixinguinha who crossed the line between popular and erudite or concert musicians. It was without any irony that Pixinguinha could comment on Villa Lobos, one of Brazil's well-known classical composers: "Oh I knew Villa Lobos. He was a good guitar player and used to be able to accompany us in the numbers. I really consider him a genius. He was our Stravinsky, a

Wagner. It was not a question of feeling. Music has nothing to do with sentimentality. I want to see the material knowledge."[47]

The Oito Batutes' conquest of Paris had been a turning point in the beginning of the widespread acceptance of popular musicians. To perform there was symbolically important in Brazil not only for one's career but also for the acceptance of the type of music one performed. But the visit to Paris alone was not enough in the midst of growing patriotism and the focus on promoting the Brazilian nation. This is where French intellectuals and their relationship to their Brazilian counterparts from the 1920s and 1930s played a critical role. French intellectuals of the 1920s became new avant-garde *flânuers*, but after the destruction caused by the Great War, Europe was not enough.[48] The logical step, as Gendron convincingly argues, was the absorption of exotica from foreign lands: bringing that to the new military-cultural complex or going out and living in the developing world in search of new inspiration.[49]

While Pixinguinha and his group were performing in Brazil, the modernist cultural revolution spearheaded by intellectuals in São Paulo began to encourage Brazilians to look inward and to appreciate their own culture. Many of these intellectuals (who called themselves modernists) had also traveled to Paris and had strong Francophile tendencies. Thus, French interest and acceptance of Brazilian popular culture validated the modernists' own patriotic quest. Although black and other non-European traditions initially appealed to the Parisian crowds because of their exotic qualities, exoticism need not necessarily be one-dimensional. This is particularly true for those such as Baker and members of the Oito Batutes who, given the options, gained personal power and legitimacy as a result of these performances and were able to transform that power into a creative force. Moreover, just as French and other European intellectuals began to give increasing attention to North American jazz artists, others were inspired by Brazilian idioms bringing unprecedented attention to Brazilian popular culture. In many cases, French intellectuals who traveled to Brazil cemented the Franco-Brazilian bonds. One vivid example was the case of Darius Milhaud, secretary to Paul

Claudel, the diplomat and minister of the French League in Rio de Janeiro from 1916 to 1918.[50]

Milhaud became friends with Villa Lobos, Alberto Nepomuceno, and other classical composers in the city, and he also became interested in Brazilian popular music, noting the ambivalence that many classical musicians held toward their talented popular counterparts. In an article published in the São Paulo journal *Ariel* in 1924, Milhaud called upon classical musicians to pay more attention to their popular counterparts and the idioms that they performed, particularly the *maxixe*, sambas, tangos, and *cateretês*, all of which to him represented the most original expression of Brazil. While in Brazil, Milhaud met some of the most important popular musicians, bought many of their musical compositions, and composed a number of works inspired by his Brazilian experience.[51]

Of his Brazil-inspired work, "Le boeuf sur le toit" (The ox on the roof) is perhaps the most well known, but there were others, including "Saudades do Brasil," (Longings for Brazil) "Souvenir do Rio," (Souvenir from Rio) "Les danses de Jacaremirim" (The Jacaremirim dances) "Dans les rues de Rio" (On the streets of Rio). In his 1922 composition "Saudades do Brasil," a *suite de danse* for piano published in Paris, Milhaud included twelve movements, each dedicated to places in Brazil, most of them neighborhoods in Rio. The local people and geography were inspiring, leading him to one of the most creative times in his life. Four years earlier, he had collaborated on "Dans Les Rues de Rio" for voice and piano with Claudel. Divided into two parts, Milhuad's short work included the poetry of Claudel in "Le Rêmoleuer" and "Le Marchand de Sorbets."[52] Milhaud had rendered his highest tribute, although his compositions were not simply imitations but new French creations as a result of exchange in a process that has taken place among artists for centuries. Yet the story of "Le boeuf sur le toit" has generated controversy about the nature of the exchange, particularly when it involves the now familiar formula of well-placed musicians with access to the means of communication being inspired by unknowns or poor musicians who are not able to generate an income from their own performances.

"Le boeuf sur le toit" was a ballet composed by Milhaud in collaboration with Jean Cocteau in 1919. The ballet, in the form of a farce created and arranged by Cocteau, was wildly popular, giving the name to a popular bar in Paris. According to Maurice Sachs, the bar quickly became one of the most fashionable nightspots in Paris and remained so through the late 1920s. So popular was Le boeuf sur le toit in its heyday that Maurice Sachs claimed in 1928: "other justly famous restaurants whose names are still remembered by all or that are still open and will remain so for a long time seem to have existed only before or after the old Boeuf." Musicians who played in other Parisian venues gathered at Le boeuf sur le toit to play after they had finished their paying gigs. Various restaurants and cabarets in various French and Belgian cities apparently adopted the name.[53]

Le boeuf sur le toit achieved such legendary status that it ended up becoming a symbol for Paris in the 1920s and led to the common misconception that Milhaud's score had been named after the bistro rather than the other way around. In *Notes Without Music*, Milhaud clarified the sources of his inspiration: "I called this fantasia *Le boeuf sur le toit*, which was the title of a Brazilian popular song."[54] This song was, in fact, the Brazilian tango "O boi no telhado" by José Monteiro (Zé Boiadêro), launched during the 1918 carnival season.

"O boi no telhado" begins by calling the *mulata* to join him: "Let's go *mulata*. Come with me / Let's go see carnival / I want to enjoy myself with you / No other party can compare."[55] Moneiro's tango takes the male perspective with an invitation to the *mulata* to join him in the festivities of carnival. The song relies on motifs from Brazilian northeastern folklore, although it makes no direct reference to the ox on the roof. Like its Argentine counterpart, the Brazilian tango emerged as a hybrid musical form with deep connections to other Afro-diasporic musical traditions. According to Mário de Andrade, at the turn of the twentieth century the popular Brazilian tango, which was also referred to as the Brazilian *habanera*, incorporated African rhythmic influences.[56]

Although Monteiro's composition was relatively unknown in Brazil and the composer is hardly remembered, his work and the works of other popular Brazilian musicians captivated the French and found their way into the Parisian vernacular in unexpected ways. Milhaud's appreciation and passion for Brazilian popular music allowed him to play a small but important role in exporting Brazilian tunes, but he was hardly alone. French novelist Georges Bernanos, who went into self-imposed exile in Brazil in 1938, returning to France after World War II and then going on to Tunis, had also lauded what he called Brazil's spirited intelligence. Blaise Cendrars made Brazil his second spiritual home and had an enormous influence on the modernists, even publishing some of their works in Paris, including *Pau Brasil* by Oswald de Andrade. In Paris, Cendrars had come into contact with a few young Brazilians, including Tarsila Amaral and Emiliano Di Cavalcanti. One year later, he headed for Brazil, where like Milhaud before him, he came into contact with popular musicians whom he often introduced to the Brazilian cultural elite.[57]

The surrealistic poet Benjamin Péret, who married Elsie Houston in Paris in 1928, also moved to Brazil. In addition to founding Brazil's Trotskyist party with his brother-in-law in 1930, he dedicated himself to the study of popular music and religion, particularly *Macumba* in Rio and *Camdomblé* in the Northeast and in São Paulo, publishing many of his views in the *Diario da Noite*. In many ways, Frenchmen like Milhuad, Cendrars, and Péret helped Brazilians cast a positive light on their popular traditions. This coincided with Freyre's studies of the historical influences of Africans on Brazilian culture and the development of mass media. The technological innovations came not from France, however, but from the United States with entrepreneurs such as Fred Figner, a Czech American who opened up the recording studio Casa Edison, and filmmaker Wallace Downey. Nonetheless, French intellectuals' role in highlighting the contributions of popular musicians in general and Afro-Brazilian musicians in particular cannot be understated.

Unfortunately, although black Brazilian contributions were widely recognized as fundamental to Brazilian popular music, black Brazilians were not the major benefactors of the music industry profits. Brazil's popular music industry was not unique, however. Black musicians and composers in the United States were systematically marginalized from the larger lucrative white markets until the late 1950s. Brazil's case was distinct, however, since the United States did not celebrate or recognize the black experience as the foundation of its popular musical traditions. Still, even these facts only partly explain the complexities of the era that witnessed thousands of productive collaborations.

Conclusion: Blackness, Urbanism, and Modernity Beyond Paris

A growing urban population, expanding capitalism, and the introduction of recording studios and radio stations were the three ingredients necessary for the forging of a new era of Brazilian popular music that was initially performed by and was based on an urban lifestyle inspired by urban Afro-Brazilians. New technologies developed side by side with a host of local urban forums, allowing for a rich dialogue across racial and class lines. With international attention and patriotism, performers who had entered the popular music spheres were able to take the urban sound to the mass market. Borges Pereira argues convincingly that the thematic content of the first successful musical numbers (recordings, in the theater, and on the radio) gradually shifted from rural themes such as those in "Luar de sertão" (Moonlight in the drylands) and "Tristeza do Caboclo" (The Caboclo's sadness) to urban ones such as those in "Feitiço da Vila" (The Vila's spell) by Noel Rosa and Vadico and "Na Pavuna" (In Pavuna) by Almirante, to name just a few. This shift was neither chronological nor absolute. Urban themes, and in particular black themes, that used phrases and slang from the urban masses will forever be a part of the Brazilian musical tradition from the 1920s onward.[58]

Afro-Brazilian pioneers and others working in the predominantly Afro-Brazilian environments had left their mark on Brazilian society. Musicians such as Pixinguinha, Chiquinha Gonzaga, Sinhô, Donga, and others continued to be important references for contemporary musicians. The growing working and middle classes were in search of entertainment, and an increasing number of performers from the working classes found new opportunities. Bourgeois society was also at a crossroads. Members of the elite would be slowly won over by Brazilian popular music. Blackness remained symbolically important for the mass audiences, particularly as an indicator of the country's roots and historical legacy and in the Brazilian language and musicality. Black performers were more than willing to share their black masks. That Brazilian society was prejudiced and discriminated against blacks illustrates that the music industry was not immune from the larger societal trends. The aesthetics and the face of popular music would be slowly stratified and divided into distinct class forums with racial connotations.

CHAPTER TWO

Afro-Brazilians and the Early Popular Music Forums of Rio de Janeiro

Cada macaco em seu galho
(Each monkey on its branch)

———————————— Popular Brazilian saying

For more than two decades, President Getúlio Vargas, who rose to power with popular support in 1930, courted musicians and performers. Vargas had been the author of the federal law of 1928 that established the payment of royalties for musical compositions, a law that the Brazilian Society of Theatric Authors (SBAT) would ask to be strengthened and enforced in 1933. One year earlier, in 1932, thanks to Pedro Ernesto, his then ally and mayor of Rio, all of the established carnival groups received funding from the government. Thus began what Sérgio Cabral has called "the great love affair between carnival and Getúlio Vargas," which lasted until 1956, when the samba school Mangueira honored him in the carnival parade.[1]

Under Vargas's watch, musicians became professionals, and radio and cinema technologies advanced, as we will see in chapter 3, but they could not have developed without the organization and creativity of

Afro-Brazilians. Black and *mulato* musicians responded to the emerging technologies and played active roles in a number of venues created by commercial interests. At the same time, Afro-Brazilians organized within their own forums to celebrate their collective identities, their neighborhoods, and their country. The emergence and development of Rio de Janeiro's samba schools, the *teatro de revistas* (popular revue theaters), and the casinos, the three major forums for musical expression, were in turn crucial to the development of Brazil's unique urban popular music sound and aesthetic that would be later disseminated in the mass media. Blackness, or Africaneity, played varying roles in each forum. The social history of these forums must be understood in the context of three important historical tends: patriotism, the developing labor and migration patterns in the city of Rio, and the shifting demography of Rio's musical scene.

Popular Music and Patriotism

First Lady Darcy Vargas attended the famous carnival balls at the Municipal Theatre and invited popular singers to social receptions at the president's residence, helping to dispel the prejudices of those who continued to look down on popular music as an unworthy form of entertainment because of its connection to the black underclass.

The emotional words of Vargas's friend Oswaldo Aranha, after attending a 1933 performance led by the great black Brazilian musician-composer Alfredo da Rocha Vianna Filho (Pixinguinha), can only be understood in the context of the struggle of acceptability of popular musicians: "I can only have words of praise for what I have just heard: people from my country, music from my country. I am one of those who always believed in the true Brazilian national music."[2]

Throughout the Vargas presidency, musical history unfolded side by side with political tragedy. As the government clamped down on the press through the national security law in 1935, it afforded musicians the space to create the first film musicals. The classical maestro Heitor Villa-Lobos best explained the Vargas government's relationship with music: "To utilize the sortilege of music as a factor of culture and civics and integrate it into our very lives and in the national conscience."[3] Vargas worked well with sortilege and ambiguity, and he understood the power of the people's music like no other Brazilian leader. Yet he was not naive enough to let it develop on its own accord. After the creation of the Estado Novo (New State) in 1936, the Department of Press and Propaganda censured performances, from radio to carnival to theatrical revues, although the agency was not above dialogue or partnerships with well-situated artists such as Villa-Lobos, who could help promote what pundits called "Brazilness."[4]

The Vargas government facilitated the exchange between classical performers and popular artists, but the impetus came from the artists themselves, inspired by national talent and looking for opportunities for creation as well as remuneration. The lines between classical or erudite music and popular aesthetics began to blur, although distinctions would forever remain. Formally trained lyrical singers such as Elsie Houston, who was also an avid researcher of black cultural influences in Brazil, performed popular music at home and abroad.[5] This was also true of Olga Praguer Coelho, Bidu Sayão, Vicente Celestino, and others. Alfred da Rocha Vianna Filho, for example, was a virtuoso, at home in any genre. Villa Lobos, "the Brazilian Mozart," as he is often called, was one of the most ardent promoters of popular music, at times fanatically vigilant in his exploration of authentic Brazilian sounds. He would be joined by a host of others, including Francisco Mignione, Lorenzo Fernandez, Camargo Guarniere, and Radamés Gnatalli, all of whom received inspiration from Afro-Brazilian popular music in general and many Afro-Brazilian musicians and composers in particular.[6]

The climate established under Vargas allowed musicians, vocalists, composers, and producers, to collaborate in ways not possible earlier. The results were revolutionary and varied, forging multiracial Brazilian sounds performed and celebrated by blacks and by whites only one generation after the abolition of slavery in 1888. Under Vargas, new industries and new ways of thinking about music and Brazil were possible. New legislation allowed composers to begin to claim royalties, although this would take decades to be universally respected.

Meanwhile, new recording technologies made recordings of percussion instruments, played almost exclusively by popular musicians, possible.[7]

With new technologies emerging, it was easy to see how the Vargas era was a time of "firsts" for the music industry, and a time when politicians and entrepreneurs capitalized on the country's rich and varied musical tradition. Vargas had been sincere when he remarked that he wished that he were as popular as the young *mulato* crooner Orlando Silva, one of the most popular performers of the 1940s. The president understood why it was important to support popular musicians since he, like the musicians, was in the process of forging a new relationship with the nation. Like them, he became a depository for emotions in addition to a political force in an era in which the popular masses were just beginning to organize politically as full citizens for the first time in Brazilian history. Brazilian musicians, especially instrumentalists and interpreters of popular Brazilian music, congregated in Rio de Janeiro, transforming the city into a musical kaleidoscope.

These developments give credence to José Ligeiro Coelho's ideas that Africanisms in Brazil necessarily transcend race-based discussions. Indeed, throughout the African diaspora, including in the United States, African diasporic musical traditions continue to influence the musical performance of peoples of all backgrounds. In *The African Heritage of White America*, for example, John Edward Phillip illustrates that some Africanisms in the United States, including language and instruments such as the banjo, are as common among whites as blacks. Melville J. Herskovits has also documented unclaimed Africanisms in white and black populations in music, religion, and eating practices. Shared cultural traits did not translate into social integration in Brazil, as the case of Rio de Janeiro vividly illustrates.[8]

Labor Patterns, Migrations, and Rio's Musical Forums

Rio de Janeiro, the socially divided and economically depressed ex-capital of Brazil, remains, as the 1936 André Filho tune exclaims, a *cidade maravilhosa* (a marvelous city), a depository of national and international fantasy, an important cultural cradle of South America, intimately connected to Brazil's literary, theatrical, and musical history. Although Rio's natural landscape and geographical beauty have helped the city to earn its distinction, it is Rio's constructed political importance that has curiously allowed the city to develop into a vibrant cultural South American mecca, a position that slowly eroded after the move of the capital to Brasilia in the 1960s.

On January 1, 1502, Portuguese explorer André Gonçalves made his way in to the Guanabara Bay, thinking it was the mouth of a river. He marked this erroneous perception by naming the place for the river and the month, Rio de Janeiro (the river of January), in Portuguese. The name was officially changed to honor the infant Portuguese king after Estácio de Sá routed the French colonists out of the area and established the city of São Sebastião de Rio de Janeiro. The focus on Salvador de Bahia, the colony's political capital, meant that Rio remained largely underdeveloped until 1763 when, in the midst of the Enlightenment, Rio became the new capital. The city was given another burst of life in 1808 when Dom Pedro of Portugal fled Napoleon's invasion of the Iberian peninsular. To the mostly African and mixed-raced people of the city, he added more than 1,500 nobles and members of the court, eventually elevating Rio from colonial capital to the capital of a newly formulated colonial empire (the United Kingdom of Portugal, Brazil, the Algarves, and the Guinea Coast of Africa).[9]

Royal patronage in the newly created imperial capital meant that cultural institutions would begin to flourish, even in the class- and race-based society in which slavery played a central role. By the time Brazil became a republic in 1889, Rio had developed into a major urban center, thanks to urban engineer Francisco Pereira Passos. Between 1900 and 1910, the city was transformed and many of its central buildings torn down and remodeled after the grandeur of Paris. Rio's geography did not lend itself to the grid model or urban development of the Hispanic American cities, but the city did have a political, economic, cultural, and religious center where the Senate, the Chamber of Deputies and the Municipal Congress, the Military School and its barracks, the port, and the churches were all located. The official edifices of national culture could also be found there: the Academy of Belas Artes, the National Library, and the Municipal Theater.[10]

The official institutions were largely responsible for the population growth that Rio experienced at the turn of the twentieth century. As the population increased, so did the possibilities for leisure. Thus, downtown Rio and its environs became the logical locale for the major popular theaters and musical venues. The first radio station was established in the city's center, as was the first cinema house. Less formal musical and theatrical developments occurred in private homes, in plazas, or in the many cafés and nightclubs spread among the neighborhoods around the center of the city: today, Lapa, Gambôa, Santa Teresa, Catumbi, and those slightly farther afield such as Rio Comprido, Vila Isabel, Estácio, and São Cristovão. Add to these the many neighborhoods that would spring up in the favelas, or *morros*, that would dot Rio's landscape.

In a country such as Brazil, where labor supply outpaces demand, urban centers are magnets for middle-class and poor migrants. Brazil, as many writers have explained, is a coastal country, not only because of its extensive Atlantic coast but also because the majority of its inhabitants live in cities by or near the ocean.

The patterns of internal migration have tended toward the large cities of the Southeast, particularly Rio and São Paulo, draining the small towns and municipalities of the interior of the country, and intensifying the economic and cultural dependency on the coast. This pattern was particularly obvious after the abolition of slavery in 1888 and the creation of the republic one year later. Rio drew migrants from all over Brazil and, together with the port of Santos in São Paulo, also attracted immigrants from across the Atlantic. Between 1919 and 1930, 3,337,723 Portuguese immigrated to Brazil, the majority of them to Rio. There were other immigrants as well: Spanish, Italian, Turks, Poles, Germans, Syrian-Lebanese, Russians, and Japanese make up the most significant groups.

While Rio attracted many individuals from many professions, dentists, medical doctors, salesmen, plumbers, carpenters, and bricklayers could find jobs almost anywhere. In most places, to be a musician or a performer was not a profession. Even in Rio, until the late 1930s few could dedicate their time to pursuing music as a profession. Still, many performers understood that Rio was the place to go if they were to have any chance of finding gainful employment. The possibilities were certainly greater in the radio and recording industries, whether as soloists, interpreters, members of choruses, or regulars in the orchestras. There were other venues, including theaters and nightclubs, as well as the casinos that tended toward national and international tourists.

Ironically, throughout the first decades of the twentieth century, the government, the press, and the elite viewed popular musicians with a certain suspicion, almost as vagabonds, and local authorities frequently harassed them well into the 1930s. Middle-class families continued to send their sons and daughters to learn the piano, but a career in popular music was unthinkable. Social values had begun to change in the late 1920s, however. The modernist revolution based on the "Week of Modern Art" in São Paulo in 1922 was about to introduce new values and ways of thinking about Brazil. Still, Rio's neighborhoods remained socially and racially stratified. The country's capital had begun to spread out from what would be called the Zona Norte, the Northern Zone, beyond to the more middle-class Zona Sul, the Southern Zone, and even toward the modern neighborhood of Jacarepagua.

The growing favelas would help to shape the social system in Rio from Copacabana in the Zona Sul to the northern regions of the city. The musical talents shaped the popular culture of the neighborhoods and intensified local identification that contributed to carnival groups, forces that the Vargas government would utilize for the formation of Brazil's patriotic, if not nationalist, stance. From 1930 to the end of the 1950s, Rio attracted Brazil's greatest talents. The city also became a springboard for international careers.

The Demography of the Carioca Musical Scene

By the 1930s, music had become a public spectacle through the institutionalization of carnival, and through various organized bands such
as the Corpo de Bombeiros (Fire Brigade) and the military.[11] Initially,
however, many poor Carioca amateur popular instrumentalists and
vocalists performed and created in private, away from the gaze of local
authorities, in their own homes among friends or from time to time
in the homes and yards of well-to-do benefactors. When they did perform in public, it was in local plazas, on neighborhood street corners,
in theaters, or in specially designated locales such as those that would
later be transformed and become the headquarters of samba.

The emphasis on performing in public spaces meant that the
musical profession consisted largely of men until the 1950s, and the
professions' lower-class beginnings in the racially stratified capital
city meant that popular music performances were not held in too
high esteem. Musicians were often viewed as synonymous with male
malandros who, in the Carioca middle-class imagination, were often
seen as street hustlers who disturbed the peace, as Ruy Guerra and
Chico de Buarque's *Opera do malandro* so vividly portrays.[12] Moreover,
popular music performers were often stigmatized, particularly in the
first two decades of the twentieth century. By the time the *malandro*
reached Hollywood in the form of an animated parrot called Joe
Carioca, he was significantly gentrified.[13]

With the creation of the Estado Novo in 1936, the Vargas administration would encourage musicians to perform and record so-
called edifying music that would celebrate values such as hard work
and patriotism. At the same time, the state began a campaign of
censorship, and it started keeping tabs on musicians. Indeed, in the
1940s Brazilian authorities began to amass a rich database on popular
musicians in the Delegacia Especial de Segurança Política e Social
(DESPS; Special Headquarters for Political and Social Security). Police
records provided social, biographical, and personal information on
the vibrant and diverse instrumentalists who made up the rank and
file of Brazil's musical industry, although, curiously, the police did not

collect information on singers, who tended to come from the middle or lower middle class.

The Regular Musicians

Documents by the privileged in society help write most national histories. They leave the documents behind that allow historians to reconstruct their past activities. In general, this also holds true for Brazil. At the same time, Brazilian insecurity and distrust of the popular classes in general and popular artists and musicians in particular meant that the state collected information on the workers who performed, organized, and helped create the gems of the "Golden Age of Radio." While the police could not collect information on all the informal musicians, many of whom juggled other jobs and left no written documents, the police archives nonetheless give us an insight into the small group of musicians who by the mid 1940s had started to become professionalized and define themselves as "musicians."

Despite the foundational contribution of blacks to the history of Brazilian popular music, by the end of the Estado Novo in 1944, most of the instrumentalists born between 1886 and 1922 were overwhelming white, or considered themselves white. The environment remained overwhelming male, and despite the importance of migrants to the Carioca milieu, 40 percent of musicians who registered with the police were born in the federal district, and 15 percent came from the state of Rio de Janeiro. This indicates that the hegemonic position of the Carioca in the creation of Brazilian popular music in the federal capital was no myth. Other states appear in the record, particularly the neighboring states of São Paulo and Minas Gerais, but the numbers from other states are small.

Vargas was largely responsible for helping to bring respectability to musicians, but so were the upper- and middle-class *aficionados* and performers, foreign and local intellectuals who associated with popular musicians in and around Lapa and in other locales around the city. The experiences in the United States and Brazil are more similar than

TABLE 1. Musicians Registered with the Special Headquarters for Political and Social Security, by State

Acre	1	Pará	19
Alagoas	27	Paraiba do Norte	7
Amazonas	4	Paraná	6
Bahia	57	Pernambuco	39
Ceará	9	Rio Grande do Norte	13
D.F.	587	Rio Grande do Sul	39
Espiritú Santo	18	São Paulo	133
Maranhão	12	Santa Catarina	7
Minas	128	Sergipe	28

Source: Delegacia Especial de Segurança Política e Social (DESPS), National Archives, Rio de Janeiro.

one might imagine. While North American segregation constructed an artificial hurdle that prohibited talented musicians from playing or rooming together—with grave penalties for black performers—talent, determination, and moral authority forced exceptions. Many black performers, such as Lena Horne, performed in all-white clubs, breaking barriers through their exceptionalism. Still, personal humiliations and awkward situations endured. Racially mixed bands could often secure gigs in clubs willing to take the risk, but invariably the members of these bands had to sleep, eat, and socialize in separate establishments. Whites could "step down" and frequent black establishments, but blacks could not "step up" and enter white establishments.

Despite the total refutation of racial democracy and the role of *mulatos* and *mulatas*, Degler's model of "neither black nor white" offers a more nuanced picture of the racial politics of performance and segregation in Brazil, particularly because of the distinction between the public and the private sphere, or what Roberto da Matta has described as "the house" and "the street."[14] Other scholars have argued that the carnivalesque nature of Brazilian public spectacle also allowed for racial intermingling and a certain degree of racial harmony. Light-skinned black performers often received preferential treatment over darker-skinned artists, particularly as singers or bandleaders for the radio, the cinemas, and the casinos, all of which were so closely linked to the tourist economy. But such preferential treatment was hardly absolute and depended on talent, genre, and occasion. Moreover, the idea of a light-skinned person being classified as "black" depended on a series of other factors.

A survey of major instrumentalists in the diverse media based on popularity, appearances, and income from the end of the 1920s to the late 1940s reveals far too few Afro-Brazilian singers, however. At the same time, two of the most popular vocalists, Orlando Silva and Sílvio Caldas, were what Degler would have called "neither black nor white" and felt ambivalent about their racial identities. There were few black women. Of the total number of musicians registered with the police, 765 were listed as white, 16 as *moreno*, only 2 as *mulato*, 460 as *pardo*, and 178 as *preto*. A close examination of photographs included in the archives reveals that musicians, like the broader society, were not immune to the whitening ideal, although it is important to point out that police officers often chose the racial identity of the musician. Nonetheless, for a vast number of musicians who registered as *pardo* (brown), for example, it is difficult to determine phenotypic or somatic features that distinguish them from those who declared themselves *preto* (black). On the other hand, it is difficult to determine to what degree, if any, fame or social background played a role in racial identification. Most, although not all, musicians were part of the lower classes. Income levels varied considerably, as did the places where musicians performed. Pixinguinga, one of the pioneers of the musical scene, for, example, is listed as *preto*.[15] Viewed a different way, approximately 54 percent of the registered musicians were classified as white, while 46 percent were classified as nonwhite. Despite the racial differences, most musicians shared similar cultural repertoires and would have been familiar with similar if not identical Afro-Brazilian musical traditions.

Although patriotism dominated the Vargas era, many foreign musicians and producers played significant roles in the formulation of authentic Brazilian sounds. This included pioneers of the radio industry such as the Czech-born Fred Figner and Leslie Evans, the American producer at RCA. The names of foreign instrumentalists also appear in the police archives, but these performers were mostly settled immigrants, probably Jews, from Poland, Italy, and Germany.[16] The contribution of these foreigners are often lost in the social history of a country and a city that witnessed the development of uniquely Brazilian social spaces that allowed for the emergence of a musical legacy.

Brazilian popular music, however, has always been somewhat dependent on a musical cycle associated with secular and religious holidays of the calendar year. Carnival was one of them. Moreover, from around 1900 to the early 1950s, specific social spaces helped provide inspiration, employment, and a sense of community to groups of individuals associated with the musical world. Today, many of these spaces are legendary and have taken on lives of their own, although they are deeply connected to the changing demographic and social trends of the time. Three social and creative forums deserve special attention: the samba schools, *teatro de revistas*, and the casinos. Each served the musical world in Rio not only as performance venues but also as places for exchange and inspiration, and each would dialogue in different ways with the emerging mass media technologies that would make it possible for thousands of Brazilians to consume popular music. By the mid 1930s, the radio, together with the recording studios and to a lesser extent the cinema, would ironically begin to influence the musical performance within the city's social spaces.

The Social History of Musical Forums

Social spaces, like people, influence one another. Rio's social spaces were organized according to distinct codes that determined who entered the social spaces and who performed there. Class, racial, and gender considerations influenced these codes. At the same time, selected musicians and performers flowed among social spaces with relative fluidity. The existence of a "provisional middle class" was predicated on an understanding that performers could adapt to different forums and to the appropriate behavior that audiences expected. Nonetheless, the casinos, the *teatro de revistas*, and the samba schools influenced each other and other important social forums, including local town squares, cafés, nightclubs, restaurants, and the very institution of carnival. The growing and diverse population of the city fueled the built environment. More working bodies meant wider markets, multiple sources of inspiration, opportunities for experimentation, and thus new forums for performance. This in turn meant more consumption, more production, and more investment, creating a cycle that would benefit Rio de Janeiro as long as it remained the capital.

Today, older Cariocas look back to this "Golden Age" with a nostalgia that Portuguese speakers call *saudade*. But *saudade* invested in emotional memories often disregards the complexities of history. Rio's cultural scene was full of contradictions, as its forums collaborated with one another to squeeze undesirables—many of them black Brazilians—out, or at least to determine the parameters of popular Brazilian aesthetics at a time that Walter Benjamin has called the age of technological reproduction, all the while celebrating Brazilianness. Rio's oral tradition of carnival, the revue theaters, and to a lesser extent the casinos remained just as important as the technological advances in cinema, radio, and recordings that would allow for the widespread dissemination of popular music.[17]

The population boom and the social characteristics of Rio's populations elucidate, if nothing else, how the oral tradition of the growing urban classes created important cultural forums. According to the 1920 census, there were 30,635,605 inhabitants in the country, rising to 41,236,315 in 1940. By the 1940s, Rio de Janeiro was still the country's most important cultural and political center, but the state was divided into two political areas: the federal district and the state district, both with close to 2 million people. By 1940, the state's population had advanced to more than 3.6 million people, slightly less than the northeastern state of Bahia, with more than 3.9 million people, and less than the 6.7 million people in the state of Minas Gerais and the

7.1 million people in the state of São Paulo. The federal district of Rio was relatively small but culturally and politically powerful.[18]

The number of newspapers and magazines, both of which raised awareness about the cultural activities and helped consolidate a sense of community in the city, was impressive. In 1933, the federal district boasted the largest concentration of newspapers and magazines in the country: 189 in Portuguese and 6 in foreign languages, including English, German, and French. The entire state of Minas had 212 different newspapers and magazines, and São Paulo had 312.[19] There were only fifty-six registered periodicals in the state of Rio outside the federal capital. Thus, Rio loomed as a cultural mecca for entrepreneurs of all types but especially in the booming industry of communication.[20]

The period between the two world wars brought unprecedented opportunities to Brazil. Since the abolition of slavery in 1888, migration to the cities by black Brazilians, Rio in particular, had increased. After World War I, immigrants from Italy, Spain, Germany, Portugal, and the recently defunct Ottoman Empire contributed to the growing population density of Brazilian cities. Rio was caught up in the quest for modernity and valued the contribution of its new European immigrants above the indigenous underclass, particularly blacks, many of whom had been free from slavery for many decades before 1888. New streets were being carved out of the mountainous landscape. Old ones were being transformed into avenues. The ports were bustling with the coming and going of cargo and travelers. This, in turn, created a bustling economy around the ports based on respectable jobs in the military, customs, and the police, reserved mostly for whites and light-skinned blacks.[21]

That was only the beginning. There were few odd jobs anywhere for the masses of poor blacks from the state and for the growing number of Afro-Brazilian migrants who had filled the city after abolition and the Guerra de Canudos (1896). Many did their best at carving out a living on the margins of the city in the growing favelas. Vendors of all types hawked their food, clothing, and bodies for a pittance. After dark, prostitutes descended upon the ports like vultures, joined by drug hustlers, *malandros*, and a host of performers and musicians whose raw talent merged in countless social spaces that have been lost to history. Then there was the middle class of bohemian life—not associated with the ports themselves but with the cafés and cabarets that dotted the city from Praça Tiradentes and its environs of the neighborhood known as Lapa, which inspired such diverse poets as Noel Rosa, Carlos Drummond de Andrade, Lima Barreto, and Vinicius de Moraes. Some establishments had long traditions and faithful clients. Others were more fleeting: bars turned into stages and itinerant circuses, for example.[22]

Rio was also where most of Brazil's popular music was being produced. The fact that all the major forums had congregated there meant more opportunities for musicians and performers from all over the country. But Rio was not the only locale that attracted artists. Recife and Salvador, cities in the northeast of Brazil, attracted technology and performers and became regional centers of cultural production. Rio's newspapers, however, covered and reported the local, national, and regional news and personalities, connecting the elite to what Anderson has called an "imagined community" in a country still largely illiterate.

Musical production was on the rise, and the composers' union, the Brazilian Society of Theatrical Authors (SBAT), had become big business. Although the SBAT had not officially included popular music composers in its title, the union attempted to fight for the social rights of its members. In 1935, the SBAT registered a total of 925 musical compositions to receive royalties. Of that number, 312 were sambas and 238 *marchas*, illustrating the growth of popular music over classical and other forms.[23] *Marchas* and sambas circulated during carnivals like close family members, although the former, as its name indicates, would prove easier for the neighborhood carnival groups to march to. Indeed, samba has evolved into different styles—*samba breque, samba canção, pagode*, bossa nova, and samba reggae—all with some connection to African musical traditions. The basic *marcha,* or *marchinha*, on the other hand, has not transformed as much but rather has continued to play an important role in preserving the songs from the early part of the twentieth century. Like Christmas carols celebrated and institutionalized by the Western Christian calendar, the *marchas*, mostly in vogue during Rio's protracted carnival season, preserve tunes written decades ago.[24] Carnival competitions for the best *marchas* captured the sentiments of the popular classes and often commented on current events in comical and sarcastic ways, to the delight of revelers.

Afro-Brazilian culture, issues related to blackness, popular culture, and patriotism constituted important themes in the *marchas* of the 1930s and 1940s. In 1931, for example, Lamartine Babo and the Valença Brothers's "O teu cabelo não nega" (Your hair gives you away) managed to discuss race and hair, praise the *mulata*, and celebrate Brazil.[25]

Merriment and misery were interconnected, however. Why else would carnival thrive among a population so stratified? In the 1930s, carnival was much more than the contemporary *sambódromo*, the edifice-avenue Marqués de Sapucaí carved into central Rio's landscape by Oscar Niemeyer that galvanizes the international media. Moreover, the concept of carnival depended on local *ranchos*, or carnival groups, in addition to the emerging samba schools that provided outlets for amateur musicians and virtuosos. The Brazilian office of the musician, if it can be called that, it must be remembered, has its historical roots in slavery, since enslaved Africans not only sang and performed among themselves but also were responsible for performing for their masters. Afro-Brazilians created bands, orchestras, and other groups that allowed them to demonstrate their knowledge of European practices as well as African ones. Many had learned music by ear. Others had studied it. Throughout the period of slavery, black musicians had filled local homes, plantations, and public forums with music that enthused locals and international travelers.[26]

To call this the carnivalesque is to understate the obvious. This was not only misery masked so well as merriment but authentic diasporic celebration in the face of terrible conditions, a process that Sidney W. Mintz and Richard Price have called the creolization of African culture in the Americas. Abolition brought a new dynamic and the movement away from forced performance to the stage, where the circus and the *teatro de revista* would be fundamental, although other social spaces would influence them. Not surprisingly, the *teatro de revista* quickly emerged as a more "dignified" form of "high" popular culture, enjoying a golden age at precisely the same time as the "Golden Age" of Brazilian popular music and the "Golden Age of Radio"—in the midst of the Vargas regime.[27]

The moral and social decadence of slavery had managed to safeguard cultural traditions and even forge new ones. Under the new republic, however, while these new traditions provided opportunities for expression, merriment, and employment, they could not do away with misery. Moral decay gave way to official and unofficial corruption and unprecedented urban poverty and misery. Freedom came at a price, and it was not the elite who paid. Like the Rio of today, where merriment, beaches, and carnival exist side by side with violence, favelas, and intense social inequalities, the Rio of the 1930s was a center of crime.

Minor crimes and infractions were greater in São Paulo, but in 1937, for example, the Distrito Federal, or Federal District (D.F.), registered 5,694 serious crimes compared to 2,733 in São Paulo and only 383 in Minas.[28] The number of infractions in Rio, including loitering and gambling, was relatively small compared to the rest of the country. In 1937, 2,787 total infractions occurred in Rio, for example, compared to 65,892 in São Paulo. The picture is reversed for serious crimes, including murder and assault, however.[29]

Misery and sickness were also a part of city life. In 1939, Rio registered 5,439 deaths due to tuberculosis, by far the leading cause of death, compared to diarrhea and stomach problems among children (3,719 deaths), and heart and circulatory problems (3,545 deaths).[30] Rio, the city where merriment and misery have intermingled for centuries, continued that tradition during the "Golden Age of Radio," which gave birth to a number of forums, including samba schools, popular theaters, and casinos, where musical experimentation and collaboration flourished. Lyrics, compositions, and performances included biting social and political commentary side by side with comedy and purely pleasing entertainment. The most public of these forums were the samba schools.

The Samba Schools

Rio's carnival today is only loosely associated with the traditional religious holiday culminating in Fat Tuesday. The preparations begin many months earlier, as do the marketing, training, and organizing. The official contemporary parades have grown to such an extent that officials are obliged to ignore the beginning of Lent on Ash Wednesday commencing the forty days of fasting and sacrifice. Today, the Parade of Champions culminates the weekend after Ash Wednesday, when the top six samba schools march through the Avenida Marques de Sapucaí celebrating their placement with a victory lap.[31]

Although the samba schools dominate modern carnival, the neighborhood conglomerations, called *blocos* or *bandas*, remain central to the city's merriment.[32] They not only play a contemporary role but also constitute one of the principal forums by which the carnival songs of old, principally the *marchinhas*, continue to flourish in some cases, almost a century after they were originally composed. During the founding stages of the recording industry, carnival served as a primary inspiration for composers and performers. The variety of Brazilian musical genres that contributed to the merriment is striking, although the way they have been characterized has not always been consistent. Even today, Brazilians often evaluate a genre by moving about and feeling the rhythm with their bodies before they decide whether they like a tune or not.

From the end of the 1920s to the mid 1940s, the samba schools provided an important social, cultural, and political space for Cariocas to congregate, create, and perform music that they considered aesthetically pleasing and socially edifying. The development of the samba schools must nonetheless be considered in the context of the other emerging forums for musical expression during the development of Brazilian modernism that would eventually call for the middle-class revolution of Getúlio Vargas. By the 1930s, the samba schools brought talented performers, instrumentalists, and dancers, the majority of them Afro-Brazilian, together for celebration but in an informal atmosphere of free-flowing collaboration. Situated in the *suburbios* or the *morros*, the samba schools would also become social spaces for drinking and merriment, like the bars and cafés of Lapa. And like the casinos and other houses of entertainment, the samba schools attracted local, national, and international observers. The differences between these forums were nonetheless substantial.[33]

In the tradition of popular empowerment, the samba schools represented an Afro-Brazilian attempt to dialogue with the nation, since most *sambistas* were absent from the major radio stations. Poor urban musicians, composers, singers, and dancers, the majority of whom were black, created musical conglomerations called *escolas de samba*, or samba schools. The name of the first, Deixa Falar (Let [Us] Speak), indicates the founders' desire to have their voices heard. In actuality, the creation of samba schools such as Deixa Falar, which emerged in the neighborhood of Estácio in 1928; Estação Primeira Mangueira, formed in 1929; and Portela, established a few years later, represents a change in the development of samba organization and not necessarily a beginning. According to popular musical researcher and writer Haroldo Costa, musical groups were called *blocos* before they were called schools. Afterward, the schools that performed well in the organized performance held in the meeting ground of Praça Onze (Square Eleven) were officially recognized as *ranchos*.[34]

Praça Onze was the meeting point to exhibit talent during the carnival season—particularly since the *ranchos* were not allowed to march down Rio Branco, where the elite carnival floats paraded. In 1932 Mario Filho, at the newspaper *Journal Mundo Sportivo*, promoted and came up with the criteria to judge the first official competitions in Praça Onze. Nineteen groups participated and agreed to be judged by a jury that mostly included white well-known Brazilians associated with Brazilian cultural production, such as the writers and journalists Orestes Barbosa and Raimundo Malgalhães Jr., the modernist dramatists and theater directors Eugênia and Alvaro Moreyra, and the politically connected Fernando Costa. Although judges like Orestes Barbosa could easily be considered a part of elite intellectual circles, his involvement with popular Brazilian circles was not atypical of the Carioca Brazilian milieu. Barbosa learned how to play guitar at an early age, and in addition to publishing journalistic articles, poetry, and books, he cowrote and composed popular music tunes with a number of musicians, including Afro-Brazilians such as Heitor dos Prazeres, Wilson Batista, Ataulfo Alves, and Sílvio Caldas.[35]

The official competitions established rules and traditions that would have a lasting effect on Afro-Brazilian official performances. Gentrification, popularization, nationalization, and social intermingling all occurred simultaneously as Brazilian musicians and artists of different racial and class backgrounds became familiar with similar references. How else could the white Barbosa cocreate a song entitled "Nega, meu bem" (1931)? The 1932 competition, which Mangueira won, also changed the behavior of musical performance with an organized singing section, *a comissão de frente* (lead commission), a percussion session consisting of *tamborins* and *pandeiros*, and later the *surdo* and the *porta bandeira* (flag holder).[36]

While it is tempting to trace the African impact on the use of instruments and the evolving rituals of Brazilian samba, doing so brings a number of challenges. First, while the African diasporic influences have been convincingly documented by a number of scholars, any linear or direct ties to Africa and African customs undermine the agency and adaptability of Afro-Brazilians to evolving political, social, economic, and cultural environments. Second, African music was heterogeneous despite the general importance of music and dance to most African cultures. Africans and black Brazilians not only continued to pass down their customs and practices from generation to generation to their black, *mulato*, and white progeny, they also learned and borrowed from each other and other traditions depending on local dynamics. The emergence and changes in samba are but one testament to that.

Afro-Brazilians participated in the evolution of Brazilian musical practices and celebrated their Africaneity while simultaneously contesting their marginalization and what Maria Isaura Pereira de Queiroz has called their "domestication."[37] Samba school names were only part of the dialogue and contestation. Deixa Falar, the first samba school, was founded in 1928 but did not participate in the competitions in

Praça Onze in the 1930s. The pioneers of the first school included the black composer Ismael Silva and the *mestiço* composer Nilton Bastos, both of whom would have an important impact on the emerging radio and music industries.[38] By the early 1930s, the "students" from the samba schools had already begun to perform in theaters. In 1933, for example, samba players appeared in the São Jose theater, the same year that the schools organized themselves into the Samba Schools Union (UES) and approached the city mayor, Pedro Ernesto, for funding, a move that would push the samba schools along the road to officialdom and recognition as a legitimate expression of popular culture in Rio. For its part, the city utilized samba, carnival, and the samba schools to attract tourists.[39]

In 1933, the newspaper *A Nação* (later *O Globo*) became the major sponsor for the carnival competition, but it was the UES and not the newspaper that came up with the rules for the competitive performance that included criteria such as best harmony. Other newspapers elected their own samba queens and kings from the popular classes. In conjunction with the UES, the newspaper *A Rua* chose a *Cidadão Samba*, or Samba Citizen, who had to live in the *morro*, know how to dance and play a variety of instruments, and be an active member of a samba school. The UES also established an important rule that kept the competition in Praça Onze local and thus decidedly more black, at least initially: participants in the parade had to be members of the samba schools, for example, and wind instruments were prohibited, a carnival tradition that continues until this day. New instruments nevertheless emerged, including the *surdo* and the *cuica*, along with a host of new samba schools with satirical names: So the Year Comes, Come as You Can, Talking Neighbors, Let Us Work Out, Stay Firm, and At the Last Minute, among others. They appeared in a collegial competition that was divided into groups A, B, and C.[40]

The samba schools became a training ground for a generation of Carioca musicians and for migrants from around Brazil who had made their way to Rio. Under Vargas, they also become a mainstay of Rio's cultural life and an important sector of popular culture in Brazil. With reason, the major singers on the radio and in the record industry and cinema relied on the talents of many of the musicians and composers of the samba schools. The existence of such schools, and Praça Onze in particular, would become the subject of a host of musical tunes, including the Grande Othelo and Herivelto Martins 1942 number that lamented the plaza's destruction in 1941.[41]

Europeans and Americans visiting Rio, along with Brazilian intellectuals, would often make their way to the favelas of Rio to meet the popular musical geniuses. In 1942, Orson Welles would try to re-create the energy of Praça Onze as a cinematographic vignette in a film on the black influences on Rio's carnival. His film was never released because, according to Welles, neither Brazil nor the United States was interested in a film that focused exclusively on black people dancing and singing. Despite the national and international snub, for most of their history the samba schools remained a distinctively Zona Norte phenomenon. The performers maintained a direct link to the gatherings and parties of the Bahianas, Tia Ciata, Tia Sinhá, and others, but they also emerged to become creative musical forces contributing to other arenas such as the popular theater.[42]

From the Circus to the *Teatro de Revistas*

Popular theater reflected the taste of the masses, was connected to popular music, and would become a fertile ground for scouts from recording studios. Rio today has a rich assortment of theaters, ranging from the baroque style of the Municipal Theater to small and inconvenient theaters such as the Teatro Cândido Mendes tucked away on a side street in the midst of Ipanema. Others in Cinelândia and throughout downtown Rio serve as movie theaters for modern-day American blockbusters or skin flicks.

Popular theater in Brazil has its roots in the circus, another forum that provided thousands of musicians with employment. Afro-Brazilian performers such as Assis Valente, Aracy Cortes, and others learned elements of the trade from their experience in the circus, where the clowns, singers, and other musical performers were part of the main attractions. The theatrical revue had become an eclectic Brazilian genre that benefited from the experience of the circus, including live musical numbers from vaudeville, burlesque, music halls, and variety and comedy shows. By the 1930s, the revue eventually became the most important venue for musicians, singers, and performers, and Rio was its capital. With influences from the French cabaret, Rio's *teatro de revista* was particularly sarcastic and malicious, full of comedy and double entendres.

Rio was the national haven for popular theater, attracting singers, dancers, musicians, and writers. According to the SBAT, in 1935, in the midst of Brazilian musical development, the federal district reported a total of 968 theatrical representations, with the state of São Paulo reporting 42 and Minas a mere 4.[43] Revues were the most popular genres, often ephemeral but registering social and political concerns through skits and musical numbers. The revues were also one of the principal art forms reviewed by the Vargas censors, particularly after the creation of the Estado Novo in 1936, although as in other countries, the censors did not catch subtext and disguised references. Moreover, the state ended up becoming more of a moral police force that took out any reference to sex, antisocial behaviors, and overt criticisms of the government. Audiences relied on revues for satirical commentary on politics, society, and local and international events. The organization, emotions, and aesthetics of the revue succeeded so well that these components were later adapted to live radio performances and to the cinema.[44]

The revues *Alô alô Madureira* and *Alô alô Copacabana*, for example, reflect the fascination with radio jargon. *Alô alô Madureira* begins with a song about Bahia, one of the Brazilian states where the African cultural legacy is most pronounced, and a typical artistic theme that many singers would insert into their performances. But there were other themes and icons from the 1930s Carioca milieu that would find their way into the musical productions, comedy, and other performances. Many were stereotypical, such as the *nêga maluca* (the crazy black woman) or the *turco* (the Turkish merchant) inspired by the merchants from the area of Rio now known as the Sahara and who might have been Lebanese or even Jewish.[45]

Radio performers were no strangers to the theater, although the local theatrical performances were not as lucrative economically. The plotless presentations of the theater revues developed side by side with texts from other forums, and plays, musical productions, and individual compositions often moved from the revue theater to the radio, making the necessary modifications to appeal to the distinct audiences. Both forums continued to be nourished by the experiences of the famous private parties of the *tias bahianas*, as well as the circuses. Of all the major national radio singers, Alves was the only one to gain his first experience in revues in the 1920s, before he became a radio personality. The darling of the popular theater was the daring *mulata* Aracy Cortes, who had worked with the versatile black pioneer of the circus, Benjamin de Oliveira. Cortes, who would also have some success on the radio and in the recording business, was most at home in the intimate, spontaneous local forums that she helped fashion.

In 1935, one year before the Vargas coup that created the Estado Novo, the D.F. registered a total of 968 staged revues, an average of 3 per day, not including dramas or other types of theatrical productions. Of those, The Brazilian Institute of Geography and Statistics (IBGE) registered forty-two new revues, which represented a staggering number if one compares it to the number of new revues on Broadway or off-Broadway that open each year. Unlike their New York counterparts, these revues attracted mostly local audiences and only occasionally international spectators. More important, however, they brought artists, musicians, and singers to the federal capital in search of opportunity.[46]

Revues in theaters around Praça Tiradentes, Praça Floriano, and other selected places near the center of the city played a significant role in what Evelyn Fuquim Werneck Lima has called the democratization of the public. Because of their low entrance fees that varied according to the seat's proximity to the stage, individuals from all social backgrounds were able to view quality performances within a given space. The revues and the performers, in turn, became references for a diverse urban population. This experience contrasted significantly from the upscale audience of the casinos, where fewer Afro-Brazilian performers would shine or present their own creations.[47]

The radio and recording industries helped validate the creations of urban musicians, most of whom worked at other jobs for a living, had little access to the recording industry, and had never set foot in a radio station. Those responsible for order helped keep these social worlds separate. As radio stars emerged singing the compositions of popular composers, the police continued to enforce at will "vagrancy laws," bust parties in the Zona Norte, and arrest musicians and confiscate their instruments. As late as 1938, for example, Dorival Caymmi reported that he had to travel with his guitar hidden so that he would not be mistaken for a vagabond.[48]

At the same time, it is clear that the idols of the radio played a critical role in convincing the elite of the value of popular music, and by extension the importance of black popular culture to national culture. Ironically, the aesthetics and face of popular music as it emerged on the radio and in the recording industry were not as representative of the popular classes as one might have imagined. Indeed although the symbolism of blackness played a central role in the musical performance on the radio few blacks became household names until the middle 1940s. Blackness was represented by and large by non-black vocalists. In utilizing masks to represent blackness, Brazilian performers and Brazilian popular music in general gentrified the popular tastes in select forums in a process that necessarily meant making the bourgeois taste more popular. Thus, with the help of figures like Mário Reis, Carmen Miranda, Aurora Miranda, Francisco Alves, and others, Brazilians forged a popular music sound and aesthetic that were examples of social syncretism at its best.

That Brazilian society was prejudiced and discriminated against blacks illustrates that the music industry was not immune from the larger societal trends. Yet it is important to underscore that Brazilian society could not and did not exclude black musicians, composers, and performers from the construction of the commercial aspects of Brazilian popular music outright. For many, popular musicians were seen as the authentic bearers of a national tradition and were appreciated and relied upon with such frequency that whites and blacks shared the same social space, both public and private, with such ease that it would have alarmed any performer, black or white, in the United States of the same era. Cohabitation did not mean equality, however. As one older black Brazilian musician jokingly remarked, "We can sing together. We can dance together. We can even sleep together, but at the end of the day we know who's going to get the recording track."[49]

The complexity of Brazilian social interaction in an artistic environment can only be fully grasped on a case-by-case basis. All generalities are not only nuanced by the poignant exceptions but also are related to the realm of emotions, faith, and good contacts. The same must be said of the participation of women in the industry. The music industry was not kind to them. Of the 1,474 musicians registered with the DESPS, less than 5 percent were women. The major radio idols were mostly men, although white women such as the Miranda and the Batista sisters made important contributions. Despite the hundreds of recordings inspired by black women, the first female black radio or recording idol, Carmen Costa, would not emerge until the second half of the 1940s. This assertion becomes complicated, however, when one considers light-skinned black women who may or may not have referred to themselves as *mulatas*, including Araci de Almeida, Aracy Cortes, and Angela Maria.[50] Thus, an examination of the role of black singers in promoting blackness in Brazilian popular music merits further study.

Casinos

Of all the live performance venues in Rio de Janeiro, the casinos represented the most glamorous, and thus the most class and race restrictive. Even then, casinos were not totally off limits to blacks and featured a number of light-skinned black performers. The casinos' musical stages were well funded since the casinos had a steady stream of investors who came to gamble. They were also the most international of the forums, appealing and accessible to international and national tourists and the wealthy Cariocas. The casinos also featured international acts from Latin America, Europe, and the United States. Musical numbers in the casinos differed significantly from the *teatro de revista*, a genre that appealed more exclusively to a Carioca or national taste and often offered commentary on local events and personalities or the samba schools that organized around the carnival season. Glamour and glitter were important in a city with a social hierarchy marked by race and class differences, and the casinos provided both. This meant that the performers in casinos were mostly white until the late 1940s.

Among the most important casinos were the Cassino da Urca and the Copacabana in the Zona Sul, Icaraí in Niteroi, and Quitandinha in Petrópolis. Traditionally, they excluded *sambistas* and performers from the lower classes who could not fit in. This changed in 1939, largely through Sílvio Caldas, who had become one of the elite of the performing world and who protested against the policies that barred black performers from performing in casinos, particularly during the Sunday gala performances.[51]

Of all the casinos, the Cassino da Urca was undoubtedly the casino most frequented by international visitors. Situated in the then posh seaside neighborhood of Urca, the casino abutted Guanabara Bay in a post-card setting that has made it into many international films. Today, Urca, whose name comes from the company that initiated the development of the neighborhood, is known for its safety because of the military compound near Red Beach (Praia Vermelha) and as the primary tourist attraction because of Sugarloaf, which affords visitors an impressive view of the city. The old casino, which has long since disappeared, had in 1933 replaced the Hotel Balneário, built one year earlier, and became a hub of South American international musical scene.[52]

In its heyday, the Cassino da Urca hosted the Miranda sisters, as well as national and international stars such as Josephine Baker Lucian Boyer and Mistinguette. Linda and Dricinha Batista performed at the Urca in the 1940s and would be followed by others, including Marlene, Angela Maria, and a host of crooners and big band leaders. Comedians such as Grande Othelo, one of the few black Brazilian performers, and the white humorist Manuel Pêra, who could be typically Brazilian and appeal to international audiences, joined them, allowing for the representation of local humor. Although few black singers secured contracts to perform in the casinos, Afro-Brazilian-based and -inspired rhythms and icons were staples in the nightly performances.[53]

In the early 1940s, a string of American and Mexican performers also made appearances in Rio's casinos. Of the Mexicans, Tito Guizar is worthy of special mention since he would later perform in the 1940s Hollywood musical *Brazil* with Aurora Miranda, featuring the music of Ary Barroso. But there were others as well. In 1941 alone, Pedro Vargas, José Mojico, Augustín Lara, and Toña La Negra (Black Toña), who helped popularize boleros such as "Cielito lindo," "Maria bonita," "Vereda tropical," would perform at the casino. The casino also saw its share of performers from Argentina and the United States: Martha Eggert and Bing Crosby were only two of them.[54]

Casino owner Joaquim Rolla converted the Cassino da Urca into a magical world for musicians, and the neighborhood of Urca soon became a place of residence and a haven for singers, musicians, dancers, and others connected to the casino. According to producer and entertainer Carlos Machado, the Urca was one of the few establishments that contracted its workers for a fixed period of time, giving some artists an unprecedented level of stability, although contracts were often exclusive. The Urca also represented a level of glamour often outside of the reach of the average Carioca, yet it was the center of the social scene, bringing together interpreters and performers from the favela to the global. Still, the owners and directors of the casino were preoccupied with projecting a bourgeois image of sophistication and modern style.[55]

Rolla's publicity department was one of the savviest, and advertisements for his properties appeared in newspapers and magazines in a versatile public relations campaign. Thus, when Rolla announced the opening of the new seven-floor Icaraí Hotel and Casino (now home to the Federal University) in Niteroi in 1939, the entire nation knew. Apartments, hotel rooms, and suites occupied the top seven floors. The ground floor housed a restaurant, a cinema house, a grille room, a dance floor, a stage, and a section for gambling. The interior designers had covered the ground floor with artificial gardens and lakes. Rolla, a white *mineiro* who originally invested in the construction business, was destined to become one of the most important names in the casino industry in southern Brazil. A man of little formal education, Rolla relied on gambling for income, but he was no gambler. His major interest was in the music, the orchestras, and the shows of the house. This interest allowed him to mix with the clientele and the artists and to rub elbows with foreign visitors, politicians, and performers from all over the world.

By the mid 1940s, Rolla had built an empire using the formula of tourism, gambling, and musical shows. In addition to acquiring the Casino Hotel in Niteroi, the Quintandinha Hotel Casino, and several other resorts in the Rio-Minas axis, he was also responsible for transporting artists and clients from one establishment to another. The history of Rolla's empire mirrors that of most empires that become too big, and the construction of the Quintandinha was emblematic of this. The casino was located outside of the center of Urca and Copacabana's bustling nightlife, yet protected within the beautiful mountains of Petrópolis in Rio de Janeiro's imperial city named after Emperor Pedro I. The construction, which began in 1941, took three years to complete.[56]

The casino's inauguration was a major event and featured some of the greatest musicians of Rio de Janeiro, among them Grande Othelo, Príncipe Maluco, and Ray Ventura and his orchestra. The fun did not last, however. On April 30, 1946, the Brazilian government of General Eurico Dutra, Vargas's former war minister, closed all casinos, "considering [them] contrary to the moral, juridical and religious tradition of the Brazilian people." This move would negatively impact the country's cultural and social traditions, not to mention the job rate among a significant portion of the musicians and performers, including singers, dancers, actors, and comedians. The casinos closed, but theoretically the bars, cafés, and shows could continue. Yet it was clear what drew the clientele to these musical venues and how they were funded. Smaller and less exclusive cafés and bars continued to thrive for decades, but the era of the grand casino revues had ended.[57]

Even though the owners of the casinos were connected to the Vargas government, for months prior to the closure critics of the casinos had been condemning the gambling and the crime and moral decadence that they claimed the casinos brought to Rio. Even though the decree had only abolished gambling and not the shows, because the funding was cut it might just as well have abolished musical entertainment as well. Many musicians found employment in other forums. Others left Brazil altogether. By the end of the World War II, Brazil had transformed into a more urban, internationally significant nation. The Vargas regime's transformation from a dictatorship into a democracy signaled a new spirit of the times in 1945.

Conclusion

When Vargas stepped down as president in 1945, the cultural symbols of his generation were already in decline, a foreshadowing of what was to come. The casinos had been abolished, the *teatro de revistas* would go into decline, and the samba schools had been transformed and became a part of the city's official carnival program. Another decade would pass before the transition would be complete. The Vargas generation had witnessed the development of the radio, record, and cinema industries, which meant that popular music found vehicles that would extend its life.

Although Vargas had helped to institutionalize a new way of thinking about Brazilianness and had provided the political goodwill without which the diverse musical forums would not have emerged, these forums were racially and socially codified. Black musicians largely performed in "black spheres of performance," along with some whites. On the other hand, white performers, along with some nonwhites, occupied "white or middle-class spheres," which usually meant more opportunities for social and economic gain. Although these spheres were racially coded in pre–World War II Brazilian society, it is important to reiterate that some blacks did perform in spheres that were known as "white," and many poor whites performed in forums considered "black." Despite the unequal economic power of the social spheres, performers across forums often worked with one another, although it is not true, as Lisa Shaw reports, that "samba was defined by the socio-economic rather than the racial backgrounds of its creators."[58]

By the 1930s, Rio had become the undisputed center of Brazil's popular music industry. Under Vargas's cultural patriotism, Brazilians forged a sense of nationhood in which popular culture in general and popular music in particular took center stage. Blackness and Afro-Brazilians played a fundamental role in the construction of the musical forums around the city, although blacks were better represented in the local forums with fewer economic opportunities. As technologies developed and Brazilian popular music became more global, Africaneity would continue to play a central role, and the place of Afro-Brazilians remained paradoxical.

CHAPTER THREE

Race, Class, and Technology in the Promotion of the Popular Brazilian Sound

> Mass forms of music now exist, less because a large number
> of recipients have the same musical needs than because
> these needs become similar, transcending all ethnic, national
> and social barriers, since the individual here can be a recipi-
> ent of music only in association with others.
>
> ———————————— Peter Wicke, "Rock Music: A Musical Aesthetic Study"

Under Getúlio Vargas's patriotism, many Afro-Brazilian performers did not always articulate or see their social position in society through the lens of race or class. On the one hand, a snapshot of life in the 1930s—in almost any café or bar in Lapa or the center of the city—could have served Gilberto Freyre well. The ease with which black, white, and *mestiço* Brazilians intermingled, or at least congregated in the same place, illustrated a harmony and social energy difficult to find in the United States, for example. On the other hand race and class played significant roles in the way musical forums emerged, and they played determining roles in shaping how Brazilian popular music would be performed in the media.

By the 1930s, technology had made it possible for Brazilians to consume and experience popular music en masse. While blackness remained central to Brazilian popular music performances, as in the case of the casinos, commercial interests would play an important role in determining who would perform. The consuming masses, which were largely Afro-Brazilian, were also important actors. Pervading social mores and a general sense of what Lucia Lippi Oliveira has described as Brazil's inherited inferiority complex nonetheless meant that white performers would be more likely to perform and represent Brazil in the two major media: the radio and the cinema.[1] The historical relationship between mass audiences and performer in Brazil begs for more nuanced conclusions, however.

This chapter argues that while radio and cinema privileged white performers over black performers in general, both technologies continued to celebrate and propagate blackness and Afro-Brazilian rhythms. Moreover, while white performers were more likely than their Afro-Brazilian counterparts to reap economic benefits on the radio, the Brazilian radio consecrated a number of *mulato* performers as veritable icons. Black performers made their appearances, although they were significantly underrepresented as ambassadors of the Brazilian popular sound. The scenario within the audiovisual media of cinema further illustrates Brazil's anxiety over black representation. In Brazil's first major studio musicals, Afro-Brazilians are largely absent, although, again, Afro-Brazilian rhythms were not.

The intersection of race and class in the social history of the Brazilian media cannot be understood without further discussion of the idea of a provisional middle class and the complex ways in which Brazilians attained privilege. Nor can the wooing of the mass audiences and the acceptance of popular music as a national jewel be fully grasped without an understanding of the role of politics in the social history of Brazilian popular music.

Blackness and Cultural Politics

By the end of 1930, a new, more sophisticated samba style was in fashion, and Afro-Brazilian themes and language remained a part of it.

White and black performers had already mastered a diverse repertoire that included eclectic tunes such as the misogynist and audacious "Malandro," the transgressive racialized samba "Mulata," and the fox-trot "Eu quero uma mulher bem preta" (I want a very black woman), as well as more laudatory and civic-minded tunes such as "Rio chic" (Chic Rio) and "Meu Brasil" (My Brazil).[2] Already in the late 1920s, the *malandro*, the street trickster who was usually black or *mulato*, had become a presence in popular culture and in musical compositions, and Francisco Alves, a white performer with popular legitimacy and radio's top performer, was one of the first to sing about him. Ironically, during the Estado Novo's quest for order in the late 1930s, the *malandro* became a target of a moral campaign of the Vargas government, although as early as 1929 Alves had also begun to record music in which the *malandro* speaks about leaving his old lifestyle behind.[3] The Vargas program against chaos and the propensity toward order necessitated a strong stand against *malandragem* and a vilification of the *malandro*, almost always with racial, if not class, overtones. Criticism of the *malandro* was a way to encourage work and physical exercise in an age when technical manpower and health were seen as keys to modernity.[4]

Popular musical compositions such as Ataulfo Alves and Felisberto Martins's "O negocio é casar" (Marriage is a must) are typical of this tendency,[5] as was "Eu trabalhei" (I worked) by Roberto Roberti and Jorge Faraj, which celebrated work through a worker's voice that exclaimed, "I worked with pride!"[6] Vargas, the leader of the 1930 nationalist revolution, was often referred to as "the greatest worker."[7] Songs such as the 1935 *marcha* "Mulatinho bamba" (Smart little mulatto) emphasized the "good *mulato*" as opposed to the *malandro* and these tunes were heard on the radio daily.[8] At the same time, state officials, intellectuals, and radio singers continued to appropriate the vocabulary of the *malandro*. Vargas's own images as president, often in a suit and wearing a Panama hat, were adaptations of the *malandro*—a Brazilian character who was ambitious, self-reliant, and independent, and who knew how to get by.[9]

A close analysis of the *malandro*'s habits, styles, and preoccupations in songs such as Wilson Batista's "Lenço no pescoço" (Handkerchief in the pocket) and Noel Rosas's "Conversa de botequim" (Bar talk) reveals the *malandro*'s discourse is one of self-preservation, similar to the idea of "*dar um jeito*" (find a way to get by), which is considered by many to be a national Brazilian trait, and thus resonates with Brazilians across classes. The *malandro* is an actor with a mask; he dresses impeccably like the members of the bourgeois class, but he often lives in misery, and relies on others since he cannot afford a cup of coffee or a newspaper.[10]

Controversial songs, whether in support of or against the *malandro*, then as now, attract attention in the media. As late at 1935, for example, Almeida Azevedo, a journalist from *A voz do radio*, called for the censoring and sanitizing of sambas so that they could fill people with pride. She blamed the radio stations for not cultivating good taste and in the same breath praised singers such as Maria Calú who "although inspired by barbaric African music was able to come up with melodic music full of expression."[11] In light of this prejudice, it is no surprise that white Brazilian performers would eventually be consecrated as the kings and queens of popular music on the radio. White performers were most likely to be closely associated with the new governing class, for instance. The Vargas government, and particularly first Lady Darcy Vargas, played a key role in promoting the importance of Brazilian popular music. Although most of the musicians with whom she associated were white, in highlighting the contributions of popular music, she also celebrated the Afro-diasporic influences on Brazil.

First Lady Darcy and the Radio Stars

The year 1939 ranks as an important watershed in Western history. In August, Nazi Germany and the Soviet Union signed a nonaggression pact, paving the way for Germany's invasion of Poland nine days later. But there is no law that says that human disaster need affect celebration and merriment, and 1939 was a watershed in the history of Brazilian popular music. On July 28, Darcy Vargas would organize one of the most important musical events that demonstrated how far popular music had developed.[12]

The event was held at the Municipal Theater, the sacred space for "serious" theater, where foreign and national companies performed classical concerts, opera, and ballet. In May 1945, the Teatro Experimental do Negro (TEN), led by Abdias do Nascimento, was the first black group to appear on stage there. Like most black performers, popular musicians had been unofficially barred from those spaces. All of this changed because of a show organized by the first Lady of the republic to benefit the poor children of Rio. Although U.S. cultural influences had already begun to take root in the radio big bands and in the technology used for recording, the French cultural presence remained prominent, and Paris continued to serve as an urban cultural reference. This was seen in the title of the show, *Joujoux and balangandás*, the French word for jewels and the colloquial Brazilian word for jewelry, respectively. The first Lady hoped to show off the metaphorical gems of Brazilian popular music, and she was going to utilize the radio stars to do so.[13]

Although proceeds for the show, billed as a celebration of popular music, would benefit charity, this was a spectacle for high society and illustrated how far popular music had come. The popular musicians would be selectively represented, and both race and class would be considerations. Artistic director Alexandre Azevedo enlisted the talents of orchestra leader Radamés Gnatelli, classically trained but equally at home in popular music and an important musical director of the recently inaugurated Sociedade Civil Brasileira Rádio Nacional, known simply as Rádio Nacional. Gnatelli called upon three of the most important popular composers of the time: Lamartine Babo, João de Barro, and Ary Barroso. Mário Reis, one of the few upper-class men who became a performer of the people's music, was also crucial, however. He would be the principal act of the evening, singing with his virtually unknown partner the theme song "Jouxjoux and balangandás," composed by his friend Lamartine Babo. As this occasion marked Reis's return to the stage, Babo also composed "Voltei a cantar" (I returned to sing), a song that would mark Reis's reentry into the world of popular music.[14]

Reis could not have been the only star at such an important event, however. Carmen Miranda and the Bando da Lua would surely have been invited, but they were literally singing and dancing to another beat in the United States with the blessing of the Vargas household. Francisco Alves, still at the top of his career, was not on the program, nor was Aurora Miranda, even though she had performed at the exposition held by the Vargas government in January 1939. That same year, both sisters appeared in *Banana da terra*, when Carmen had introduced the *mulato* Dorival Caymmi's "O que é que a Bahiana tem."[15] Given the buzz that Caymmi had created, it was important that he perform. After all, part of the show's title had been borrowed from one of his compositions. He belonged there although he had no connections to the network of composers and performers from Catete, the middle-class Zona Norte, or the Zona Sul. He was not a Carioca, nor was he white. He appeared dressed in his black suit and black bow tie and tried to re-create the gestures that Carmen Miranda had immortalized in *Banana da terra*, some of which he had probably taught her. His presence was an exception, but as his granddaughter Stella confirmed, his participation opened the doors of high society to him. The show was repeated three more times that winter, once two days later on July 30 and then again on August 11 and 16.[16] The show had been a resounding success and had cemented popular music's arrival, initiating a new phase of radio, a technology that had begun to transform Brazil two decades earlier.

The Emergence of Radio and the Provisional Middle Class

To characterize the growth of radio in Brazil only as a technology misses its most important social and cohesive dimension as a new national forum of political, cultural, and economic exchange that would transform and become a reference for Brazilians across the country. As Bryan McCann perceptively reports in his *Hello, Hello Brazil: Popular Music in the Making of Modern Brazil*, "radio came to Rio de Janeiro before Christ," referring to the Christ statue at Corcovado that would later become a symbol of the city and nation.[17]

TABLE 2. Radio Stations in the Federal District, 1939

STATION	YEAR FOUNDED	OWNERSHIP
Serviço de Radio-Difusão Educativa (MESP)	1923	English
Rádio Clube do Brasil	1924	Brazilian
Rádio Sociedade Mayrink Veiga	1926	Dutch
Rádio Educadora do Brasil	1927	Brazilian
Rádio Sociedade Guanabara	1933	Brazilian
Rádio Cruzeiro	1934	Brazilian
Rádio Difusora do Distrito Federal	1934	American
Rádio Jornal do Brasil	1934	English
Rádio Tupí	1935	English
Rádio Ipanema	1935	Brazilian
Rádio Transmissora Brasileira	1936	American
Rádio Vera Cruz	1937	Brazilian
Rádio Nacional	1936	Dutch

Source: IBGE, Anuário Estatístico do Brasil (Rio de Janeiro: IBGE, 1939/1940), 1121.

National cohesion aside, as radio developed, it relied on foreign capital to market its products to the growing urban masses. The first radios emerged in the early 1920s, and by 1937 there were a total of 1,489 registered stations in Brazil, with 13 in the federal district and 10 in the city of São Paulo. The intellectuals of the 1920s modernist movement who spoke of Brazil's ability to consume and assimilate foreign customs could easily have pointed to the radio to indicate how Brazilians took foreign capital to create cultural products that were uniquely Brazilian and appealed to the masses.

Not only was Rio the capital of Brazil, it was clearly the capital of radio. The city became the center of social and cultural exchange and a crossroads of internal, regional, national, and international migrations. Diverse performers descended around the Bahia de Guanabara and its outskirts. Technological advances after World War I had changed the cultural scope in a country that was largely illiterate and stratified by race and class. While the 1940 census indicated that at the end of the 1930s less than 6 percent of the Brazilian homes had radios, that figure jumped to almost 47 percent in the state of Rio de Janeiro, and 63 percent in urban areas in the state. The new device created, demarked, and, in some cases, destroyed social spaces and forums.[18]

Although nonwhite populations made up the majority of the masses, the small white middle and upper middle classes were the major owners of the new apparatus. This did not mean that blacks did not consume radio programs, only that fewer Afro-Brazilians owned radios. Afro-Brazilian language and rhythms, icons as we have seen, formed the foundation of Brazilin popular music that would slowly take over the Brazilian radio airwaves. Yet the new technological spaces made little room for black representation at the highest level. As the radio and recording industries elected their icons, few Afro-Brazilians were among them, and most of them were *mulatos*. Ironically, many whites would also face prejudice for performing what many considered black music.

In 1923, the Carioca intellectual and university professor Edgard Roquette Pinto had the foresight to establish the Rádio Sociedade do Rio de Janeiro's headquarters in the Brazilian Academy of Sciences. Brazilians such as Pinto would not necessarily have been pleased with the explosion of popular music on the radio because, as late as the early 1930s, many middle- and upper-class listeners continued to look down on popular music. Moreover, Pinto had envisioned the radio as an edifying, educational technology. Inventions are curious phenomena: once created, their destiny is separate from their creators, as the great scientist Albert Einstein would later lament. Pinto had not invented the technology, however. Nor was the modern radio a Brazilian technology, despite Father Roberto Landell de Moura's registered patent in the 1890s. While music was linked to radio from its inception, in the beginning the preferred genre was not popular music. Official radio broadcasting began in Brazil on September 7, 1922, with the inaugural address of President Epitácio Pessoa at the International Exposition of Rio de Janeiro. On that occasion, operas were transmitted from the Municipal Theater and the Teatro Lírico through loudspeakers at the exposition, in Niteroi, Petrópolis, and São Paulo, in addition to the personal receptors given to various dignitaries present at the exposition sites.[19]

Opera and so-called erudite music soon gave way to the taste of the masses, although in many cases the same musicians were employed, having been lured by the cultural and economic promise that the rise in prestige and acceptance of popular music entailed. Ademar Casé's program at Radio Philips registered that change. The Casé program, which began in February 1932 as a four-hour show on Sunday afternoon with two hours of popular music followed by two hours of concert music, quickly became a popular music program that lasted until midnight, with supplemental programs on Tuesday and Thursday evenings. Good national art alone does not spur mass consumption, particularly in a postcolonial society accustomed to looking to Europe for its cues. Four other forces were at work, all coming about after the Week of Modern Art in 1922, to encourage Brazilians to look inward: affordable radios, publicity, leisure, and the growing discretionary income among the working and middle classes.[20]

Despite the varying use of radio, including for education and information, by 1939 the transmission of music and musical programs constituted the bulk of radio programs broadcast live. Even so, Brazilian radio could not have survived without the record industry. Records accounted for the vast majority of transmissions throughout the country, particularly at small radio stations that did not have the budget to contract live orchestras or performers. Record companies were indispensable even for those who could. At the same time, recording studios made ample use of the radio to promote their new releases and very often to entice listeners to buy record players. For a few performers, such as Carmen Miranda, Francisco Alves, Mário Reis, and others, exclusive radio contracts were often forthcoming with exclusive recording contracts, followed by shows and excursions around the country and abroad.

Although radios first served exclusively educational purposes, their entertainment value soon became clear. The 1932 law that sanctioned advertisements on the air was a watershed in the history of the medium's growth. In Rio, Dutch-founded Rádio Mayrink Veiga became the major force in the 1930s, before the appearance of Radio Cruzeiro in 1934 and Radio Tupi in 1935. Rádio Nacional, the station that was modeled after networks in the United States and that would set the tone for mass communication until the arrival of television to Brazil in the 1950s, was also created in 1935.

Records had emerged in Brazil as early as 1902. The first popular recording artists were instrumentalists such as Manuel Pedro dos Santos, or Baiano, who recorded his *lundu* and Afro-Brazilian precursor to the samba, "Isto é bom" (Zon-O-Phone), at Casa Edison in 1902. Still, pursuing a musical career was as inconceivable for the middle class of the Zona Sul as it was for the members of the working class who were employed as manual laborers and played music for leisure. Musicians often performed for a recording, but they only received a one-time flat fee with no rights to future revenues. When Amadeu Silva signed the typed receipt that read, "I received 30 *mil reis* from Fred Figner for exclusive and irrevocable rights to record and distribute his compositions world wide," for example, there was no doubt as to the relationship between the hired worker and the recording company.[21]

Baiano, Manoel Evêncio da Costa Moreira (better known as Cadete), Nozinho, Mário Pinheiro, and Eduardo das Neves constituted the first group of instrumentalists who worked for Figner at Casa Edison. A few years later, Baiano recorded melodies without lyrics, a style that developed as much due to technological limitations as to aesthetic taste. But Baiano would also record the first samba, "Pelo telefone." Thus, singing on records emerged with force thanks to the new, subtler electromagnetic system of sound recording, and later on with the invention of the microphone.[22] Like Sinhô, none of these men would have described themselves as black, although they knew and were often associated with Afro-Brazilian musical forms, and inhabited the shared diverse Afro-Brazilian musical venues from the circus to the theater to the multiple spaces around "Little Africa" and downtown Rio.

The development of radio from the 1920s through the 1930s meant an expansion in opportunities for musicians from diverse backgrounds who would be called upon to forge community ties beyond the immediate local boundaries. Three simple words, "*Alô alô Brasil*," would begin the process, as a radio speaker addressed audiences who could be sitting in front of him or her or listening to the radio miles away. Audiences witnessed the performers, singers, presenters, and humorists inventing a Brazilian mass-media tradition. Radio station owners and program producers would gradually utilize elements from the theatrical revue, employ local humorists, and utilize the talents of local musicians and singers while relying on the internationally based recording industry.[23] Parlophone, Victor, Odeon, Brunswick, Columbia, and Gramophone (the last two joined in 1931 to became Electric and Musical Industry [EMI] of London) produced records for a culturally hungry urban population. Odeon, Parlophone, and Columbia had by that time won a large share of the Brazilian market.[24]

Both radio and recordings recognized the influence of African rhythms on Brazilian popular music, and that influence was heard in the programs that multiplied on radio station after radio station. Of the 12,586 registered radio musical programs at the end of the 1930s, 8,513 were dedicated to popular music, 1,036 were vocal concerts, and 2,093 were operas or chamber music performances. Ironically, while the vocal performers changed in each category, Brazilian musicians had become so versatile that many instrumentalists performed in all three genres, defying observers who insisted on concrete demarcations between popular music and the so-called erudite music.[25]

Rádio Mayrink Veiga had been the undisputed producer and promoter of Brazilian popular music in the 1930s, and it offered white singers such as Francisco Alves lucrative contacts over the years. With a voice that could not have been overlooked, Alves sang all the genres of the day, whether they were national or foreign: sambas, *marchas*, *toadas*, *canções*, *valsas*, *hinos*, fox-trots, tangos, and many others. César Ladeira, the then artistic announcer for Rádio Mayrink Veiga, had baptized Alves with the title "the King of the Voice" for his versatility and unmistakable vocal timbre.[26]

In the more prestigious radio stations, performers, musicians, and later actors broadcasted in auditoriums carefully constructed to please a live audience sitting a few feet away from the stage and a radio audience throughout the state and sometimes in other parts of the country. Going to the radio auditorium was akin to going to the theater, except there was much more fanfare in the radio auditorium. In addition to the performers and crew, radio stations employed announcers, commentators, and animators who would encourage the audience to clap and who in São Paulo were called "*macacas de auditório*" (auditorium monkeys).[27]

Throughout the 1930s, the social environment of the radio stations and the publicity industry around it became the focus of Carioca gossip. An entire industry emerged, complete with advertisers, photographers who published intimate portraits, and in-depth interviews in a host of publications from the dailies to the more elaborate vanity magazines. Radio stars were created, and fan clubs emerged in a frenzied environment that forged national tastes and aesthetics. Radio, more than any other medium, was responsible for creating what Anderson has called an "imagined community," which was in theory neither black nor white nor *mulato* but which in practice reflected the ideals of a modernist generation, a new reality that showed the intermingling of the popular and erudite.

Rio's network of radio stations attracted and relied on talented instrumentalists and Afro-Brazilian pioneers. Pixinguinha, one of the most talented and admired musicians of the era, was the orchestra leader at a number of radio stations, including Rádio Mayrink Viega and Rádio Nacional, but as his biographer, Sérgio Cabral, affirms, Pixinguinha was never good with money. He was so popular that a *cachaça* was named after him, although he never gained a penny for it. But talent alone was not enough. As elsewhere, to make money one had to be well connected and prepared to navigate the system to one's advantage.[28]

Newcomers from other cities to Rio, like migrants everywhere, had an additional and immediate motivation. Away from home, talent and drive urged them on, particularly those who could offer something that the local market desired. This was the case with Dorival Caymmi, who, like many Bahians, moved to Rio with zeal and the hope for opportunity. Though migrants landed in Rio from all over the country, Bahia occupied a special place in the city's musical imagination. Despite his initial difficulties and the separation from his family, Caymmi embraced Rio's people and its musical scene. Contacts in the music business secured him an appearance on Lamartine Babo's program Clube das Fantasmas (The Phantom's Club), which went on the air at Rádio Nacional at midnight. In his initial radio appearance, he sang the first of his *músicas praieras* (beach music), "Noite de temporal" (Stormy night), about a fisherman who does not go out to sea.[29]

Caymmi performed at a number of radio stations, including Rádio Tupi and Rádio Transmissora, where he would make 200 *mil-reis* a week, a handsome sum for the time.[30] Musicians were slowly becoming professionalized thanks in no small part to the pioneering Casé program that began on February 14, 1932, on Radio Phillips. It was the first radio variety show that practically took up the entire afternoon. Rádio Mayrink Veiga had ushered Brazilian popular music into its "Golden Age," but the creation of Rádio Nacional transformed the industry and took it to its peak—until the invention of television. Founded in 1936, Rádio Nacional had became a leading force by 1938, a position it held until the early 1960s when the military government replaced talented musicians and producers at the station with their cronies.[31]

Indeed, the 1936 inauguration of Rádio Nacional would change the radio scene in Rio forever. The Rádio Nacional studio was a technological wonder, and it came to represent the best of Brazilian radio, particularly in the 1940s and 1950s. Rádio Nacional, which belonged to a media conglomerate that owned a number of important publications, including the newspaper *A Noite* and the magazines *Carioca*, *A Noite Ilustrada*, and *Vamos Ler*, took the live radio audience to another level. Today the radio station is housed in an unimpressive building at the end of Avenida Rio Branco, opposite the marine compound, near Praça Mauá, recognized in 2003 as a national monument by President Luis Ignacio "Lula" da Silva. A glass curtain isolated the musicians and orchestra behind the stage, while singers performed in front of a filled auditorium as programs were broadcast live.[32]

Rádio Nacional's success did not come without its costs. Its standardization and sophisticated symphonic sound, modeled after orchestras in the United States, practically put an end to improvisation and experimentation with Brazilian percussion instruments by the late 1940s. Henrique Foréis Domingues (Almirante), leader of the Bando de Tangarás, had been a pioneer and innovator in the 1930s. With the help of more sophisticated technology, the band introduced a new percussion sound on records by including original Brazilian instruments.[33] Rádio Nacional's orchestras substituted the percussion instruments for metal instruments. The new technology helped produced a clear and more precise sound but one that did not differ from the orchestral sounds of New York or London. Rádio Nacional's orchestras also adopted the U.S. American big band sound, thus mandating a given number of saxophones, clarinets, and trombones. In reality, this style during and after World War II was an example of U.S. cultural imperialism at work and affected countries throughout the Western Hemisphere.[34]

The majority of radio's popular music programs in the late 1930s and 1940s had evolved into guaranteed successes, and not only because of the extraordinary talent. Studio audiences were sympathetic because the seats were full of passionate fans who had taken the time to clip out their invitations from fan magazines or newspapers. Audiences also included invited guests, politicians and their spouses, and relatives and friends of those appearing on the radio. It was, as Cariocas say, "*todo de galo*," with a dress code that made sure that everyone was well dressed and on his or her best behavior. Soon, the live performance seemed like a gala at the Municipal Theater in Rio or at the Met in New York City. People were dressed to the hilt, and in the winter months it was common to see women in their fur jackets and fur hats and men in double-breasted suits or tuxedos. White performers like Alves mirrored or perhaps set the aesthetic standard for singers as well as musicians.

Performers were a reflection of their audiences, and all prepared for a ritual in which each one created images of what the other wanted. Those who could not afford the proper attire simply borrowed or rented items for these occasions. Even Dorival Caymmi, who had come to Rio from Bahia in the late 1930s, had to borrow a suit from his friend Paulo

Tapajós to be able to perform. Caymmi aside, such social codes kept the audiences and the performers middle class and decidedly white—or at least apparently middle class and white looking. To call this discrimination tells only part of the story in a country where class and racial barriers can often be traversed by acquiring appropriate signifiers, including specific modes of behavior and dress that tried to maintain the provisional white middle-class aesthetic and mores.[35] The provisional aspect has to be emphasized, as this was performative, whether one was a spectator or a performer. Moreover, the "magic" of radio forged a sense of national community across color, class, and region.

With reason, radio programs would begin with an announcement from the master of ceremonies, known by the English word "speaker," usually directed at the audience listening at home or in some private establishment. From the beginning to the end of a program, the aim was to maintain the audience in a constant state of excitement— connected to the performance through music, orchestras, comedy numbers, and in-house animators.[36]

The emotional excitement of the radio programs shed no light on the social and economic dynamics being played out. In his study of radio programs in São Paulo in the 1940s, João Batista Borges Pereira demonstrated the exclusion of Afro-Brazilians from the highest levels of radio production, including from the administration and the coveted role of speakers. Rio's dynamics were similar. On the other hand, blacks and *mulatos* were well represented both in the radio audiences and in the amateur programs where performers sang for little or no remuneration.[37] Nonetheless, the auditory nature of radio meant that Brazilians largely visualized connections of an imagined community—although images, particularly photographs in the vanity press, helped consumers to construct images of their icons.

Radio Wooing the Nation: Black into White

Population growth, industrialization, and foreign investment were on the rise, and Brazil was expanding economically. Ademar Casé, a white Brazilian, was also blessed with good timing. The month after his program went on the air, the Vargas government approved the use of commercial advertisements in the radio industry. In addition to music announcer, Casé became a successful publicist, attracting ads from a host of businesses, which in turn allowed him to attract greater talent and hence a larger part of the growing listener market. He brought together talent from all over the country, baptizing them with names that essentialized their personalities. At the same time, like any industry, there were social codes and rules that kept poor people and the majority of Afro-Brazilians at bay.[38]

Whiteness was not necessarily a prerequisite for national popularity, however. Many black singers, dancers, and comics performed live on Brazilian stages for radio with white stars. The list of black instrumentalists was long, although as in national broadcasting in the United States, black musicians were often sponsored by white performers. What African American entertainer Sammy Davis said of early black performers on the radio in the United States might also apply to Brazil: "We could not do it ourselves because we were outside of the system. It's always someone inside the system that has to say, 'Let's open it, let's let them in.'" North American segregation institutionalized these practices so much so that whites not only put on black masks by performing in blackface but also by imitating black speech and dance and co-opting a host of musical styles from jazz to the blues. In many cases, co-opting, as I have discussed, was not the appropriate description for artists who claimed Afro-Brazilian customs as their own.[39]

Brazil's social pattern of race relations and "fronting," which privileged white performers in the entertainment world in a less aggressive manner but was present nonetheless, intertwined with notions of class and patriotism. White performers such as Carmen Miranda, Francisco Alves, and Mário Reis did not necessarily believe that they were performing black idioms that were separate from their own cultural experience. At best, they saw themselves as celebrating and promoting Brazilian culture. At worst, they were shocking bourgeois society by performing lower-class cultural practices. Both Carmen Miranda and

Almirante actually performed in blackface on stage. They were excellent performers according to most accounts, and Brazilians loved Miranda especially. The popularity of her "black performances" in Brazil is reminiscent of the "black performances" of white U.S. actors on the 1930s radio soap opera *Amos 'n' Andy*, except neither of the U.S. actors grew up being so intimately influenced by Afro-diasporic traditions.

While blackface was common in the United States and was specifically related to segregationist policies codified in law, in Brazil the practice of blackface was neither widely used nor widely accepted. Passing as black in performances in Brazil was much more complex. Brazilian white performers passed as blacks by assuming the black voice without blackface. In so doing, black idioms became Brazilian. In an overwhelming number of recordings and radio performances, white interpreters assumed the black voice. Carmen Miranda does this explicitly in "Boneca de pixe" (Tar baby, 1938) and "O que é que a Bahiana tem" (What the Bahiana has, 1939). In her performances of the latter in Brazil and abroad, Miranda transformed the dress and headdress that the mostly black working-class Bahian women wore into a bright and colorful gentrified costume for the stage. Despite the outer appearances of gentrification, Miranda's performance did not cease to be genuine—her live and radio audiences recognized that. Her charm and movements, particularly the use of her head, hands, and hips, indicated that her body had been shaped by Afro-diasporic customs. The very possibility that white Brazilians like Miranda could represent and claim blackness in an authentic manner signals a distinct Brazilian mode of thinking of and perceiving of blackness from that in the United States.

A host of male performers from diverse backgrounds also assumed the voice of the black *bamba*, the *malandro*, or a host of other characters that Carioca audiences would have recognized. In addition to Almirante's performances with Miranda, songs such as "Vadiagem" (Bumming around, 1929) and "Meu burracão" (literally, My hole-in-the-wall, but referring to a house in the favelas, 1933), which hail the pleasures of the bohemian lifestyle and life in the favela, were two poignant examples. The Brazilian concept of racial co-optation by performers is complicated by the presence of many *mulato* or *mestiço* performers such as Orlando Silva and Sílvio Caldas, who followed similar practices in their live and radio performances, and thus merit further attention.

Neither Black nor White: Blackness and the *Mulato* Singers

Mulato performers were no strangers to the radio stations of Rio de Janeiro, and were readily welcomed, sometimes as honorary whites. This was particularly true of light-skinned *mulatos* such as Sílvio Narciso de Figueredo Caldas and Orlando Silva. Self-proclaimed *mulatas* such as Aracy Cortes and Araci de Almeida encountered more resistance, although this had as much to do with their own attitude and their refusal to give into the dominant gender expectations in the public domain, as we will see in chapter 5.

Caldas, on the other hand, became an important player on the musical scene, although to call him a rival of white performers such as Francisco Alves or Mário Reis is to downplay the camaraderie and competitive innovation of the era. Handsome, charming, and Carioca, Caldas was born in the working-class neighborhood of São Cristóvão, behind the Quinta da Boa Vista residence and abutting the neighborhood of Engenho Novo. He was a smooth crooner, what Brazilians called a *seresteiro*, who seduced the popular masses but also conquered those from the upper class. He, too, complicated the distinctions between "high" and "popular" culture, like a jazz musician or a Broadway singer.[40]

Caldas had worked as a mechanic and a taxi driver before he became a professional singer for Rádio Mayrink Veiga in 1927. He loved singing as a child, and like many of his peers, he sang for the radio without remuneration. His first radio contract came in 1929 from Rádio Sociedade, and recording contracts soon followed, first with Brunswick, then with Victor. Caldas might have been as well known as Alves had he the forceful personality and drive, and had he been white, although race, in his case, was only one contributing factor. A light-skinned *mulato* or *mestiço*, the same term that Sinhô preferred, Caldas was known as the "Caboclinho Querido" (Dear Caboclo), a title given to him by the speaker, Ademar Casé. He was also called "the Elegant Malandro," a title laden with class and racial connotations and just as euphemistic as the first. At times, he also used the name Mário Vieira to make money in other venues or to avoid technically breaking exclusive contracts. Caldas was also a composer—his fame as a pioneer of the "seresta" earned him his other popular title, "Brazil's serenader."[41]

Following in the footsteps of Caldas was another *mulato* singer, Orlando Silva, who would become so much more popular that he earned the moniker "the Singer for the Multitudes."[42] Born in 1915, Silva, who also came from a humble background, had to conquer many obstacles before he became a household name. His story, told in the 2004 musical directed by Antônio de Bonis, *Orlando Silva: O cantor das multidões*, represents one of the most fascinating stories of the musical world of Rio de Janeiro.[43]

Although popular artists in general were still viewed with a certain amount of disdain by the upper classes, this did not stop them from rubbing elbows with the political and cultural elite who appreciated their newly found wealth and power. Silva's popularity had become such a force to reckon with that President Vargas reportedly remarked to Silva that he envied his popularity—to which Silva responded, "But no one is more popular than you, president." Vargas retorted, "But no one is as popular as you are and doesn't have enemies."[44]

Silva's life, like that of many musicians, was intimately linked to the political events that occurred during the Vargas regime. In 1937, when Silva was wooing Brazilians with his first big hit, "Labios que beijei" (Lips that I kissed), Vargas was about to close Congress and establish his dictatorship. Five years earlier, Silva had worked giving change to riders on the municipal buses. He was a poor *mulato* teenager, slightly unkempt, who often wore his dingy bus uniform after work hours. When Silva performed, he was always impeccably dressed, as if he understood that projecting an image of sophistication was as important as his voice. Or perhaps he did it to distance himself from the dirty teenager on the bus?[45] The widespread success of nonwhite entertainers such as Silva and Caldas indicates that "blackness" was not necessarily a decisive barrier to success on the radio and the growing media outlets connected to it. Talent, success, and adherence to given aesthetics and behaviors all made entrance into the provisional white middle class easier. But one's status was never absolute or permanent, as Silva himself would later discover when he fell on hard times.

Of the female singers, two *mulata* radio performers deserve special mention: Araci de Almeida and Angela Maria, both of whom are discussed in detail in chapters 4 and 5. Aracy Cortes also made her mark on the radio, but as we have seen, her domain was clearly the popular theater. Of the two performers, Almeida came the closest to being a national radio icon in the early 1930s. Like her male counterparts, she was closely connected to the popular composers, although she reportedly composed a few tunes herself. Nicknamed "the Samba in Person" by the newspaper *A Modinha*, Almeida released her first record, "Em plena folia" (In the midst of the merriment), with Columbia in 1934, although it was her recording of "Palpite infeliz" (Unhappy beat) by the talented Noel Rosa that won her widespread praise two years later. According to her contemporary David Nasser, Almeida had a critical eye and was one of the few female performers who participated in the process of creating sambas.[46] Almeida, who was often voted "most popular singer" by radio fans, had made significant inroads into the world of radio, although she was not able to become a casino performer or an international ambassador.

It is equally as difficult to claim race as the only explanation of Almeida's status as it is to disentangle race relations and attitudes from her life and upbringing in the downtown neighborhoods of Rio de Janeiro. What is clear, however, is that the next big *mulata* radio star, Angela Maria, did not appear on the Brazilian airways until the late 1940s and early 1950s. By that time the demographics of radio performance had become much more multiracial, as had the audiences. Like many of the musicians, Maria came from humble beginnings and began working at an early age before entering the world of radio.

One of her first professional experiences was as a singer in the popular nightclub Dancing Avenida before being invited to sing at Rádio Mayrink Veiga.

In addition to the *mulato* performers, the list of black male singers and interpreters was not short. Along with the many pioneers mentioned in chapter 2, they included Ataulfo Alves de Souza, João Paulo Batista de Carvalho, Matheus Nunes (Cacovelho), Jamelão, Nelson Cavaquinho, Mário Ramos (popularly known as Vassourinha), Otávio Henrique de Oliveira (Blecuate), Francisco Ferraz Neto (Risadinha), and José Tobias de Santana, and duos such as the Dupla Verde e Amarelo, comprised of Erasmo Silva and Wilson Batista.

Afro-Brazilian performers in general nonetheless experienced a glass ceiling. Indeed, few performers had the opportunities and thus the impact on or rapport with Brazilian audiences as did white stars such as Carmen Miranda, Mário Reis, Francisco Alves, and Aurora Miranda, widely regarded as the four most important singers on radio in the 1930s. There were, however, exceptions. Afro-Brazilians such as João Paulo Batista de Carvalho, for example, carved out a place for himself by bridging the folkloric with the popular with his *pontos de umbanda.* Nelson Cavaquinho, who, like Cartola, sold his compositions cheaply to interpreters, began to perform as a soloist in the 1940s, although he would be associated with the samba school Mangueira. Not until the 1950s would he and many of the black singer-songwriters enter the mainstream media, now consecrated as the "Old Guard." By then, Cartola and his wife, Zica, had founded his bar, Zicartola, where many of the Old Guard were introduced to a new generation of intellectuals.[47]

At a concert in Leblon in 2003, Jamelão, the singer of choice for Porto Alegre composer Lupicínio Rodrigues in the 1940s and 1950s, revealed his thoughts about his position in the music world. It could easily extend to a host of black performers from the 1930s and 1940s who would only be recognized by the children and grandchildren of their contemporaries decades later: "I've seen a lot of bad times, and I've seen a lot of good times. People who did not want me to perform and people who wanted me to perform. They're all gone and I'm still here." Indeed, Jamelão, singing sambas in the new millennium, had survived most of his generation by some fifty years, and despite the early economic exclusion, he viewed the 1930s and 1940s radio era as critical to his career. Jamelão and other Afro-Brazilian performers could not be as positive about the early cinema.

National Cinema and National Icons

The arrival of musical cinema to Brazil would take away much of the masses' ability to construct their own image of the national community. Indeed, the silver screen would play no small role in catapulting the emerging white radio stars to the status of icons. Despite the early contributions of black producers and actors such as Benjamin de Oliveira during the silent film era, and the continued contributions of Afro-Brazilian pioneers to musical scores, blacks would be largely absent from the silver screen until the late 1940s.

Cinema, unlike its ancestor, the theater, is, as Walter Benjamin argues, an alienating technology, which removes the spectator one step farther away from the performer. At the same time, this distance augmented the perception of performers as stars and legends, which in turn created interest in the performers and ultimately forged an imaginary sense of intimacy. This process is central to Hollywood film production but also is symptomatic of film in countries like Brazil, although on a much smaller scale.[48] With an expanding urban population, however, cinema did not replace theater but supplemented it as a form of entertainment. Like the recording industry, its reliance on capital—in the case of Brazil, foreign capital—limited and indeed placed the control of those images in the hands of a small group of individuals. Brazilian cinema production from the turn of the century to the 1940s did not reflect the diversity of images, music, and dances that often surfaced in the rudimentary but eclectic theatrical productions in the *teatro de revista*, in the circus, and certainly in the samba schools. Working artists and performers, nonetheless, found small ways to use the new technology to their advantage.[49]

The imported film technology and the new movie houses in Rio quickly adapted to the Brazilian milieu. Outside of the cinema houses, vendors set up their makeshift carts to sell candies, sweets, and other snacks to the audience entering the movie houses. Upon entering, moviegoers passed through a lobby (as they do today) before entering the viewing room that would turn dark when the film began. During the silent film era, musicians were employed in both areas. Instrumentalists and the occasional performer were strategically placed in the lobby before the film began. More fortunate musicians would have a secure stable job in the orchestra playing the score that accompanied the film. Pixinguinha, who had broken racial barriers on numerous occasions, was one of the most versatile instrumentalists of his day, and was one of the lucky ones. The most famous musical performers, however, were singers like the Miranda sisters, Mário Reis, and Francisco Alves, who actually appeared on the silver screen.[50]

In 1918, Pixinguinha played a number of musical instruments with the Cinema Palais orchestra on Rio Branco and Rua Sete de Setembro. The owner, José Gustavo de Matos, like many shop and theater owners, temporarily closed down the establishment because of the Spanish flu, which had caused thousands of deaths in the city. After the scare had passed, Pixinguinha and others returned to the Palais, but this time to play in the lobby with the Oito Batutes, performing regularly throughout the 1920s, including the memorable two-week contract with the dance couple Greenlac and Drayton at the Odeon Theater.[51]

As we have seen, the Oito Batutas had four talented black players: Pixinguinha, Donga, China, and Nelson Alves, and their visibility, nationally and internationally, was unprecedented for popular musicians. The cinema proved hospitable to them and countless other musicians who filled the lounges and entrances with live music before the talkies would make the cinema less of a social affair. For many instrumentalists, the lobby represented another vibrant place for performance and experimentation. Some cinema houses also contained well-equipped stages that were used for concerts or musical presentations when films were not being shown.

At the same time, the cinema had helped make white performers such as Carmen Miranda and Mário Reis and other lesser-known performers larger than life. Artists who received top billing, such as Miranda, did not perform in cinema lobbies in Brazil, although she did perform on the stages of many cinema houses in and outside of Brazil. In Buenos Aires, Miranda performed for a month at the Cine Broadway in 1931. The following year, back in Brazil, she appeared at the Cine El Dorado, and in 1933 at the Cine Odeon.[52] As singers emerged as stars on the silver screen, many musicians would also be displaced from the lobbies and the orchestral pits where they accompanied the silent films. Some would move from the orchestra pits on to the screens as performers, usually accompanying singers, who would be the bigger stars. Before the early 1940s, few of these performers were Afro-Brazilian, however. While new technologies always replace workers, they also provide opportunities for others who can educate themselves and adapt to the new environment. Musicians are no exception. The new foreign talkies required dubbers and relied on studio musicians. More opportunities emerged when Brazil began to make its own talkies. As in the United States with *The Jazz Singer*, the first American talkie in 1927, Brazilians flocked to Brazil's first major musical in 1930, *Coisas nossas*.

Foreign imports still dominated the market, a phenomenon that has continued until the present day. At the same time, Brazilian productions throughout the 1930s were met with positive reviews from the public. In a media for the urban public that appealed first and foremost to the visual senses, glamorous performers and interpreters received top billing, although they could not have succeeded without the instrumentalists and performers behind the scenes.[53]

In 1935, the same year of the press's strike against censorship, João de Barro and Alberto Ribeiro directed the film *Alô alô Brasil*, starring Brazil's top interpreters, comedians, and entertainers, including Carmen Miranda. Miranda followed in a film with Mário Reis and a host of other popular musicians called *Estudantes* (Students). In this film, Miranda plays a university student who charms a host of her male classmates with her personality and voice. *Alô alô carnaval*, produced by Wallace Downey and directed by Ademar Gonzaga one year later, continued in the tradition of *Alô alô Brasil* and featured a cast of Brazil's most endearing performers: Carmen Miranda, Francisco Alves, Mário Reis, Aurora Miranda, Luis Barbosa, Almirante, Alzirinha Barbosa, the Bando da Lua, Dricinha Batista, Heloisa Helena, the Pagã sisters, Joel Gaucho, Lamartine Babo, Muraro, Jaime Costa, Barbosa Junior Pinto Filho, and Oscarito, none of them Afro-Brazilian.[54]

Restored in 2002, Downey and Gonzaga's film presents a moment in history—before the pressures of copyright and agents—that would be difficult to match today. That so many performers came together for one event was unprecedented. Carmen Miranda impressed audiences with her appearance, but she was not alone. The young Dricinha Batista, singing "Pirata da areia" (Pirate from the sand), appeared in a short skirt that would have scandalized some viewers. Mário Reis's "Mimi" was meant to woo audiences, as the camera follows him and flashes on the faces of female onlookers. The humor was often risqué: jokes from Almirante and Lamartine Babo, with drag numbers and comical and sensual dances by men and women.[55]

Notably absent, however, was Araci De Almeida, one of the few *mulatas*, albeit light skinned, who was, in fact, invited to participate in the production. Almeida refused to appear in the film dressed as a maid singing Noel Rosa's "Palpite infeliz" as the directors had requested.[56] Almeida's position is understandable given the power of the silver screen and the dangers of typecasting a woman who was not white. Besides, all of the other female singers appeared in fantasy costumes or in attire that was decidedly bourgeois. Carmen Miranda, for example, appeared twice in the film. In her first appearance, she interpreted Oswaldo Santiago and Benedito Lacerda's "Querido Adão" (Dear Adam), a song that dialogued with the 1935 hit "Eva Querida" (Dear Eve), a *marchinha* written by Lacerda and Luiz Vassalo and recorded by Mário Reis. The intertextuality of popular musical performances was indicative of a close-knit musical world of interpreters, lyricists, composers, and instrumentalists who used a number of media to express themselves.[57]

What most people remember about *Alô alô carnaval*, however, is the finale with Carmen Miranda and her sister Aurora interpreting

"Cantoras do radio" (Radio singers). The fact that the directors chose to end a film with a tribute to the radio indicates that cinema, although more powerful in projecting larger-than-life images of the emerging idols, had not yet attained the status and power of the radio. Decked in their golden tuxedos in a style reminiscent of Marlene Dietrich, the sisters not only sang the glories of the radio but also highlighted their own role as pioneers of film and radio at the same time. Gonzaga captured the voices and images of Aurora and Carmen with three separate cameras. The sisters smiled and moved from side to side on Cinêdia's makeshift stage, creating a final product that was most certainly a precursor of the music video.[58]

Afro-Brazilian *sambistas* would only begin to appear in the film musicals in the mid to late 1940s, paralleling the changes in the radio industry and society at large. By the 1950s, popular music and its Afro-Brazilian connection emerged in a variety of national films. Films in the 1940s, such as *Caí do ceu* (I fell from the sky, 1946) and *Está tudo aí* (It's all there, 1949), featured Afro-Brazilian performers, including Ataulfo Alves, Apolo Correia, and Déo Maia. *Orfeu Negro* (Black Orpheus, 1959) in some respects represented a culmination of Brazilian directed films that featured black musicians. Ironically, the director, Marcel Camus, was French.

Black Orpheus would take bossa nova, the new Brazilian popular music, global. In a change of historic trends, the film mostly featured the music of white Zone Sul composers but included on-screen appearances by a host of talented black performers, including Cartola.[59]

The most important film of the generation was nonetheless *Alô alô carnaval*, which was released in the same year that Vargas announced his new government, called the Estado Novo. Although it would not have a negative impact on musical films, censorship became a way of life after the creation of the Department of Propaganda (DOP). Musicians, dancers, and others were registered with the political police's Delegacia Especial de Segurança Política e Social (DESPS) from 1933 onward. In April 1938, the chief of police organized an archive to record information about any individual or institution that might pose a threat to the public order. The government was most concerned about the infiltration of Communists among the working classes, and, as in the United States under McCarthyism some years later, the Brazilian government kept close watch on artists and intellectuals.[60]

National "stars" like the Miranda sisters, Alves, and Reis were hardly viewed as threats, however, and their notoriety kept the police away. Vargas, his wife, and others in the Vargas government nonetheless saw in the popular musicians and performers possibilities to promote patriotism and to bolster their own relationship with the people. The Vargas government had played a significant role in brokering, supporting, and promoting Carmen Miranda's trip to the United States with the Bando da Lua in conjunction with the 1939 World's Fair in New York City.[61]

State support of popular music was crucial to the widespread celebration and acceptance of Brazilian popular music by the late 1930s. The relationship between the state and musicians was never one-dimensional. Privately owned radio companies, recording companies, and film studios also played a significant role in shaping the popular Brazilian sound. At the same time, organic relationships among the musicians, and the creations and inventions that resulted, were at the center of the new Brazilian sound. In many instances, creations and partnerships defied racial and gender norms, but in many forums the social relationships accommodated themselves to the stratified social realities of Brazilian society.

Conclusion

Individual stories and exceptions complicate easy categorizations, yet three basic generalizations help us understand Brazil's complex musical world: No black performers became major musical stars or performers during the first stage of mass media, from 1929 to 1940; black composers, performers, and musicians collaborated extensively with singers and entertainers who made it in the spotlight; and the hierarchy of the musical cultural landscape was racially and socially divided. Whites were the owners of the means of production, including radio auditoriums, theaters, casinos, cafés, and the stages of the silent movie cinemas, *casas de chope*, and nightclubs.

Racial intermingling, however extensive, was inevitably one-way. White performers often entered areas where poor blacks lived and worked, including favelas, with relative ease while looking for composers, performers, and musicians. Only on rare occasions did poor black performers and composers enter the white world of the radio auditoriums, recording studios, and casinos or on the stages of the best theaters. Yet to call these performing spaces "white" is not entirely accurate without an explanation of the complex racial and class codes in Brazil and the idea of the "provisional middle class." Moreover, it is important to consider the many exceptions: Pixinguinha, Dorival Caymmi, Grande Otelo, Heitor dos Prazeres, and the young black *paulista* performer Mário Ramos de Oliveira (known as Vassourinha), who begin his career on the radio at age twelve and died tragically before his twentieth birthday.

Black vocalists and instrumentalists played crucial roles in the provisional middle class, and most social spaces were largely free of racial tensions. Audiences accepted and often welcomed them with adulation, giving credence to the Freyrian myth that Brazilians did not harbor any racial prejudice. This was particularly true of the Brazilian urban spaces where Brazilians were not trying to impress international audiences or where large investment was not at stake. Indeed, technological developments benefited white performers more than their black counterparts.[62]

At the same time, established nonblack performers and interpreters such as Mário Reis and Carmen Miranda were instrumental in providing limited but important opportunities for black performers. The actions of others, such as Almirante, who insisted on recording with popular musical instruments (including the *tamborims*, *cuicas*, *surdos*, and *pandeiros*), benefited black performers as well. Almirante's band, however, was identified as all-white male performers—although some of them were possibly *mestiço*-who came from middle-class backgrounds and who performed without remuneration, not wanting to disgrace their families and accept money for their performances like common musicians.[63]

In many respects, the 1930 revolution that broke out in Rio Grande do Sul, Minas Gerais, and Paraíba in protest of the March election results was the beginning of the change that made the intermingling and the appropriations possible. Getúlio Vargas established his authority as the new president of Brazil one generation after the abolition of slavery, at the precise moment when intellectuals were propagating new ideas of Brazil.[64]

In an era without television, and where radio had not yet become ubiquitous, carnival was one of the great media of communication, although it brought the performers few economic benefits. A good song or rhythm could have little impact or it could become a staple, defying the ephemeral nature of popular culture. The merriment of carnival was juxtaposed to the growing censorship of the Vargas government and especially the campaigns against vagrancy and loafing. These campaigns benefited those singers, particularly white males such as Mário Reis and Aloysio de Oliveira, who were viewed as "upstanding citizens." At the same time, the bourgeois world began to take notice of Brazilian popular culture, and white performers helped to bring popular forms into their circles. These changes were also reflected in the cultural populism of modernist writers and thinkers such as Mário de Andrade, Carlos Drummond de Andrade, and others.[65]

Interclass and interracial camaraderie notwithstanding, white performers benefited disproportionately in a market in which both the supply and the demand for entertainment were expanding. This situation fostered creativity and experimentation, allowing white singers such as Francisco Alves to continue performing and recording while running his own show, introducing new talent to Brazilian audiences. Moreover, in this environment, talent, love of music, creativity, and partnerships across class and racial lines created unforgettable recordings and performances, fueling the nascent patriotism so important to the Vargas regime. Perhaps more important, for the first time "decent families" heard, appreciated, bought, and sponsored popular music at a time before the concept of MPB, the official mainstream term for popular Brazilian music, became fashionable.

CHAPTER FOUR

Race, Class, and the Making of "the King"

Cariocas and people from all over Brazil mourn the unexpected death of Francisco Alves, "the King of the Voice," the popular singer who was always the soul of the guitar, the radio man who knew how to sustain the rhythm of his national expression for decades after decade, as the greatest singer of all times.

———————— *Díario da Noite*, September 29, 1952

Kings and queens have not governed the people of the United States or Brazil since their respective colonial periods. Revolutionaries dismissed George III of the House of Hanover during the American Revolution in the 1770s, and the Spanish and Portuguese colonies of South America routed out the Iberian monarchs by the 1820s. The peoples of both continents have, nonetheless, inherited a fascination with royalty and continue to use royal titles to distinguish perceived greatness or superior talent in any given field. Popular music is no exception.

The royalty of popular music, like actual kings and queens, exercise a given control over the masses. Unlike traditional royal titles, which can be passed down through families from generation to generation, popular music titles are specific to generations and rely greatly on the media for validation. In societies where Afro-diasporic customs entered national culture from the bottom, royal titles in the early social history of popular music were necessarily influenced by both race and class. In the musical world, the ascent of Francisco Alves, "the King of the Voice," the first star of radio, and a trailblazer at the forefront of a group of musicians who took Rio's popular culture to the nation, is symptomatic of those influences.

This chapter utilizes the life and career of "the King of the Voice" to help us understand the racial and class dynamics of the early social history of Brazilian popular music. Alves's engagement, collaborations, and dialogue with Afro-Brazilian pioneers and traditions illustrate that no popular musical king in Brazil could have been crowned without black subjects. At the same time, the complex relationship between white king and the nonwhite masses was not one of mere exploitation. Alves's collaborations with black and *mestiço* composers and musicians and his singing partnership with Mário Reis, who was white and came from the elite classes, indicate that he played a dual role of popularizing black tunes as well as helping to gentrify the emerging national tastes.

Indeed, Alves was a respected elder and patron to many black musicians who would have major influences on Brazilian popular music. An examination of his family and circle of friends, his connection to Afro-Brazilian pioneers and other musicians, his partnership with Reis, and the social circles in which they moved sheds light on Brazil's social history and popular music.

There are many social parallels between Elvis Presley, the North American "King of Rock and Roll," and Brazil's "King of the Voice," although the latter was long deceased when Presley received his title. Presley had grown up near and in the segregated black neighborhoods of Tupelo, Mississippi, where some houses were often reserved for white families, and was accustomed to hearing black gospel music, among other genres. According to biographer Peter Guralnick, if you lived on the street where this music was heard, you "breathed it in as natural as air—after a while you got used to it, it became yours, too."[1] While U.S. segregation imposed a different mode of social interaction and thus celebration, the issue of cultural sensitivity of artists and the importance of the social environment applies equally to Brazil.

Alves, the son of white Portuguese immigrants, grew up in a neighborhood with Afro-Brazilians and was intimately familiar with many Afro-Brazilian musical genres. He was an important transitional figure who captivated the attention of the white elite and earned the respect of the black and *mestiço* popular classes with whom he lived, worked, and celebrated. Alves became the consecrated white *malandro* of samba because he sang about that lifestyle. He helped to gentrify and nationalize the *malandro*, and remained at the center of the popular music industry for almost three decades. Chico, as he was affectionately called, understood his importance, but he also understood his limitations as a performer, and he made decisions that illustrated that he understood the peculiarities of Brazil's social structure.

Alves's Family and Friends

On September 27, 1952, Francisco Alves died in a horrific car crash as he was returning to Rio from São Paulo. Fire had ravaged Alves's car, and the flames had consumed his body. His death was a reminder of that generation's mortality, its dreams, its aspirations, and its fading worldview. He had been the subject of hundreds of radio programs and journalistic articles throughout his life, but would be no more. With his death, the complicated transfer into memory began.[2] The tens of thousands of people who turned out for his funeral paralyzed the city, creating a national spectacle. "Francisco Alves's voice is gone but we hear it now more than ever," the magazine *Manchete* reported. The lines in front of the municipal congress building stretched for miles, as crowds waited to glimpse the body laid out there. Radio stations throughout the city further heightened emotions by broadcasting his famous songs, reminding Cariocas of the voice that was sure to be immortalized.[3]

Alves's life and achievements, his popular attraction, and his social goodwill shared many parallels with the city of Rio de Janeiro. Born to

Portuguese immigrants on August 19, 1898, Alves was a native Carioca, a son of Rio de Janeiro, and people in the city turned out to mourn their loss. Chico, as we have noted, grew up in a neighborhood of Portuguese immigrants, listening to *fados* and being exposed to Brazilian rhythms. He had lived on Riacheulo Street in Lapa, the bohemian center of the city during a golden era of Brazilian popular music, and had studied at the Colegio da Ajuda.

Lapa in the 1930s and 1940s can be compared to Harlem in the 1920s, when artists and intellectuals descended upon the cafés, bars, and cultural establishments to exchange ideas, and when musicians experimented with a host of influences to create unforgettable American tunes. But Lapa was much more. It was a multiracial, multicultural neighborhood of international immigrants and migrants from all over Brazil. It was also a center of prostitution, of *malandragem* (slumming), of poetry, art, music, and other forms of entertainment. "A Lapa," the tune composed by Heriveltto Martins and Bendito Lacerda, described the neighborhood as the Federal District's best spot on the map and "the neighborhood with four letters where so many *malandros* lived and where so many valiant ones died."[4] Madame Satã, the notorious black transvestite performer, self-proclaimed *malandro*, and longtime resident of Lapa, describes the neighborhood in similar terms: "I loved my beloved Lapa. Everything awful in my life happened there. But all the love that people had for me also came from Lapa."[5]

Alves and a host of other musicians and singers were influenced by the activities of the neighborhood. In his 1972 memoir, Madame Satã explained that the "*malandro* was the man who attended the serenades and who hung out in the bars and the cabarets. The *malandro* never ran away from a fight even if it was against the police . . . and he respected others." Satã, who moved to Rio from northeastern Brazil practically as an indentured servant, documented his social marginalization and ill treatment in Brazilian society on many fronts. Nonetheless, he emphasized the camaraderie among *malandros* and musicians in Lapa, where he befriended and shared experiences with black and white musicians such as Noel Rosa, Heitor dos Prazeres, Cartola, Nelson do Cavaquinho, Francisco Alves, Araci de Almeida, and others.[6]

Satã understood the social codes of the street as well as those of the "provisional middle class." Even though performers like Satã understood the prevailing social codes, this did not mean that they followed them. Satã constructed his own nontraditional family and saw no contradiction in being a *malandro* and a transvestite who performed mostly female songs in Lapa's cabarets and cafés. Unfortunately, like so many disenfranchised black men throughout the Americas, Satã ended up in a cyclical pattern of confrontations with the law, which culminated in a conviction for murder and landed him in jail.

Whether black artists like Satã chose to perform exclusively in underground and bohemian locales because they would not have been have been accepted into the provisional middle class is unclear. Many nonetheless believed that they could get by employing their very own sense of *Jeitinho*, by relying on contacts in the fluid world of popular musical performances where they often came into contact with more renowned musicians, intellectuals, and artists.

Although Alves had become a household name long before Satã was jailed, he had also come from humble beginnings and was no stranger to tragedy. His sister had succumbed to Spanish flu, which had ravaged the city during World War I. In addition to the privilege of whiteness, however, what separated Alves from the many displaced Afro-Brazilian performers of downtown Rio was his secure family structure, a social element frequently absent in discussions of race relations. Chico's parents, and particularly his father, like many parents of the time, did not want their son to become involved in the life of musicians. At age eighteen, he found a "respectable job" working in the Julio Lima hat factory, an experience that would help foster an understanding of working-class values, including an appreciation for the emerging popular music.[7]

Alves had many friends who were musicians, and soon he began to earn a reputation as an amateur singer, performing at the *roda de sereteiros*, at birthday parties, at weddings, and at receptions. These experiences ultimately led him to the radio and recording studio. The white tenor Vicente Celestino was one of the early singers in the theater and had been the model for upcoming performers. His loud, operatic voice was perfectly suited for performances before amplification revolutionized the music industry. Before there was amplification, musicians had to play loudly, and singers had to project their voices throughout theaters and performance halls in order to be captured by the sound sensors of the gramophone. In many cases, singers had to scream. Thus, loud, operatic, bellowing voices such as Vicente Celestino's captured audiences for generations.

As Alves reported to his friend David Nasser: "Vicente Celestino [was] the tenor of two generations and the absolute idol of my youth. . . . His voice was one of the most beautiful of Brazil. His gentleman-like presence on stage, his abundant hair, his unflinching and arrogant gestures, made him the most powerful lord of the national stage."[8] Alves's adulation for Celestino's style, voice, and presence was augmented because he knew that Celestino, whom many called "the Brazilian Caruso," was one of the few singers who made his living exclusively from singing, a feat that Alves himself would later attain. Alves's praise of Celestino was not without racial implications. The code words "gentleman-like" and the reference to his hair indicated that Celestino was both white and middle class and thus a worthy model to emulate. Moreover, Alves understood that he could not simply copy or emulate verbatim the style and voice of the poor *malandros* of his neighborhood, who were unappreciated by paying audiences.[9]

From Student to Elder

As in the case of thousands of performers, music would provide Alves with the opportunity to escape the working-class lifestyle that afforded so few opportunities for economic advancement. His first major performance was in the 1921 musical revue *A Dor é a mesma* (The pain is the same).[10] By that time, Alves had acquired a reputation for being a dedicated performer with a large bellowing voice like his idol. As he developed his own individual style, he incorporated thematic elements of the popular classes to catch the attention of people in the growing

LEFT: Ataulfo Aves from album cover from the 1970S. Source: Author's collection.

BELOW: Ismael Silva and group of "*pastoras.*" Source: Funarte.

Ismael Silva.
Source: Funarte.

Sinhô. Source:
Author's collection.

ABOVE: Pixinguinha.
Source: Funarte.

RIGHT: Wilson Batista.
Source: Biblioteca Nacional, Music Division.

BELOW: The Oito Batutes.
Source: Biblioteca Nacional.

RIGHT: Poster for film *Alô alô carnival.*
Source: Funarte.

BELOW: Carmen Miranda and Aurora Miranda in *Alô alô carnaval.* Source: Funarte.

Araci Córtes. Source: Funarte.

Mario Reis rehearsing with musicians. Source: Funarte

ABOVE: Carmen Miranda as Bahiana.
Source: Author's collection.

LEFT: Carmen Miranda as Bahiana2.
Source: Author's collection.

BELOW: Sinval Silva.
Source: Biblioteca Nacional, Division of Music.

ABOVE: Carmen Miranda with Grande
Otelo and Angela Maria, 1954.
Source: Funarte.

RIGHT: Linda Batista and Grande
Otelo. Source: Funarte.

BELOW: Dorival Caymmi.
Source: Biblioteca Nacional, Division of Music.

ABOVE: Angela Maria from album.
Source: Author's collection.

RIGHT: Angela Maria and Louis Armstrong.
Source: Biblioteca Nacional, Music Section.

BELOW: Francisco Alves, center, with
Orlando Silva to his right.
Source: Biblioteca Nacional, Music Section.

capital, working with various white and Afro-Brazilian performers and composers. By 1928, he had already recorded 143 songs, and he became known for his laudatory songs about the bohemian life of Rio. Three decades later, after a long career on the radio and a discography that included 383 sambas, 166 *marchas*, and more than 400 other recordings of various genres and themes, his death would have a major impact on many Brazilians.[11]

Early in his career, Alves—with the help of talented composers such as Sinhô, and local bands and instrumentalists such as the Grupo dos Africanos (Group of Africans)—had delighted audiences around Brazil with recordings and performances that celebrated Brazilianness with humor, criticism, and lyricism.[12] As a performer to mass audiences, he often affirmed patriotic sentiments and racial stereotypes in songs such as the 1927 *marcha* "Os canoeiros do Norte," which celebrates the Brazilian *caboclo* or *mestiço* from the northeast as the prototype of the Brazilian nation, and the 1928 *embolada* "Nego D'Angola" (Angolan black man), which indirectly and sarcastically comments on Brazil's Africaneity. Others songs such as the 1937 samba "Mulata cor de jambo" (Light-skinned mulatta) equates the *mulata* with Brazilian sexuality and nationality, and the explicitly sexual fox-trot "Eu quero uma mulher bem preta" (I want a very black woman) references Josephine Baker's appeal to Brazilian men: "I want a nice black girl / very naked, very naked / She has to be sweet-smelling / Very naked very naked," as part of the song went.[13]

Although Alves often performed to audience expectations, by all accounts he was a generous man, and thus had many friends in and outside of the popular music industry. He worked and performed with Brazil's great composers and musicians, many of whom he had helped along in their careers and many who had imitated him as he had once imitated Celestino.[14] Many women counted themselves among Alves's protégés, including Araci Teles de Almeida and Linda Batista.[15]

Araci de Almeida, who, as we have seen, earned the moniker "the Samba in Person," released her first record with Columbia with Alves's help, in 1934, although it was her recording of "Palpite infeliz" (Unhappy beat) by the talented Noel Rosa that won her widespread praise two years later.[16] Ironically, Aracy Cortes, the *mulata* pioneer of the theatrical revue, had also been important in Alves's life. Cortes had worked with the novice Alves for the theatrical company São José, which specialized in *burletas* and theatrical revues. She would cross paths with Alves throughout her career, even saving him once from being fired. Nonetheless, she was the reigning star of the revue, and the first to sing many of the major compositions of the 1930s, including "Aquarela do Brasil," Ary Borroso's most important homage to Brazil.[17]

There was no precise formula for success in any major forum of musical performance. Rapport with the audiences was fundamental, and different forums appealed to different demographics. Marketability and pervading social conventions worked against women in general, particularly outspoken women like Cortes and Almeida, but they also worked against blacks and poor people. Aracy Cortes, often referred to as a *mulata*, not only reigned supreme in the revue but also fared reasonably well on the radio and in the recording industries, making almost 250 records from the 1920s to the 1950s. Like Alves, Cortes never quite made it in the casinos, however, nor did she appear in film musicals.[18]

Afro-Brazilian women such as Almeida and Cortes had been fortunate to work with Alves, but they had not reaped the rewards of a mainstream performer to the extent that he had. Alves, a handsome and talented white male willing to work and network, benefited from the rules of the game as he also helped others. While Alves was a major presence in the national cinema, he, too, had not transferred that success to the casino scene, although he had connections with the musicians and composers as well as with recording and publishing companies. He also worked with many of the members of the first bands to make records.

The original arrangements of the Bando de Tangarás (Tangarás Bird Band) were simple and initially deeply influenced by music from what Brazilians called regional bands, although members of the band had also grown up hearing the Afro-Brazilian rhythms around the neighborhoods. Three of the teenage members (Almirante,

Braguinha, and Henrique Brito) knew each other from the high school in Tijuca, and they were joined later by Noel Rosa from the nearby neighborhood of Vila Isabel. All of the members, with the exception of Almirante, who played *pandeiro*, played guitars at a time when the guitar was still not yet fully accepted among the middle classes. Almirante and Braguinha also sang.[19] The 1929 invitation to make a record at Odeon meant that the composing experiments of the Bando de Tangarás would be responsible for one of the first recorded urban group sounds.

In subsequent years, Victor, Odeon, Parlophone, and Columbia would dominate the market as they competed for local talent.[20] More important, however, these foreign companies were the emerging capitalist hierarchy in the Brazilian popular music industry. This meant that the multinational companies would benefit most, followed by local publishers and then the star performers. Afro-Brazilian composers and musicians who had created the works reaped few rewards. Copyright laws, or lack thereof, played a significant role in Afro-Brazilian disenfranchisement, as did middle-class desires to appear modern.

The Alves-Reis Partnership

When Mário Reis set foot in the popular musical milieu, he became known as "the Elegant Gentleman of Samba" because of his refined style but also because the media knew that he came from the upper class. Although Reis, like Alves, often sang about the risky life of the *malandro* and other popular class themes, he projected a bourgeois style in dress and appearance. Alves's partnership with Reis resulted in the most celebrated male duo of the time, and helped to cement the widespread acceptance of popular music by middle-class audiences. That they were both white males was no coincidence. Reis's upper-class background, coupled with his good looks and his remarkable talent, afforded him opportunities and choices unavailable to many other performers of his generation.

Reis's soft voice was perfectly suited for the new age of microphones and amplification, and many consider him a precursor of the spoken songs of bossa nova. But his social connections undoubtedly helped him bring Brazilian popular music to the elite. Brazilians of all walks of life were comfortable with the image that the duo projected in an era in which Brazil wanted to project itself as modern, which meant on par with Europe and the United States.[21]

Alves and Reis could only have had such power in a stratified society in which power is guarded by the few. They did not intend to exploit poor musicians for their own benefit, at least not consciously. But who they were mattered. Although Reis spent a shorter period of time performing in the popular musical arena than Alves, his contributions were more decisive in bringing cross-class respectability to popular musical production. Reis had crossed class lines, and to a certain extent racial barriers, at a considerable risk to his prestige and his standing in society. It was a risk that paid off. That he is remembered even today as "the Elegant Gentleman of Samba" speaks volumes about attitudes Brazilians harbored about popular music, samba, and popular performers. What an irony that at the end of the twentieth century, samba, which has been shunned by many of the urban poor in favor of *partido alto*, *pagode*, reggae, and hip hop, is experiencing a renaissance led by the middle classes of the Zona Sul in Rio de Janeiro.

Reis was connected to the Brazilian elite in many ways. His family had economic and political connections, although he had his share of tragedy during his adolescence. His father, Raul Meirelles Reis, died in a railway accident when Mario was seventeen, and the family soon thereafter committed his mother to a mental institution. In 1910, his family moved from the neighborhood of Rio Comprido to Tijuca, home of the América Football Club, which would become a central part of the family's social life. Although it is a cliché to associate Brazil with "samba and soccer," in Reis's case the cliché rings true, since his family's association with football (soccer) brought him into contact with the youth in the surrounding neighborhoods, including Andaraí, Grajaú, and Villa Isabel. According to Reis's biographer, Luís Antônio

Giron, a number of men from the musical milieu, including Noel Rosa, Carlos Galhardo, Sílvio Caldas, and Francisco Alves, were avid supporters of the América Football Club, which came to be known as "the club for artists."[22]

The title was no exaggeration, as history would soon reveal. In 1920, Mário Reis's father was elected president of the club. The secure, private, and intimate space of the club cultivated an extended family of fans who missed no opportunity to revel in a secure and familiar environment. The celebrations before and after games, birthday parties, Christmas, New Year's Eve, carnival and *festas juninas* provided ample opportunity to come together frequently. In these environments, Mario and his brother, João, not only fraternized with other football and tennis players of their class but also with friends and club fans from all social backgrounds.[23]

The club also sponsored music festivals that brought together many artists from the surrounding neighborhoods. In the early 1920s, Mario had begun to take guitar lessons, and these festivals provided him with a familiar and amateur forum to sing and to hear others perform. Like other great performers, Mario certainly had talent, but he also found himself at the right place at the right time. These amateur celebrations brought together many talented musicians and composers who would later make an important impression on Rio de Janeiro's musical scene. Henrique Foréis Domingues (Almirante) was one of them. João de Barro, or Braguinha, was another. Although both musicians wrote and sang about Brazil's *mestiço* origins, and many Brazilians may claim that Almirante, in particular, has "one foot in the kitchen," a phrase used to note the African ancestry of many white Brazilians, to call either of them black or Afro-Brazilian is to misunderstand Brazilian society. Although they celebrated Brazil's black and *mestiço* roots, and experienced and were culturally formed by the pervading Afro-Brazilian cultural traditions, both belonged to the more middle-class circles and thus had access to education and media, although they were not as privileged as Reis.

Reis and his male cousins also enjoyed the privilege of being voyeurs at more public spectacles in the surrounding neighborhoods and particularly in Lapa's bars and cafés. He respected the performers and enjoyed their music, but he did not necessarily fraternize with them. According to Astrea Braga, wife of João de Barro, Reis seemed "to come from another planet, moving among the common folk like a god."[24] Braga's view was not universal. Francisco Alves understood Reis's appeal and had a hand in bringing him into the public's eye through his connection to the popular maestro Sinhô, who had recognized Reis's talent.[25]

By the mid 1920s, Sinhô had already published music and was a respected composer of the *teatro de revista*. Still, the meeting between Sinhô and Mário Reis in A Guitarra de Prata, a music store in downtown Rio, in 1928 was beneficial to both. Reis found in Sinhô an excellent guitar teacher, and Sinhô found a voice that he considered perfect for his compositions. Together they created a new way of performing samba, or as Mozart de Araújo intimated, a "new way of singing," as if Reis was speaking softly rather than singing, making him clearly one of the precursors of bossa nova. Ironically, Sinhô's contact with Fred Figner, owner of Casa Edison, led to Reis's first studio experience and the beginning of his recording career.[26]

Reis's first recording was Sinhô's 1928 composition, "Que vale a nota sem o carinho da mulher" (What is a note without a women's affection?). The song would set the standard for the singer's entire repertoire. Sinhô had written the music and the lyrics, even though the latter are credited to Avlis Bésoj. The sentimental words of the composition, combined with the intimacy created by the guitar, found its perfect form in the voice of Mário Reis, who announces each syllable with detailed perfection. "Amor! Amor! / Não é para quem quer" (Love! Love! / It is not for he who wants it), the singer almost laments, in three stanzas full of colloquialisms that mass audiences would have appreciated.[27]

Sinhô's first recording with Reis had two guitars, one played by Reis and the other by Donga, another Afro-Brazilian musical pioneer. It is unclear whether Sinhô actively pursued his partnership with Reis because of the latter's social standing and thus huge potential.[28] That Reis brought respectability to samba is certain, but "respectability" meant acceptance by those who establish the social rules. Moreover, this newfound respect has to be understood within the social, racial, and economic context of the time, when singers and performers in general faced prejudice and when society as a whole associated musical performers with bohemia and immorality. Reis's presence allowed middle- and upper-class audiences to gain insight into the genius of the Brazilian popular classes at a time when many knew more about the customs of London and Paris than those in their own backyard.

Francisco Alves used the typical social code words in describing Mário Reis: "O rapaz de boa aparência" (A guy with a good appearance), which meant that he was not only good-looking but was white and not poor. It would be a phrase used by countless employers throughout the twentieth century to warn prospective black applicants that they need not apply.[29] Reis highlighted the image of the *gran fino*, an elegant gentleman-musician with a pedigree who exuded sophistication and style. This image appealed to many in the middle and upper middle classes, but it also attracted those from the poorer classes who perceived performers or radio as unreachable—even though they were singing popular music. To make matters worse, as Reis began to bask in the limelight, his mentor's health deteriorated. Sinhô finally succumbed to tuberculosis on August 4, 1930, on a boat from Ilha do Governador, where music producer Fred Figner had bought him a house. Unlike Alves's funeral, there were no crowds at his funeral. Neither Alves nor Reis made an appearance, and the city hardly skipped a beat. Benedict Anderson has shown us the importance of newspapers to nation building. Prior to the radio, they were also important in celebrating heroes and in registering deaths. The news of Sinhô's death, however, made the dailies too late. His funeral service was hurriedly organized and publicized too late for those interested in attending.[30]

Reis was not only a product of his economic privilege. Like Carmen Miranda and Alves, he would become a radio idol. As radio moved from its initial educating purposes to mass entertainment, Reis represented "civility," as the many accolades and descriptions that appeared in the press attest.[31]

The Expanding Social Circles of Popular Music

Mário Reis had helped to bring the elites into the popular main-stream. The 1930s were called the "Golden Era" for many reasons, and popular music would not have been noticed unless intellectuals and the elite had not been a part of it. There were also many economic opportunities for the poor as well as the rich. New radio and record-ing stations tried to meet the demands of the market, thus giving opportunities to musicians and performers in record numbers, and creating and meeting a new demand for entertainment. The era was golden because of the quantity and quality of productions, but it is important to emphasize that compared to the performers, the producers of popular music benefited disproportionately.

Discrimination is measured not only by attitudes, preferences, and prejudice, which have always worked against the poor and blacks throughout the Western Hemisphere, but also by economic exclusion. A large body of research has already shown the endemic exclusion in manufacturing, agriculture, and a number of other sectors based on race.[32] While the empirical evidence on the music industry is scant, most observers see contemporary music as one of the few sectors that has provided opportunities to a diversity of men and women and thus must necessarily be less exclusionary and more representative of Brazilian demographics.

The development of favelas and popular music in Rio de Janeiro is a more complicated story. Yet the experiences of the Bahian Dori-val Caymmi and the Carioca native Noel Rosa help us place Reis's contribution to Brazilian popular music in perspective. Caymmi, an Afro-Brazilian from Bahia, arrived in Rio in 1938, when the radio and recording industries were well developed but still expanding, and thus still on the lookout for new acts and talent. Songs about the Northeast remained in vogue, but that would not have been enough to allow Caymmi to break into the musical world. He, too, had contacts and talent and moved with musicians in the urban spaces of downtown Rio. All of these factors helped when producers were looking for a new act to replace Ary Barroso's Bahian number in the film production of *Banana da terra* in 1939.

Caymmi would be the only Afro-Brazilian to perform in Darcy Vargas's *Joujoux and balagandãs*, an unprecedented fund-raising event of 1939 that featured the most celebrated performers of Brazilian popular music alongside amateurs. The event would also represent a comeback performance by Reis, who had taken a hiatus from performing. Among a star-filled ensemble of talented musicians and performers, Reis was at the very center of the program that signaled the marriage of the Vargas administration with popular music.[33] Caymmi would go on to have a long and productive musical career that overlapped with the new group of Bahians—Gilberto Gil, Caetano Veloso, Gal Costa, and Mari Bethânia—who would take the Southeast by storm in the 1960s.

The fact that Caymmi was a middle-class migrant to Rio from Bahia and thus able to sidestep some of the social barriers ought not to be ignored. Indeed, Caymmi was a vital presence in the second decade of the Vargas era, when many more Afro-Brazilians entered the entertainment ranks at the highest level. It would take another generation to change the overarching class considerations, which maintained the middle-class bourgeois aesthetics and dress codes in radio auditoriums and other important performance spaces. Moreover, the remuneration for singers and interpreters outpaced those for popular instrumentalists and composers. At the same time, the popular success of composer-performers such as Dorival Caymmi, Hector dos Prazeres, Ataulfo Alves, and Noel Rosa did not necessarily translate into economic success. This was particularly true for Noel Rosa, whom many Brazilians consider the most poetic of Brazilian composers.

From a social perspective, Rosa's and Reis's lives were worlds apart, despite the similarities in race. They might have moved in similar social circles if Rosa had decided to finish medical school. But Rosa's unique experience, his innate poetic talent, his suffering as a result of a birth defect, and his penchant for merriment would take him down a different path. Even though he came from a middle-class background, Rosa had been an integral part of Rio's bohemian nightlife, sharing a multitude of experiences with the *bambas* of Lapa. Reis would lead a life of exclusion and luxury in the Zona Sul long after Rosa died of tuberculosis in 1936, leaving "a great lacuna because he was a great animator of the Brazilian samba," according to the newspaper *A Modinha*.[34]

The social differences that separated Reis and Rosa were often bridged during the rituals that surrounded performances in public forums around the country, giving the illusion that all performers were equal. This dynamic musical world brought together individuals of diverse social, racial, and regional backgrounds along with artists with different dispositions and goals. The group Ases do Samba (Samba Aces)—comprised of Mário Reis; Noel Rosa; Romualdo Peixoto (Nonô), the only Afro-Brazilian in the group; Peri Cunha; and Francisco Alves—is a case in point. Organized in 1932 and managed by Alves, the Aces embarked on a tour of southern Brazil that would include stops in Porto Alegre and Florianopolis, cementing their roles as national icons. Reis and Alves were the leading vocalists, but they relied on Rosa's talent, wit, and poetry; on Peri's expertise on mandolin (*bandolim*); and on Nonô's wizardry on piano.[35]

On stage, they were all applauded as veritable stars of Brazilian popular music. Off stage, social distinctions were clear. Although they were all paid equally, Reis's and Alves's status meant that they could stay in more expensive hotels, eat in more expensive restaurants, and socialize within different circles. When the band arrived in Porto Alegre, for example, Reis and Alves checked into the Grande Hotel, one of the most comfortable hotels in the city, while Rosa, Nonô, and Cunha stayed at one of the inexpensive *posadas*. Never mind that they were comrades or that Nonô had been recommended to Alves by Reis. Arrangements like these were commonplace, and musicians seemed to accept them as the natural order of things.[36]

All things are not equal in life. Nor are they in death. We mourn when individuals are ripped away from us. The irony is that in many cases of the musicians in the 1930s and 1940s, the very city and environment that nurtured and inspired them were unable to aid them. This was certainly true in the case of Noel Rosa, whose talent, although well known and widely honored, never granted him the economic standing of that of a white elite such as Mário Reis or even an Afro-Brazilian such as Dorival Caymmi. Some may argue Rosa did not desire such economic standing. He was a musician's musician, and performers appreciated his wit, his ingenuity, and most of all his compositions.

When Rosa died of tuberculosis in 1937, the industry to which he had already contributed was steadily growing. The *Diario Carioca* proclaimed it best on May 5, 1937: "Yesterday, the *carioca* people lost one of the most perfect interpreters of its poetry."[37] Rosa was an intuitive poet and a keen observer of life, particularly among the poor people of the city. He understood the need to produce poetry that reflected the beauty and musicality of the real lives in the favelas and of the poor Cariocas, who were marginalized from the official media conceptualization of the Brazilian nation. His genius in musical creativity and popular poetry did not translate to his lifestyle, however, where he was often reckless with his health and particularly with alcohol. Rosa frequently wrote compositions utilizing the Afro-Brazilian voice and rhythms, but unlike Alves, or even Caymmi, he refused to adopt the values of the provisional middle class, preferring to live the bohemian life that he sang about in many of his songs.[38]

Rosa's life contrasted directly with Mário Reis's discreet image. Yet both artists had collaborated on numerous occasions and had contributed in multiple ways to the vibrancy and dynamics of the musical milieu of the era. Despite Rosa's influence as a composer, he was not a national idol who would bring forth the emotions that Cariocas would transfer to interpreters such as Carmen Miranda and Alves in the 1950s. Moreover, in 1936 popular music was still making its upward climb, and pedestals were being constructed. Other composers, such as Sinhô and Estacio's Nilton Bastos, had also died from tuberculosis, and their funerals took place virtually unnoticed.

By the 1950s, Brazil was clearly in the sphere of influence of the United States, with which it had allied during Word War II. The political and economic alliance was reflected in social and cultural exchanges as well. The cultural influence had begun under the guise of the "Good Neighbor Policy" with the onset of the war. Cultural producers from the United States began to import Brazilian cultural commodities and reexport them for Latin American consumption. The exchange between bossa nova and jazz was possible as a result of the alliances forged in the 1940s by Carmen Miranda, Aurora Miranda, Ary Barroso, Aloysio de Oliveira, and the members of the Bando da Lua and several other bands.

Oliveira played an important role in the development and shift of Brazilian popular musical from amateur to professional performance in the 1930s. Oliveira was one of the founding members of the Bando da Lua, one of the first professionally organized middle-class bands. The band had managed to rent a space in the neighborhood of Catete on Martins Ribeiro Street, in front of the Praça José de Alencar, and band members organized their activities in a manner untypical of Brazilian bands. The choice of space proved an important decision, since the locale served as a practicing and meeting point, and as a storage facility for instruments and clothes, along with housing a small archive. The Bando da Lua also invested in a complete sound system that gave the band a consistent and professional sound. Oliveira, who served as the band's musical director, had the most contact with other composers and performers and also chose the band's repertoire and arrangements, a role that he would play again in the 1950s and 1960s as producer for the bossa nova generation.[39]

The Bando da Lua became a sensation in Rio even without lead singers or dancers, but the band's sound was neither revolutionary nor particularly innovative. Compared to the other talent of the era, the Banda da Lua was average, but the band was in the right place at the right time and had race and class working for it. The band's repertoire, organization, and connections nonetheless earned it a reputation for solid performance and workmanship. The fact that the band members were connected to the white middle class of the Zona Sul meant that the band enjoyed exposure in the city's middle-class media. It helped that Oswaldo Eboli, better known as Vadeco, the band's *pandeiro* player, worked at the newspaper *O Globo*, allowing him to publicize the band's performances. The Bando da Lua performed in various venues throughout the city, sharing programs with vocalists although not accompanying them. That would change in 1934 when Jaime Yankelevich, owner of Argentina's Radio Belgrano, contracted the band to perform in Argentina with Carmen Miranda. This uncommon arrangement would begin a professional relationship between Miranda and the Bando da Lua that would last for more than two decades.[40]

The role of Aloysio de Oliveira, director of the Bando Da Lua, deserves special scrutiny since he prolonged his career in music as a result of the expertise that he accumulated in the United States and also because he made the successful transition from performer to producer in the midst of the bossa nova hype. Oliveira, the young amateur from Catete, eventually became artistic director of Odeon. He would not only promote new artists but also would be instrumental in re-releasing many of the old artists' songs as well.[41]

Reis's way of singing had a greater impact on the Brazilian style than many other singers because, as one reporter noted, Reis "created the way Brazilians sing."[42] President Vargas appreciated the talents of Alves and Miranda, but, socially, he had much more in common with Reis. Alzira, Vargas's daughter, had been Reis's close friend. Darcy Vargas, the president's wife, had lured him out of retirement to perform popular music for the bourgeoisie. Reis's melodious soft voice, coupled with his image and attitude, had allowed the first Lady—and, by extension, President Vargas—to join the upper classes with the popular classes in the promotion of Brazilian popular music and its musicians. It would be no exaggeration to say that through association, Reis helped to promote the works and acceptability of Brazilian musicians in a race- and class-conscious society. That visibility, as we have seen, did not necessarily translate into economic benefits for all musicians, however.[43]

As we have also seen, talent alone has never been sufficient to change one's socioeconomic position in life. On the other hand, Reis's contacts and the privileges that his background afforded him would not have aided him much if he did not have talent. The commercial dynamics were complex. Singers and recording artists lived on one side of the tracks. The mostly poor nonwhite instrumentalists, and particularly composers, lived on the other. These two sides were not strictly divided along racial or class lines but intermingled in dynamic ways that defy generalizations. Nonetheless, Reis represented the face of Brazilian popular music in a country still unwilling to economically compensate those who created its foundations. Men such as Alves were at the center of the music industry, and establishments were constructed to cater to their needs.

Other Comrades and Rivalries

The world of popular music seemed an uncomplicated one in which friendships and professional partnerships often intertwined, where the lines of competition and alliances were often blurred. Vocalists and producers sought out composers based on a variety of factors, but the reverse could also be true. Noel Rosa, talented and idiosyncratic, was often the center of musical rivalries, such as the one with Wilson Batista that ended in insult. Wilson and Rosa had written and recorded a number of songs playing with the lyrics and the style of the other, until Wilson, a talented black composer of the era, wrote a song in which he made fun of Rosa's disfigured face.

Another rivalry involved Sílvio Caldas and Francisco Alves. On this occasion, Rosa had a falling out with Alves. Inspired, Rosa, a prolific composer of sambas, wrote a melody that he entitled "Vitoria." In the malicious yet poetic style of the era, the song talked about the undoing of a partnership, presumably his and Alves's. To try to add insult to injury, Rosa had arranged for Sílvio Caldas to record it at Victor studio. As fate would have it, Alves, who had an exclusive contract with Odeon, appeared at Victor and agreed to record the composition as Caldas's back-up vocalist, creating one of the few recordings for which he was never given credit.[44]

In theory, recording contracts employed a rigid language, but in practice singers and composers and musicians found ways to break exclusive contracts and maintain a greater control over their own participation, a practice that would lead to problems when Brazilians such as Carmen Miranda and Aurora Miranda traveled to the United States. Alves knew how to use the system to his advantage, but as we have seen, he also helped others. He had a knack for identifying talent, and many sought him out. This was the case of the Batista sisters, Aurora Miranda, and Orlando Silva.[45]

The gratitude and affection that Silva held for Francisco Alves was obvious despite the disagreements they had over the course of their long relationship. At one point, Silva had become so popular that people began to accuse him of being a snob, and even refusing to shake Alves's hand at the radio station.[46] Musicians are a breed unto themselves, however, and Silva never denied Alves's influence, even after Alves's death. Through the intervention of various friends from Rádio Nacional, including Manoel Barcelo, who later opened a store in homage to Francisco Alves called O Rei da Voz, and Paulo Tapajós, Silva was contracted to take the place of Alves on his show *When the Pioneers Meet*. On Alves's old show, Silva made a successful comeback, although his battles with alcohol continued, and his health deteriorated. In 1956, Orlando Silva suffered a horrific fall, resulting in the amputation of one of his legs.[47]

In death as in life, society makes comparisons. The death of Orlando Silva in 1978 was one more opportunity for comparisons with Francisco Alves, his mentor and friend. Fittingly, Silva was originally buried on the same grounds as Alves, at the cemetery of São Jóao Batista in Botafogo: lot number 452, plot 13—although two years later his remains would be moved to the cemetery in the working-class neighborhood of Cajú. It was no surprise that Silva's death made the front page of *O Globo* and the *Journal do Brasil*, the city's two major dailies. The crowds poured into the cemetery and blocked all of the adjacent streets. The solemn fans remembered him with his hits "Labios que bejei" (Lips that I kissed), "Carinhoso," and others. They were not always sung with sorrow, the accepted emotion for a burial, but with serenity and joy, almost celebrating his accomplishment and the beauty of his voice. But this was a different era.[48]

Following in the tradition of Alves's funeral, other musicians, singers, and performers were present as Silva's burial, only on a smaller scale.[49] Journalist Sérgio Bittencourt best described the relationship among Francisco Alves, Francisco Alves, Sílvio Caldas, and Orlando Silva: Francisco Alves had a powerful voice, one that came from the chest. He was essentially a singer. Sílvio Caldas, on the other hand, had a limited voice but used it to interpret lyrics like no other male performer. He was essentially an interpreter. Orlando Silva was the synthesis of both of them. He was a singer and an interpreter.[50] Many fans and fellow performers, such as Araci Almeida, who considered Sílvio Calves "the greatest singer of all times," passionately disputed this hierarchy.[51] There was no doubt, however, that Orlando Silva saw himself as Alves's successor, if not protégé, and he had been present at Alves's funeral twenty years before his own death, visibly altered, but a symbol, nonetheless, of the connection of the old with the new.

Absent from the discussions in the press after Alves's death was the enigmatic figure of Alves's ex-partner, Mário Reis, who could choose to come and go without any risk to his position or status. Still, he was associated with what composer Mário Lago has called the "quintet of the great" from the 1930s: Carmen Miranda, Aurora Miranda, Francisco Alves, Custódio Mesquita, and Mário Reis.[52]

Alves, according to Reis, was a great musical genius who consistently reinvented himself, tried new styles, and collaborated with other promising new musicians to maintain his popularity. He had been competitive and supportive at the same time.[53] The Alves-Reis combination made history on many fronts. They could not have done it, however, without the emergence of new composers such as Ismael Silva and Nilton Bastos, who created their first major success, "Se Voce Jurar," whose release broke new ground at Odeon. A photograph of Alves and Reis appeared in the small area in the middle of the groundbreaking record, showing the two men dressed in coats and ties, their black hair slicked back with grease. Reis appeared in the background smiling at the audience as Alves, in the foreground, gazed at imaginary viewers to the left. Odeon reproduced the same photograph on the cover of the sheet music, emphasizing the duo rather than the composers, whose names (without photographs) appear at the bottom, slightly to the left. Moreover, the sheet music accentuated the often ambiguous relationship between composer and performer since Alves is also listed as one of the composers.[54]

Copyright and Copiers

Bastos had been a friend and partner of Ismael Silva, one of the founders of the samba school Estacio. Silva, as I have indicated, had left his mark on samba, on the radio, and on a host of vocalists, including Reis, Alves, and Carmen Miranda. Silva, who went on to compose a number of works with Rosa and for Reis, would outlive his partner by some forty-seven years, dying at age seventy-two in 1978. Unlike Bastos or Rosa, however, Silva, who was black and poor, would be recognized with a state-sponsored funeral because he died in an era when Cariocas were committed to celebrating and preserving their cultural heritage. His body would be laid out at the recently established Museum of Image and Sound, before being buried at the cemetery of Catumbí.

Despite the recognition in death, the experience of Afro-Brazilians composers such as Ismael Silva, Cartola, and Wilson Batista and that of poor whites illustrated that the economic relations in general and copyright laws in particular operated within a prejudiced framework that exploited black labor. Given the few opportunities available to black composers and musicians, it was better to have their works recorded and performed by interpreters such as Reis than by lesser-known performers, black or white. More problematic, however, were the deceptive plagiarisms that erased the names and contributions of unknown composers from sheet and print music. Vocalists and producers who could afford to buy musical scores benefited from this practice, while relegating blacks to less lucrative forums, where they did not necessarily reap monetary benefits from their performances.

This did not mean that poor blacks did not continue to mingle with the elite of the music industry or perform on the radio and in the theater, only that they were not necessarily as well paid or remunerated at all. Many white amateurs also did not receive payment. The creative geniuses of the poetic *morros* or *suburbios* were clearly at a disadvantage, however. Ignorance about the new system and the lack of clear and consistent laws regarding intellectual property rights worked against them. Thus, during the "Golden Age" of Brazilian popular music, there were two types of composers: those who wrote music and lyrics and those who were registered as authors of music and lyrics. These individuals were not necessarily the same because of an important middleman called the *comprositor*, a neologism formed from the union of "comprar: to buy" and "compositor: the composer," designating the person who bought music from composers.

In selling one's music, a composer gave up his or her right to record, to resell, and most important, to appear as the author, thus disallowing any future rights. The *comprositores* were often artists who recorded the music themselves or sold or gave it to other singers to record. Their names appeared as the author in the registered copy at the National Library and on the sheet music when it was published, and thus they reaped the royalties. Studios and recording companies also bought compositions directly from composers, becoming the official "composers." Nightclubs and other businesses followed this tradition, creating a complex relationship among official and unofficial composers and performers. In addition, only in some cases did the recording artists make a substantial amount of money from the compositions that they bought. The recording companies and publishers such as the Irmãos Vitale, the Magione e Filhos company, and Editora Musical RCA Leme Ltd. reaped the profits.[55]

No matter who profited, popular composers seemed to be in poor straits. This was a time in which copyrights and patents were not universal. It is therefore not surprising that poorer artists, often celebrated in the historical memory as musical geniuses, faced dire economic challenges. Ironically, these composers showcased their talents through the voices of well-placed, mostly white interpreters such as Alves and Reis, and many of these composers were delighted to do so. This relationship between performers and composers may seem unimaginable today when large media conglomerates often possess all copyrights for the majority of the artists who sign on with them.

In fact, in the early stage of development of the recording industry, registered composers, whether they were legitimate or not, still relied on the recording and music publishing companies of sheet music to have their work recognized. This prestige and recognition were rarely compensated monetarily.[56]

Brazilian popular music was growing, and for some was a thriving music business. Only a few of the great stars, among them Francisco Alves and Carmen Miranda, were able to live exclusively from a career in music in the 1930s and early 1940s. Most of the money that was made was pocketed by the top ranks of four commercial enterprises: the radios, the recording companies, owners of theaters and casinos, and the music publishing companies. Radio programs, including the most popular Casé program, even began to require that their singers present new songs on the Sunday program.[57] Ironically, on the published sheet music registered with the National Library, photographs of composers often appeared with performers. Radio and recording studios relied on talented musicians, black and white, middle-class and poor, to fill the many engagements and obligations of a demanding audience.[58]

Conclusion

Francisco Alves crossed paths with many of the great performers, composers, and musicians of his era. He was, for many, not only "the King of the Voice" but the voice of Brazil. No wonder his funeral became a national event. The procession began downtown just after eleven in the morning. A procession of vehicles carrying flowers followed the city's fire department vehicle that carried the casket. The convoy moved from downtown Avenida Rio Branco through the neighborhoods of flamengo, arriving finally at the São João Batista cemetery in Botafogo. Dionysus was present in the wild cries and the singing voices, even though they also reflected the immense sorrow of a people in mourning. At the cemetery, the uncontrollable crowd crushed many mourners. Many others received medical treatment for emotional stress or minor injuries. Police officers had to intervene to make sure that the casket would arrive at its proper destination.⁵⁹

The crowds treated Alves as if he were a saint. They wanted to see him, even touch the casket that contained his charred remains, before he would disappear forever. Those who received news that his car, now a big heap of scarred metal, was being kept outside of the city in Braz de Pina made their way there and literally tore off almost every piece to keep as reminders of their idol. At such an emotional moment, the recording companies could not resist a golden moneymaking opportunity. The studios re-released 112 of his major recordings from over the previous three decades. They would have produced more if some of the old wax originals had not already been destroyed. But some historical documents are lost forever. In the following years, many more records would be re-released, and in 2002, the fiftieth anniversary of his death, a number of CDs and publications would honor him even more. According to Norma Tapajós, wife of Paulo Tapajós, when Francisco Alves sang a song, no one else dared to sing it, much less to record it—not because he prohibited it but because no one ever imagined that he or she could do it half as well.⁶⁰

Politicians understood the power of Alves's voice. In Rio, the Municipal Congress dedicated an entire session to Alves, and politicians turned out for the burial as well. Because President Vargas could not attend the funeral, Captain José Henrique Acióli represented him, an indication of how important Alves was to the nation. Francisco Alves's body was gone, but those present felt his voice. The city, the state, and the nation had never experienced a public mourning on this scale. It was clear that popular music and its performers represented and touched the core of Brazil. Alves's life had been representative of a vivacious period of cultural growth in Brazil's history. His death, like the death of the president, was another indicator of life's ephemeral nature. Brazilians attempted to immortalize him through mourning and celebration, and memory.

Alves had unwittingly brought people together in ways that Getú-lio Vargas had desired on a political level. He had been a conduit for composers who voiced the political, economic, and social happenings of a generation. At the beginning of his career, Alves had registered the political conflict that would eventually lead to the Vargas revolution in 1930 with his recording of Eduardo Souto's humorous *marcha* "E sopa" (It's a soup). With "Retrato do velho" (The old man's portrait) twenty years later, Alves sang Vargas's praises after the former president handily won the 1950 election. The title of the Haroldo Lobo and Marino Pinto song makes reference to the return of the custom of hanging Vargas's portrait in homes, a practice that was widespread during Vargas's dictatorship (1936–1944).[61]

The nation and Vargas missed Alves, although Vargas would focus his energies over the next four years on trying to keep his enemies at bay. News of Alves's death spread around South America and eventually made its way to Carmen Miranda and the Brazilians who were performing in the United States. A little less than three years later, Miranda's death would shake the generation to its core once more, marking ever more sharply the end of the "Old Guard" and the beginning of something new.

At the time of Alves's death, a host of black composers had already begun to receive widespread attention and to be economically compensated. Popular music performance, which is supposed to be timely and ephemeral, turned out to be neither, particularly in a capitalist market where new technologies can prolong the lives of cultural texts. The cohesive forces of nationhood, which rely on historical memory, played a significant role in propagating the names of the pioneers who had passed away but who had left behind a body of texts that would become reference points for future generations. Although Reis was able to ride a new wave of interest in the 1960s and 1970s, the musical world that Reis had inhabited was long gone, and most of his friends had already passed away. He had become a recluse by choice and by circumstance. Unlike the case of Francisco Alves, Reis died in an era of cynicism, when the memory of the "Golden Age" was just that: a memory. Musical tastes had already been fractured by a host of new musical markets and by television. Brazil had already experienced the era of the famous music festivals and the countercultural revolution called *Tropicália*. Reis died in a period with new aesthetic possibilities for a generation that questioned authority.[62]

Questioning authority necessarily changes the relationship of the public with their idols and with history. Not coincidently, Mário Reis's death almost went unnoticed in October 1981. His last wish was that his casket remain closed. Neither stranger nor friend would be able to gaze upon him. None of the staff at the Copacabana Palace, where he had lived in the last years of his life, made it to his funeral mass. A handful of friends showed up at the burial at the São João Batista cemetery, where he was laid to rest less than a hundred meters from the tombs of Francisco Alves and Carmen Miranda. The magazine *Amiga* reported the attendance of six friends associated with the musical world: Carlos Galhardo, Braguinha, Carlos José, Mozart Araújo, Odete Amaral, and Sérgio Cabral.[63]

The presence of Cabral was significant. The major biographer of the "Old Guard" of the "Golden Age" of Brazilian popular music and of the radio, Cabral symbolized a generation of researchers that included Abel Cardoso Jr., from the Paulista town of Sorocaba, and Ricardo Cravo Albin, first director of the Museum of Image and Sound (MIS), which was responsible for preserving the city's musical memory. Reis's role in the propagation of Brazilian popular music was essential, both aesthetically and politically. He brought in the middle- and upper-middle-class audiences to popular music because of his interpretations. Yet it was a world that Francisco Alves had molded and over which he reigned for almost three decades. Most of the major interpreters of the 1930s and 1940s could trace some connection or relationship to Alves. Of the male performers, Reis and Alves had followed in the footsteps of Vicente Celestino, creating a new tradition of singers of the masses who would enthrall audiences for decades. Like marketers, the vocalists molded the relationship between audiences and the compositions in ways that transcended race and class.

Performers were creating and teaching the audiences while reflecting the audiences' collective fantasies and aspirations and while building a tradition, however faulty and socially prejudiced. Alves's voice was one of the first national voices of Brazil. And then came Carmen Miranda.

There were others, but their voices were the first instruments of a national community. Poets such as Wallace Stevens have given tribute to the power of the voice.[64] Brazilian voices touched emotions in a new way, through a new technology, like a Brazilian scherzo to replace and dialogue with the generation-old minuet. Despite the forces of gentrification and the often co-opting of poor black musicians, vocalists with access to the mass market continued to promote and even honor the Afro-Brazilian musical traditions.

CHAPTER FIVE

Africaneity, Performance, and the Women of Brazilian Popular Music

> . . . styles have a history, and those histories condition and
> limit possibilities.
>
> ——————————— Judith Butler, *Gender Trouble*

I f the world of Brazilian popular music were a kingdom and Francisco Alves its king, the undisputed queen would have been Carmen Miranda. Like Alves, Miranda had come from humble beginnings and had traversed racial, class, and cultural lines to captivate Brazilian audiences. Like many of her generation, she observed and absorbed the Afro-Brazilian musical innovations of her downtown neighborhood and acknowledged that she learned how to samba with the *mulatas* from the hills of Rio.¹ She also participated in the pageantry and musical performance of black music, which was intimately connected to her patriotism. As a woman, Miranda broke social norms and taboos, and like other female performers of her era, she utilized both her voice and her body to communicate with her Brazilian audiences. But unlike her predecessors and her contemporaries, Carmen Miranda learned how to separate her public performance from her private life. On stage at the beginning of her career, when few black women received steady performing contracts, Miranda utilized racial parity, sarcasm, humor, charm, and sensuality to dialogue and engage with the Afro-Brazilian musical tradition and to endear herself to the new Brazilian audiences.[2]

This chapter explores the role of Brazilian female performers in promoting Afro-diasporic and Afro-Brazilian musical forms and attitudes in the age of mass communication. We have seen how black Brazilian traditions, which established the foundations of the Brazilian popular music tradition, were initially promoted, celebrated, and adopted by white and nonwhite performers alike. Although Afro-Brazilians participated in the construction of the new Brazilian sound, white and to a lesser extent *mulato/a* and *mestiço/a* performers became the stars and the major ambassadors of Brazilian popular music in the age of mass media.

Like their white male counterparts, white female performers benefited disproportionately from the compositions and labor of Afro-Brazilian popular musicians and composers. But the female voice and body played a singular role in celebrating Brazil's Africaneity and dialoguing with the Afro-Brazilian tradition. Women like Carmen Miranda worked diligently to please their public and to perform in the popular vernacular, even though the elite would scorn them. Although *mulata* and *negra* performers such as Aracy Cortes, Araci de Almeida, and later Angela Maria and Carmen Costa may have had widespread rapport with the Brazilian masses, none of them attained the public attention or economic success of Carmen Miranda.

For talented performers such as Carmen Miranda, the production of Brazilianness and blackness functioned on multiple levels. Carmen Miranda's performances were metaphors for popular class joy and recently achieved respectability. Audiences could see and hear the popular classes in her voice, her language, and her mannerisms as she performed gender, race, and nationhood. Her performances were also celebrations of popular aesthetics and style, particularly in the movements of her body and in her overall presentation and attitude.

But when Miranda said that she had learned samba from the *mulatas*, she was not referring to specific women such as Almeida or Cortes. She was utilizing a specific Afro-Brazilian racial term so that audiences would understand her authenticity. Africaneity, like Africanism, denotes the ways and modes in which peoples and nations affected by the African diaspora acknowledge, incorporate, express, and celebrate their African cultural heritage. Given its history of racism and black marginalization, and the public disrespect of the black body in general and the black female body in particular, Brazil summoned white or "near white" performers to perform in its most important national venues, including the radio and the cinema. Carmen Miranda's unique experience and talents allowed her to answer that call.[3]

Early Female Radio Stars and Performers: From Carmen Miranda to Carmen Costa

It is ironic that the name of the first black woman (in Portuguese, *negra* rather than *mulata*) to become a major radio and recording personality was Carmen Costa. The fact that she worked as Francisco Alves's maid is indicative of the multilayered yet intimate relationships among performers in the popular musical milieu. Born in the interior of the state of Rio de Janeiro in 1920, Carmen Costa moved to the city and started working with Francisco Alves at age fifteen. Because she worked for Alves, she quickly became familiar with the world of popular music, meeting many of its major personalities, including Carmen Miranda. Like Miranda and Alves, she was attracted to the world of performance, and according to some sources, it was Alves who discovered that Costa had talent. Unlike Alves and Miranda, however, she did not enter that world with invitations, but began as an amateur, like most of the unknown Afro-Brazilian signers. Costa sang backup for many singers in various choruses and performed in many of the amateur programs and unpaid competitions sponsored by Rio's radio stations and theaters. With more experience, Costa formed a duo with the black composer known as Henricão before launching her solo career in 1942. By that time, the Brazilian popular music industry had grown considerably, and Carmen Miranda had already moved to the United States, taking Brazilian music global.[4]

The comparative role of race in the popularity and opportunities of Carmen Costa and Carmen Miranda is an important one to consider. Costa was of a different generation and could be better compared to the white singer Emilinha Borba, with whom she began her career at Rádio Nacional. In addition, performance depends so much on individual attributes. Although race is one of them, given that white and nonwhite performers benefited from the vibrant Afro-Brazilian traditions around Rio, voice and charisma were two traits that were arguably more important. Costa's voice and style, particularly before the mid 1950s, when she began to sing in a more colloquial style that used the popular vernacular, differed significantly from those of the other popular singers of her day, including Miranda. Indeed, many Brazilians have said that Costa did not have a "black style," a comment that reflects a point of view that associates blackness with a given Brazilian aesthetic quality of samba that performers such as Carmen Miranda and others perfected in the 1930s.

We do well to remember the complexity of the relationship between gender, race, and nation in popular musical performance. Black performance throughout the diaspora did not emerge in a vacuum. Black cultural practices were not, as Eric Lott reminds us in *Love and Theft*, essences deposited in black bodies.[5] Rather, when we speak of black performances or blackness in performance, we understand that these are practices understood as black, despite in many cases their *mestiço*, *mulato*, or even European origins. Throughout the Atlantic world, the legacy of black slavery meant that white commodification often shaped and influenced the activity and performance of blackness. Abdias Nascimento has pointed out the importance of the black mother, the black female lover, and the black woman's role in providing the first sexual experience for young white men, for example. While the black woman is ever present as a sexual object in the official narrative of national life and psyche, she remained invisible in the postabolition rhetoric of citizenship, hidden from the public view that privileged whiteness. Thus, a white woman who could perform "black" while maintaining the privileges of whiteness would also be compelling to audiences hungry to see themselves as modern, but desperate to celebrate what they perceived was part of an authentic hybrid cultural tradition distinct from that of Europe and the United States.

Women and Musical Performance

The position of the *tías bahianas* discussed in chapter 1 represents one type of Latin American feminism in which pioneering women worked within the confines of the prevailing society, even in "traditional" female roles, to further their own interests and those of their communities. The case of Francisca "Chiquinha" Gonzaga, one the other hand, indicates another brand of feminism in which middle-class women chose to abandon their bourgeois feminine traditions.[6] Gonzaga, who gave Brazil one of its most important carnival classics, created a scandal that had helped open the door for many female performers who would follow in her footsteps in the 1920s and 1930s.[7]

Aracy Cortes, the darling of the *teatro de revistas* who began on the stage in the early 1920s, for example, combined music, performance, and scandal in ways that Brazilians had not seen before. By the middle of the 1930s, a host of new performers, led by Carmen Miranda, who would work within the system as well as challenge it, would emerge. Other white performers, such as Dricinha Batista, Linda Batista, and Aurora Miranda, began their careers through family contacts at a very early age, never engaging in another profession for the rest of their lives. Others, particularly nonwhite performers, had to work in a host of other jobs before breaking into the growing music industry.

Only by the late 1940s did the racial and class demographics among women begin to change, as more Afro-Brazilian women attained prominence and many more women from the popular classes attained opportunities. They were not all welcomed in the "provisional middle class" forums, however. Both Araci de Almeida and Aracy Cortes, who described themselves as *mulatas* at various points in their careers, were known to hang out "with the boys" and use foul language, descriptions that did not necessarily endear them to the Vargas regime or the elite. Cortes was particularly provocative. She began her acting career in the circus with the Afro-Brazilian pioneer Benjamin de Oliveira before becoming the darling of the *teatro de revista* and a radio singer and a recording artist. As I have discussed, Cortes had already performed at Chez Nudistes in Paris and had caused a sensation when she appeared seminude, with a guitar covering her breasts. Like Josephine Baker, Cortes utilized her body in provocative ways.[8]

Although she had recorded many of the musical compositions that Carmen Miranda would later re-record and turn into smash hits, her domain was the popular revue theater. The theater was not as lucrative as the radio or the recording industry, and she never received invitations to perform in the casinos or in any of the Brazilian musical films. Race, social class, and marketability played a significant role in Cortes's fortunes. Like many of the Afro-Brazilian pioneers, she retired on a modest pension and slowly slipped out of the public's attention.[9]

As we have seen, Araci de Almeida had been another pioneer and was much more a part of the bohemian music scene than the Miranda sisters or even Cortes. Almeida, with her "boyish ways," lacked resources but not initiative.[10] By the late 1940s, *mulata* crooners like Angela Maria could become icons among radio performers because of the groundwork laid by many other women. So, too, could other women who came from humble beginnings. Examples were Dalva de Oliveira and other nonwhite singers such as Elizete Cardoso and of course, Carmen Costa. Ironically, many of these Afro-Brazilian women did not dance or utilize their bodies in the way that Miranda felt free to do. While these performance choices relate directly to individual personalities, nonwhite women nonetheless felt obliged to fit into a more limited way of performing gender in order to be accepted into the provisional middle class, at least initially.

Black and *mulata* female performers broke racial barriers during a period when more and more women began entering the labor force in general and then in the performing professions in the late 1940s and early 1950s. Indeed, by the mid 1950s women were essential components of the musical milieu, and the media often relied on sensationalism surrounding stereotypical female behavior to galvanize fans around competitions such as "the Queen of the Radio." One of the most visible rivalries that benefited radio stations was between Marlene and Emilinha Borba. Borba, who was born in the northern suburb of Mangueira, recorded her first record the year that Carmen Miranda left for the United States. Miranda had helped secure her a position at the Cassino da Urca, reserved for those popular artists like Miranda who would appeal to middle-class and foreign audiences.[11] Hailing from São Paulo, Marlene joined Rádio Nacional in 1948, also after having worked in the Cassino da Urca and before becoming one of the few performers who conquered many media in the 1950s.[12]

The popular music milieu also attracted women connected to the wealthy classes. This was the case of Elsie Houston, a classically trained performer and researcher, and Carolina Cardoso de Mello, who received her training at the National Institute of Música and later transcribed many popular compositions—particularly *choros* for the piano. Despite the fact that few formally educated women from the middle class became part of the popular music milieu, the education level of female musicians in general tended to be higher than men's. Of the musicians who registered with the police, however, less than 3 percent were women, the majority of them white. Like their male counterparts, the majority of registered female musicians came from Rio de Janeiro, although other states and countries were also sporadically represented.[13]

Of all the women, Carmen Miranda emerged in the middle of the 1930s as the most important performer of her time. Despite her Portuguese birth, she came to represent the popular Afro-Brazilian *mestiço* tradition that resonated with Brazilians from all walks of life. She took from and dialogued with past and present female performers, and made many of the Afro-Brazilian popular symbols, particularly the Bahiana, the *mulata*, and the *nêga maluca*, her own. Like Alves,

Miranda had influenced many women, including her sister Aurora, who would also become an important female musical performer. Paradoxically, Carmen Miranda's widespread success would also influence the performances of established performers such as Aracy Cortes.

Carmen Miranda and Blackness

The Brazilianness of Carmen Miranda's performance, and of that of other female performers, was at times understood and even articulated as a connection to blackness, as Elsie Houston declared when she boasted about the African roots of Brazilian rhythms.[14] Moreover, the multilayered sense of Africaneity in Brazilian popular music performance must also be viewed in the context of what Paul Gilroy has called "the syncretic complexity of black expressive cultures, which resists the idea that an untouched, pristine Africaneity resides in specific forms."[15] Writers such as Edward Thorpe erroneously defined black dance, for example, in essentialist biological forms. Thorpe characterized white dance as erect and rigid and black dance as pelvic centered, allowing a series of back-and-forth and rotating movements. Not only does Thorpe dismiss the influence of nationality and nationhood on cultural practices, but he also downplays the importance of environment in favor of biological determinism.[16]

Writing on dance in the United States, dance journalist Zita Allen points out that the imprecise, essentialist, and stereotypical use of the term "black dance" has often limited the ability of African Americans to determine what they perform. It is worth reproducing the series of questions Allen asks about the nature of black dance, and by extension black cultural practices:

Is it a black choreographer's work performed by black dancers? A white choreographer's work done by black dancers? Or a black choreographer's work danced by whites? Must it always have a "black" theme? . . . Is it found only in America, or does the label "black dance" apply to works in the repertory of Senegal's National Dance

Company or Cuba's Conjuncto Folklorico or any other company consciously trying to preserve its African heritage?[17]

Oneyda Alvarenga's reference to at least thirteen Africanisms in Brazilian music is also worth reiterating. These include the call-and-response style of singing; the breaking up of the melodic framework; the *umbrigada*, or rapid movement of the belly and pelvis dancing; the importance of drums; and a nasal tone of signing—all with direct or indirect links to various African musical traditions.[18]

The issue of whether black Brazilian dance and music can be separated from other ethnic forms is secondary to the socially constructed Brazilian reality that has historically relegated perceived black forms to the margins. The adoption of those marginalized forms practiced by the lower classes and by many avant-garde artists in the modernist era constituted a de facto celebration of what was understood as representing the aesthetics and values of the majority of Brazilians. Representing Brazil, or *brasilidade*, was as important to female performers of diverse backgrounds, including Elsie Houston, Aracy Cortes, and Carmen Miranda. The fusion of race, gender, and nationality can be best understood by examining the trajectory and interconnections of the female performers within the largely male popular musical world. Carmen Miranda's life and career provide us with a window on to the gender and racial dynamics of this world.

The Miranda Sisters and Their World

Despite the advances of women in the 1920s and 1930s, the radio era was a time when society continued to question the reputations of women in public life. For many, women involved in music were seen as easy and uncouth, and they were often compared to prostitutes. Some women took advantage of these stereotypes and indulged audiences with provocative images. Others resisted the stereotypes and made painstaking efforts to show that they were "descent girls." Carmen and Aurora Miranda traveled the latter path, at least in public. They made appearances at public performances together or with chaperones, for example, and they rarely frequented Rio's downtown bohemian night scene. This still did not win them the approval of many of the elite.[19]

During the "Golden Age of Radio," it was possible to bring the most unlikely individuals together across social lines, and "Taí," Carmen's first hit song, was certainly an example. Joubert de Carvalho was a white medical doctor from Minas and a composer. Carmen Miranda was a twenty-year-old singer from the working class looking for her big break. Their mutual interest in music brought them together. Miranda's exposure to so many important personalities in the late 1920s and early 1930s would eventually pay off. Indeed, musicians enjoyed her as much as the public did, and it was difficult to find flaws in the way she gave herself completely to her performance.[20]

In a country where birthplace can define one's status in the community, the Miranda family's situation exemplified the tensions and challenges of cross-nationality. Her parents, José Maria Pinto da Cunha (1887–1938) and María Emília Miranda da Cunha (1886–1971), were born in Portugal. Of their six children, the two oldest, Olinda and Carmen, were also born in Portugal. Amaro, Cecília, Aurora, and Oscar were born in Rio, and thus Brazilians considered them legitimate Cariocas, even though Olinda and Carmen were both small children when the family moved to Rio in 1910. Being Portuguese in Rio had its advantages and disadvantages. Gilberto Freyre's *lusotropicalism* aside, after independence, many Brazilians were determined to distance themselves from their former colonizers, whom they considered backward and decidedly unmodern. This, however, did not slow the hundreds of thousands of Portuguese immigrants who landed at the port of Santos between 1908 and 1939 to embark upon a new life in Brazil.[21]

The Miranda family lived in Lapa, the public home of musicians and actors, on Rua Joaquim Silva, number 53, and José Pinto da Cunha worked as a barber on the Rua da Misericordia, close to where the Museum of Image and Sound is now located.[22] On the radio, Carmen Miranda would be thrust into a creative world that put her into contact with musicians from all walks of life. Celebrated composers such as Ary Barroso, Andre Filho, and Assis Valente were important, but Sinval Silva, Pixinguinha, and many others would also have an impact on her, allowing her to forge an eclectic and unorthodox style that was both new and provocative.[23]

Carmen Miranda was by no means the most talented performer or singer in Brazil. She was not well studied, nor did she have a particularly unique command of the art of vocal manipulation. Yet she was an indefatigable Brazilian interpreter and performer: a package of grace, flirtation, charm, humor, and sensuality that wooed audiences, female and male alike. Radio and records were the two media that would introduce her to the public, but she soon learned how to choose her venues and the people with whom she worked. Indeed, Miranda preferred the intimate, controlled, and predictable venues like the casinos and radio auditoriums. She shunned the more popular theater revues, for example, especially after an unpleasant experience during the revue *Vai dar o que falar* (Something to Talk About) in September 1930.[24] That revue, written by Marques Porto and Luiz Peixoto, included a number of scandalous numbers, including one on Mangue, the neighborhood known for prostitution. The scene vividly showed men looking for prostitutes and included police on real horses canvassing the area. Despite the revue's general appeal to popular tastes, *Vai dar o que falar* had gone too far, leading some audience members to shout out the last name of the authors of the piece, changing it from "Porto" to "Porco" (pig). The entire experience had an emotional toll on the young Miranda, and she feared that her association with scandal might have changed her relationship with the public.[25]

Carmen Miranda was a keen observer and a quick study, able to recognize talented musicians and composers. Ary Barroso, a white musician who later earned the monikers "Mr. Brazil" and "Mr. Samba," was one of them, and Miranda understood that female performers needed well-connected composers like Barroso.[26] She was known as "the Remarkable Little One" not because of her lifestyle, but because César Ladeira had baptized her with that name, as he had done to so many emerging talents.[27] Like most of the great composers of his day, Barroso explored the role of blacks in Brazilian culture in his compositions and he nourished many careers, including Miranda's. Originally from the small town of Ubá in Minas Gerais, Barroso first performed on the radio in Rio in 1932. By then, Miranda had already recorded seven of his compositions, including "O nêgo no samba" (Blacks in samba), with Marques Pôrto and Luis Peixoto (1929), and "Isto é xodo" (This is something special).[28]

In his interview with Mario de Moraes, Barroso recalled Miranda's particular talent:

> I don't remember exactly how and when I met Carmen. The earliest music that she recorded from my repository is from 1932, "Isto é xodó." But from the first time I saw her I considered her a star with a great future. And could it be because I thought she was a great singer? I don't think so. Nor was her body anything special. Carmen was everything. It was everything together that made her the greatest thing from the Latin world as far as a popular singer.[29]

Although Barroso had worked extensively with Miranda, he had also composed for Araci de Almeida. He had also been instrumental in mythologizing the wonders of Bahia, a practice that remained in vogue for decades. Ironically, Barroso's refusal to record his "No baixo de sapateiro" for the film *Banana da Terra* had made room for Dorival Caymmi's "O que que a Bahiana tem," which would inspire the Bahiana image that Miranda would export to the world.[30]

Barroso's classic "Aquarela do Brasil" (Watercolor of Brazil) had been inspired by his boyhood on the Barrinha farm, near Uba, Minas Gerais, where he saw "the women carrying food to the tired, sweating black men working in the fields."[31] "Aquarela do Brasil," a *samba de exaltação*, or glorifying samba, was a joyous serenade to Brazil that served the Vargas government's nascent patriotism well. Moreover, "Aquarela do Brasil," until the 1960s, was one of Brazil's most popular songs worldwide.[32] Barroso's association with Miranda and other female performers granted them legitimacy, something Aurora Miranda would crave when she lamented later in life not having performed any of Barroso's songs.[33]

The Miranda family lived in the center of the city, in close proximity to the radio stations and recording industries, and were exposed to the booming music industry's products, performers, composers, and producers.[34] Demand for musical performers grew from the late 1920s, when the first radio stations were firmly established, until the early 1940s, giving hundreds of poor and middle-class hopefuls opportunities to sing and perform an eclectic array of compositions, from tangos, *lundus*, *modinhas*, and *marchas* to the consecrated sambas.[35] Aurora Miranda was one of the first to follow in Carmen's footsteps. Unlike her older sister, Aurora Miranda was a bona fide Carioca and did not have to face the ambivalent identity questions about her nationality that would later beleaguer Carmen. Like her sister, Aurora took advantage of the opportunities of the growing mass media thanks to both local ingenuity and foreign investments in the newly established recording companies such as Odeon, Victor, and Columbia.[36]

Throughout the 1930s, Aurora Miranda's schedule of radio and theatrical appearances was impressive. Aurora was not yet seventeen years old when she performed in the Sunday afternoon Rádio Mayrink Viega amateur program, a show that drew teenagers and adults from all over the country. In June 1933, she appeared with her sister at the Teatro Recreio at a festival sponsored by the newspaper *A Noite*. This was followed by an appearance at the movie house Cine Gloria with emerging talents such as Jorge Maud, Petra de Barros, the Bando de Lua, and Custódio Mesquita. In 1934, that same group from the Cine Gloria traveled to São Paulo to perform at the Teatro Santana and Radio Record before leaving for Buenos Aires. Thus, at an early age, Aurora had already been exposed to some of the most important names in the musical business, and had gained local, national, and international exposure.[37]

Carmen and Aurora often performed on the same program on the radio and in theaters in Rio, São Paulo, and Buenos Aires, as well as at the Cassino da Urca in Rio, but the Miranda sisters rarely performed together as a duo. Duos, particularly female duos, were not common in Brazil. At the same time, a number of radio surveys made it clear that both sisters attracted a substantial fan base. Aurora's experience in

the world of radio, and particularly her contact with other performers, eventually secured her a recording contract with Francisco Alves
when he was still the most important male vocalist. Alves had invited
Aurora to sing in one of the festivals that he had organized, and her
performance there led them to record Assis Valente's *marcha* "Cai cai
balão" with the Odeon orchestra, directed by Simon Bountman.[38]

"Cai cai balão" was an important watershed in Aurora Miranda's
and Assis Valente's careers. Valente, a *mulato* from Bahia, was already
making a name for himself as a composer of Christmas tunes, with
"Boas festas" (Happy holidays) and "Pão de açucar" (Sugarloaf). "Cai
Cai" (Fall Fall) was the first of a series of *festa junina tunes* (June festival
songs), including "Acorda" (Wake up) and "São João" (St. John). Like
carnival, the yearly June festivals guaranteed performers, musicians,
and composers a forum to display their talents. Moreover, Aurora's
duet with Francisco Alves assured her of a certain level of attention
and visibility not available to many other performers. The fact that she
was a talented young woman associated with a famous musical family
meant that doors were opened to her, and her association with Alves
flung them wide open. That they could both promote and sing the
works of popular black and *mulato* performers such as Valente, Sinval
Sylva, and others signaled their dialogue with the pulse of the urban
masses.[39]

Female Performance and Africaneity: The Radio and Beyond

The live performances of Carmen Miranda and her duets with her sister
indicated the extent to which Carmen, in particular, relied on her body
to celebrate Brazilian music. Her movements were an important dimension of her Africaneity, even though she would avoid any unbridled
Dionysian movements that many Brazilians historically associated with
African dance. It would not be incorrect to claim that both Miranda
sisters understood that certain forums called for "gentrification" of
styles while others did not, since much of their dancing was improvisational, although Carmen was clearly more comfortable with this latter

style. The sisters' performance of Alberto Ribeiro, João de Barro, and Lamartine Babo's compositions in the film *Alô alô carnaval* illustrate an improvisational performance style that relied on the widely recognized and popular movement of the *marcha* while highlighting the Mirandas' role as ambassadors of national music.[40]

> *We are the radio singers*
> *We are the radio singers,*
> *We spend our lives singing*
> *At night we wrap up your dream*
> *In the morning, we are there to awaken you.*[41]

I have discussed the connection of the *marcha* to the Afro-diasporic tradition. It was the slow, sanguine movement of the two sisters, and particularly Carmen's—their waists moving from side to side and accentuating the movement of the hips—that connects the Mirandas' bodies to the Afro-Brazilian dance and musical performative traditions. Moreover, as Patrice Pavis has indicated, actors most effectively confront and engage audiences through the body and the personality.[42]

José Ligeiro Coelho has called Carmen Miranda an "Afro-Brazilian paradox." He is right. She performed the Afro-Brazilian female character and thus became black, or at least an exaggerated black singer and dancer.[43] She embodied the aesthetics and patriotism of a generation of black and white Brazilians, presenting a spectacle that engaged audiences of all backgrounds. Aurora would engage Brazilians with her own recordings, but Carmen's kinetic charm and performance were in a category of their own. This did not stop Aurora from recording André Filho's 1934 *marcha* "Cidade maravilhosa," a tune that would become the "Official Hymn of the State of Guanabara."[44]

Cariocas continue to perform this song after carnival, and in other official and unofficial promotional campaigns for the city of Rio de Janeiro. Aurora had been an avid student of music even though, like the majority of the performers of her time, she had no formal training. Carmen was the trendsetter who many would try to imitate, a consummate interpreter to the point of changing the music to fit her own style. Aurora, on the other hand, saw her role as a performer in more traditional terms. Singing was her job, and she executed it with a high degree of professionalism.[45]

Despite their closeness and traveling together constantly, and in spite of the consecrated memory of the now famous "As cantoras do rádio," the Miranda sisters had different approaches to their performances. Carmen's more improvisational style, her closeness to the popular composers, and her use of her body would distinguish her most. Indeed, Aurora often found it was difficult to work with Carmen. Carmen would frequently take a song and spontaneously change the lyrics, its tone, and its choreography, thus making it completely her own, like the improvisational performances of jazz musicians. But this was the precise quality that strengthened the bonds between Carmen and her audiences.[46]

Carmen and Aurora Miranda led a new female presence in the music and performance business, but they were not members of "the environment." A certain distance was healthy for women who wanted to guard their reputations. For those who did not care, it was a different story. Aracy Cortes, on the other hand, was the type of woman who seemed not to care. Cortes constantly broke the social rules of proper gender decorum in public and in private. She made her body central to her performance and celebrated publicly and privately her connection to Africaneity and to Afro-Brazilian performers such as Benjamin de Oliveira. Carmen Miranda had been more discreet, although she pushed the limits of performance in forums intended for the middle class as well as in more popular performance venues.

The distinctions between women like Araci de Almeida and Aracy Cortes ironically had little to do with economic class and more to do with age, family background, and personality. The Vargas's government campaign against vagrancy hit the bars and restaurants not just because of the men who frequented them but also because of the women who went there. Frota Aguiar, chief of the Delegacia de Costumes, mounted a campaign against *cafetinagem* (café slumming), among other activities that the government labeled as vagrancy. He also targeted the "dancing girls," Rio's version of escorts, who hung around Café Nice, for example, mostly from the nearby Dancing Milton or Dancing Avenida.[47]

Women such as Aurora Miranda reiterate what Norma Tapajós claimed when she said that she never sensed or witnessed any prejudice against women, although their very absence in archival documents, photos of orchestras, auditoriums, and radio studios indicate that only a few women were able to make careers in the field of popular music production.[48] Unlike Carmen Miranda, Cortes, and Almeida, Aurora Miranda did eventually retire from public life to become a mother and wife, following the gender norms of the day. Reflecting on her career in the mid 1960s, Aurora Miranda claimed that she had no regrets. She had left the limelight to dedicate herself to her family. This had always been the standard story, and one that many middle-class women had followed.[49]

Women certainly understood that it was a man's world, but that did not stop Carmen Miranda from partnering with talented male musicians to secure exclusive contracts. Male colleagues surrounded her and helped to build her career while she more fully incorporated elements of Afro-Brazilian culture into her repertoire, of which her adoption of the Bahiana was the most important. Miranda's evocation of Brazilian sexuality in general, and black and mulatto sensuality in particular, was balanced with humor. At the same time, she had no compunctions about assuming the *favelada*'s or the *mulata*'s poetic voice, or becoming the storyteller or the satirist of the popular class.

Humor, Blackness, the Popular, and the Celebration of Brazil

When Carmen Miranda left for the United States in 1939, her farewell song was "Adeus batucada" (Good-bye drumbeat), written by her black chauffeur and musical composer, Sinval Silva.[50] The *batucada*, as Mário de Andrade reports, "was a popular synonym for the samba in the 1920s and 1930s."[51] Miranda's relationship with Silva was illustrative of the unique social environment in which she moved. Silva, who had been introduced to Miranda by Valente, became Miranda's confidant, her friend, and her personal chauffeur. In 1935, he composed the biggest hit of her career to date, "Adeus batucada." Like Ary Barroso, Silva had moved to Rio from Minas Gerais, and had worked in a number of jobs before becoming a mechanic. Even though Valente had introduced Silva to Miranda as someone who composed music, Silva did not consider himself a professional composer and thus was not insulted when she offered him a job as her driver. Not merely "driving Ms. Miranda," Silva quickly became her friend and musical collaborator in a milieu that often allowed for close associations across race and class lines. Friendly associations did not mean that they were socially equal, however, a reality that Silva and his family downplayed even when he visited Miranda in the racially segregated United States in 1951. As late as the 1980s, Silva received coverage from the press in Rio because of his relationship to Miranda. In the early 1990s, Silva's widow, who lived in one of the poor suburbs of Rio, had nothing but positive recollections of Miranda and what she did for her husband. Sinval Silva, meanwhile, died in relative poverty, although he was awarded with the city's newly inaugurated musical award, the Bachelors of Samba, by the Museum of Image and Sound.[52]

According to Silva, Carmen Miranda was a superstitious woman who, at the age of twenty-four, fretted over a fortune teller's prediction that she would die within two years. After receiving this tragic prediction, she asked Silva to compose a samba for her with "a bit of sadness." The result was "Adeus batucada," a song that once again equated Brazil with blackness by way of the *batuque*, a term that could refer to dance, music, or celebration. Miranda had already recorded several compositions that made reference to her love of the *batuque*, including the 1935 recording of Kid Pepe's "Se gostes do batuque" (If you like the *batuque*), which made explicit reference to the capacity of poor and simple black people in the favelas to enjoy life.[53] "She was good people," Silva insisted, as he prepared to sing among the "Old Guard" at the Opinião Theatre in 1972. "She respected simple and modest people."[54]

Despite her close ties with many black musicians, or perhaps because of them, Miranda felt comfortable playing with race, many times in ways that would horrify some contemporary audiences. She performed in blackface, for example, and imitated the language of the black working class in Rio, not unlike many of her North American contemporaries who imitated nameless black American popular performers.[55] The difference was that Miranda saw the black tradition as part of her own and collaborated and worked with black composers and musicians. Miranda had befriended many Brazilian pioneers, but she also had been generous and had made contacts with the younger generation, and many of these contacts were with Afro-Brazilians. The black comedian and performer Grande Otelo, for example, met Miranda when he arrived from São Paulo in 1935, and he went on to perform with her at the Cassino da Urca.[56]

Many female performers attended her funeral like somber sirens mourning the passing of a sister. For example, Dalva de Oliveira, who attended her funeral, had developed a strong relationship with Miranda, and she was about to ask the Hollywood star to become godmother to one of her sons. Dalva de Oliveira shared the story of female social ascension through music with Elizete Cardoso and Araci de Almeida. Like Carmen Miranda, she had come from a working-class background and eventually made her ascent to national recognition through radio. Oliveira was not a Carioca, however. Born in the Paulista city of Rio Claro in 1917, Oliveira began working as a *babá*, a babysitter, at age eleven to help her recently widowed mother. Later she took on a number of odd jobs, including cleaning and working in a factory in the federal capital that manufactured slippers. Coincidentally, the owner of the factory also owned the radio station Radio Ipanema, where she got her first break. The experience at the small radio station led to opportunities at Rádio Sociedade and Radio Phillips, in addition to performing in theaters, where she met the white Herivelto Martins and the black Nilo Chagas, then the Duplo Preto e Branco (Black and White Duet). César Ladeira later baptized the three of them the "Trío de Ouro" (Golden Trio). If duos were rare, trios were exceptionally rare, yet the Trío de Ouro went on to create and record many of Brazil's classics, particularly in the 1940s.[57]

In the early 1950s, Oliveira earned the respect and admiration of professional musicians and composers such as Villa Lobos. Critics claimed that she possessed a voice and style that many tried to imitate. Long after Carmen Miranda left Brazil, Oliveira was a leading female radio personality in the era when audiences elected the most popular female performer as "the Queen of Radio." Oliveira won the title in 1951, but fan clubs of the singers Marlene and Emilinha Borba, for example, turned a friendly competition among professionals into a feud. Following on the heels of the first radio divas were crooners such as Angela Maria, who would be one of radio's first nonwhite "queens," although as João Carlos Rodrigues affirms in his *O negro brasileiro e o cinema*, she became a star because she was a "light-skinned *mulata*, almost white."[58] But it is important to emphasize that she was not white, and this represented a change.

To say that there was no competition among performers before the era of the "radio queens" would be misleading. Competition has always been essential to capitalist radio production, and after Decree 21111 in March 1932, which allowed advertisements on the air, radio stations began to invest funds in musical productions to attract consumers. Newspapers tapped into the sensibilities of the growing urban masses in a competitive manner as well, through polls and interviews that required patrons to vote in various competitions. Carmen Miranda was among the best-paid Brazilian performers of her time, and probably second only to Francisco Alves, because she tapped into popular sentiments and embodied characters with which Brazilians were familiar.[59] Her use of the Bahiana was but one strategy in her diverse satire, where racial parity and humor and her own performance of blackness were central. As José Ramos Tinhorão reports in his *Historia social da música popular brasileira*, while the elite and upper middle class still looked toward Europe, the culture of the urban masses was about to have a national explosion, and Carmen Miranda would play a significant role.[60]

Satire and Carmen Miranda's Performance in Brazil

While Vargas's nationalist rhetoric attempted to nationalize "the popular," Carmen Miranda showcased popular black musical rhythms with lyrics that spoke of poverty and the importance of music to daily life, to race, and to patriotism. Humor, satire, and exaggeration of black and other popular rhythms were central to Miranda's musical repertoire. These performance strategies connect her to other Afro-diasporic representations, such as minstrelsy practiced by contemporaries like Josephine Baker. Humor, and particularly satire, played a crucial role in musical performance and in popular music in general. Male and female composers and interpreters relied upon caricature and exaggeration to engage their audiences, or in many cases resorted to parody, sarcasm, and irony to generate what Freud calls "comic pleasure."[61] Female performers such as Miranda, Baker, and Cortes created myriad ways to laugh about the national character while simultaneously celebrating nationhood. Lyrics and musical scores provided the framework for performance, but successful execution depended upon the personal style of singers.

Carmen Miranda succeeded in this endeavor as a Brazilian singer largely through the evocation of humor and folklore, often presenting and embodying stereotypical images familiar to national audiences. On a few occasions, Miranda lent her satirical style to social criticism in a manner atypical of her time. Her passion for the popular vernacular often led people to call her vulgar. Her "vulgarity," however, often allowed her to break racial taboos, while defying gender roles that sought to limit women's behavior. Through comedic and satirical samba tunes, rather than through other genres such as ballads or folk songs, Miranda presented the popular language, rhythms, and aesthetic qualities inherited mostly from African influences. While much of the black culture content emerged in picturesque form, she nonetheless encouraged celebration, as songs such as "Disso é que eu gosto" (That's what I like) clearly affirm.[62] Many of the songs she recorded explicitly called for a recognition of the legitimacy of popular music, and thus were an implicit criticism of bourgeois cultural values. Miranda never begged for this recognition. She demanded it in humorous ways. Carmen set an example of how to perform both race and gender before she traveled to the United States.[63]

At the same time, Miranda's role as a "gentrifying agent" of popular music must be emphasized. She served as part of a middle-class vehicle between the mostly black and *mulato favelados* and the nation. In her unconventional book based on personal interviews and conversations with Miranda, Dulce Damasceno de Brito, a journalist and friend of Miranda, displayed her own prejudice toward popular music when she emphasized that Miranda brought sophisticated gestures to the samba from the *morros* and explained that "her special style gave popular music something that it lacked: class." This comment is particularly ironic since Miranda had come from the lower classes and had lived among poor white and black residents for most of her young life.[64]

Still, Miranda's hymns to the Brazilian nation and Brazilian culture included such playful versions as "Minha terra tem palmeiras" (My land has palm trees) written by João Barro and Alberto Ribeiro, and her rendition of Amado Regis's samba "O samba e o tango" (Samba and tango) juxtaposes the rhythms of the Brazilian samba to that of the Argentine tango.[65] Despite the explicit message of national pride, both songs defy the solemnity associated with the nationalist rhetoric, which often presented Brazil in ultra-idealist imagery. "O samba e o tango" is essentially a playful nationalist battle between Brazil and Argentina in which Brazil prevails, while "Minha terra tem palmeiras," *a marcha*, presents Brazil as a land of rum, rhythm, fruit, blondes, and chocolate *morenas*, where one can "cut loose." The satire is not only found in explicit lyrical references but also in Miranda's own playful manner, and in the samba or *marcha* rhythms, sometimes lending themselves to celebratory humor, mockery, or surprise.

"Eu gosto da minha terra" (I like my country) by R. Montenegro, which Miranda recorded with the Victor Brasileira Orchestra in August 1930, lauds Brazilian civilization and the Brazilian "race," which has brought forth so many beauties and pleasures.[66] The song's unequivocal faith in Brazil, combined with its playful execution, became a Miranda trademark visible in other songs such as "Terra morena"

(Browned-skin land), which proclaims that "God is Brazilian," and "Nova descoberta" (New discovery), which describes Cabral's love affair with Brazil.[67] Such exaggerations that made Brazilians feel good about Brazil constituted a vital force of Miranda's humor, which endeared her to the public.

In the first stanza of "Eu gosto da minha terra," the singer hails the Brazilian landscape and forges in the tradition of racial democracy a sense of a cosmic Brazilian race to which she belongs. Stanza two reinforces an appreciation for popular culture such as the samba and a rejection of foreign influences, much like the nationalist-minded *antropófagos* of the 1920s modernists. Finally, she rejects exile or going abroad, to remain in her national home. Sung by a woman born in Portugal, and who maintained her Portuguese passport, this song was an affirmation of Miranda's own sense of Brazilianness.

That Miranda considered herself carnivalesque underscores her vision of herself within the satirical Brazilian musical genre.[68] On the other hand, the fact that she was Portuguese and chose to celebrate her Brazilian identity could be manipulated to promote Brazil's encompassing sense of racial democracy. Indeed, Vargas's antiimmigrant tactics, which heightened during World War II, all but forced immigrants with strong foreign identities to embrace Brazil. Thus, Miranda's evocation of a "Brazilian race" connected her to Gilberto Freyre and other theorists of racial democracy, while downplaying her foreign birth.

The adaptation of the Portuguese to the tropics, a crucial element of Brazilian pride, was certainly emphasized in Paulo Barbosa and Vicente Paiva's 1935 "Salada Portuguesa" (Portuguese salad), a simple carnival tune that acknowledged Brazil's greatness in comparison to Portugal.[69] According to Edigar de Alencar, this song was accepted as a carnival entry precisely because it gave Brazilians the opportunity to present themselves in more favorable terms than the Portuguese, yet it also allowed immigrant families such as Miranda's to again affirm a Brazilian-Portuguese connection.[70]

Nonconfrontational, frivolous musical compositions proliferated in the 1930s, thanks in part to the censorship machine of the

Department of Publishing and Propaganda and the general tendency toward national celebration. Many musicians nonetheless insisted on social commentary and criticism within a broader parameter of national pride. Carmen Miranda was among them. Her status as "the Ambassador of Brazilian Popular Music" afforded her an opportunity to comment on social relations, and to address the nation at large in a didactic manner. Her carnivalesque aesthetic elicited laughter, but challenged authority within limits.[71]

Race relations and blackness became more explicitly the subject of Miranda's 1939 duet with Almirante, "Preto e branco."[72] Constructed in the form of a dialogue, "Preto e branco" offers a the humorous look at race relations in Brazil while nonetheless criticizing Brazilians' aversion to blackness in much the same way that Mário de Andrade critiques whitening in his 1928 novel, *Macunaíma*. The song plays with Brazilian images and stereotypes of blacks and ends with the cathartic punch line:

God also made blacks white
Where? At the bottom of their feet.

Brazilian racial humor often came at the expense of blacks. While Miranda unconditionally renounced racism and her racial satire often carried a humorous social commentary, her songs frequently reinforced stereotypes prevalent in the 1930s. "O nêgo no samba," for example, which she first recorded with the Victor Brasileira Orquestra in December 1929, later released in May 1930, underscores the natural ability of blacks to dance and whites' difficulty of acquiring these "Brazilian talents." The connection to blackness and Brazilianness is highlighted not only in the lyrics but also in the body of Miranda, which seemingly contradicts the lyrics. Miranda, a white woman creating samba, remarked, for example, that "white people can't dance samba"—but this is a constructed whiteness, foreign to the very Brazilianness that the singer promoted and thus distinct from her Africanized body.

Black people's samba
Breaks the hips
Black people's samba
Has liquor in it
Black people's samba
Always on your toes
Black people's samba, my baby
Drives me crazy

In samba, white people get injured
In samba, black people move themselves around
In samba, white people don't really have much skill, my baby
In samba, blacks are born to groove[73]

In the 1935 release of the *marcha* "Mulatinho bamba" (Smart little mulatto), Miranda reinforces similar qualities in the *mulato*, only now with more sensual undertones and an emphasis on the physical beauty of a *mulato* in ways that would have been inappropriate for "descent" white women of the era.[74] The first stanza talks about the *mulato*'s unique dancing qualities, while the last one compares his beauty to the white Hollywood actor Clark Gable.[75] The singer assumes the position of a woman from the popular classes, probably black or *mulata*. The masked Carmen Miranda assumed the role of the voyeur who is seduced by the beauty and elegance of this *mulato*. Furthermore, the third stanza, "He does not carry a knife / and he neither wears a handkerchief around his neck / Nor a straw hat on his head," provides a positive image of a *mulato bamba*, while implicitly denouncing the "bad" *malandro*, who would have worn the attire the singer criticizes. Such positive appraisals were fully in step with the Vargas regime, whose condemnation of antisocial behavior among the popular classes was notorious.

Like Miranda, many of the female singers performed songs that expressed the views of various characters from the popular classes. Songs such as "Ao voltar do samba" (Coming back from the samba) and

"Rencenceamento" (The census) allowed them to express diverse emotions and sometimes to comment on contemporary events. Songs with titles such as "O imperador do samba" (The samba emperor),[76] "Gente bamba" (Bamba people),[77] and "Deixe esse povo falar" (Let these people speak)[78] underscore the importance of respect for popular music, and the importance of Afro-Brazilian cultural practices to the national soul.

The compositions of this period that make reference to blacks or *mulatos* are not altogether stereotypical, and it was Miranda's incarnation of the Bahiana and her evocation of the blackness of Bahia, seen through the lens of the Carioca, that represented her most resounding celebration of Africaneity. At times this celebration is seen in the evocation of Brazilian cultural influences, such as food, as in "A preta do acarajé" (The black woman with bean fritters), first recorded in 1939 as a duet with Dorival Caymmi. "A preta do acarajé" presented elements of the Bahian folklore in nonstereotypical terms, as if describing a scene at ten o'clock in the evening on the streets of Salvador, the capital of the northeastern state of Bahia. The song emphasized the hard work that blacks often endured to produce something pleasurable for consumption: "Todo mundo gosta de acarajé" (Everyone likes bean fritters), but "ninguem quer saber o trabalho que da" (no one wants to know how much work it takes).[79] This last line might easily apply to Miranda's own body of work and the energy and time she devoted to becoming the Bahiana, who would be permanently associated with food on her head. Indeed, Miranda often reaffirmed her patriotism and Brazilianness though food and music.

A Note on the Bahiana in Brazil

In *Carmen Miranda: Bananas Is My Business*, Helena Solberg documents how Miranda utilized the Bahiana, an Afro-Bahian symbol associated with the poor street women selling their wares in the northeastern city of Salvador, to present to Cariocas, North Americans, and then the world. Simultaneously, Miranda created a seemingly fresh and unique female personality that will forever be associated with her, although she was not the first to use the Bahiana. Aracy Cortes, the queen of the *teatro de revista*, had used the figure before her, as had Elsie Houston, but Miranda made her jovial, fun-loving, sensual, and nonthreatening Bahiana a ubiquitous icon. Co-optation only tells half the story. Moreover, Miranda's performance and celebration of the Bahiana, like the celebration of myths and icons elsewhere, became important because of the desires and visions of the audience. Miranda became the Bahiana, and through her Miranda once again claimed her Africaneity and reaffirmed her Brazilianness.[80]

The composer most associated with Carmen Miranda because of the Bahiana was Dorival Caymmi, a Bahian who arrived in Rio in 1938, but Bahia and Bahians had been important to her career before his arrival. The Bahians Josué de Barros and Assis Valente had played fundamental roles in her career throughout the 1930s, for example. Barros had radio and recording contacts, had already recorded Brazilian music in Germany, and had been instrumental in securing Miranda's first recording contract with Brunswick, after which she transferred to Victor.[81]

Assis Valente supplied Aurora Miranda with his compositions and was also a key personality in Carmen's early career. Valente's compositions, which vacillate between malicious and playful and which comment on the social conditions and practices in Rio, served Carmen Miranda's early style well.[82] "Tem francesa no morro" (1932) was particularly hilarious and malicious in the way it criticized the Carioca imitation of the French, and it shows Valente's own inclination for playing with languages:

Donê muá vu plé loner de dance aveque muá
Dance ioiô
Dance iaiá
Si vu frequente macumbe
Entrê na virada e fini pur samba

Vian petite francese
Dancê le clasique

An cime da mese
Quando la dance coméce
On dance ici on dance aculá
Si vu né pá dance
Adiê mon cherri, pardon já me vá[83]

Carmen Miranda's recognition of Valente's talent resulted in many collaborations, twenty-three recordings in all. When Miranda returned to Brazil in 1940 after her first stint in the United States, Valente had two sambas for her to record. She recorded "Recenseamento" but refused to record "Brasil pandiero!" since it made fun of the way North Americans had gravitated toward samba. Her experience with professional musicians abroad and her knowledge of the North American public meant that she had become an international performer with a reputation to uphold. The musical world did not always make it easy to mix the emotional and business sides, and in this case most reports indicate that Valente took the refusal personally. Moreover, by the early 1940s the musical world was beginning to change. A host of new composers and singers were beginning to emerge in a more competitive environment, where North American influences were apparent. As a result of this trend, Valente would eventually have a difficult time securing work as a composer.[84]

Many female performers forged close relations with specific composers. Carmen Miranda's association with a host of composers, including many Afro-Brazilians and specifically Afro-Bahians, helped catapult her to stardom, but they were not the only ones who had helped create her repertoire. Not only had she emerged in the right place at the right time, she was one of the first to emphasize, through her performance, the distinction between a performer of Brazilian music and a singer. Her instinct, her interpretation of songs, and her mocking, sensual, and playful personality with lyrics and rhythms made her the most sought after performer of her time. Despite racial exclusivity in a number of places, particularly casinos and certain radio clubs, the Brazilian collaboration across racial lines in the 1930s and 1940s implied a social flexibility unimagined in the United States at the time. Miranda's collaboration with Afro-Brazilians such as Valente and Caymmi attests to this.

Her meeting with Dorival Caymmi may have been by chance, occurring as it did because Ary Barroso had refused to let her perform his Bahian songs in the movie *Estudantes*. If Carmen Miranda needed a composition with a Bahian theme, the popular music network would contrive to find her one. Bahian themes were common among Carioca composers, and Miranda had already recorded many, including Barroso's "No tabuleiro da Baiana" (The Bahiana's tray, 1936), André Filho's "Baiana do tabuleiro" (The Bahiana with the tray, 1937), and "Nas cadeiras da Baiana" (On a Bahiana's hips) in 1938 by Portelo Juno and Léo Cardoso. Thus, Dorival Caymmi appeared to introduce Miranda to his ode to the Bahiana, a song that not only allowed Miranda to sing about a far-off place but also to slowly show audiences how her body was in fact the Bahiana.[85]

Some have argued that Caymmi was responsible for teaching Miranda how to move, but it is clear that she was adept at moving her body to rhythms throughout the 1930s. Collaboration with Caymmi afforded her an opportunity to synchronize music and body in ways that she may not have done before, beginning a practice that she would continue throughout her career. To the principal questions "What does the Bahiana have?" and "What is it that the Bahiana has going for her?" the singer responds by moving and oscillating different parts of her body as she shows off the Bahiana's charms. After 1939, Miranda would be forever associated with the Bahiana, one of Brazil's important icons of blackness.

Conclusion

After living for more than a decade in the United States, Carmen Miranda returned to Brazil in 1954 to visit her family and to recuperate from her strenuous working schedule. Brazil had already changed considerably, and black women had made important inroads into the top tier of national performers. Miranda took the opportunity to meet the newest names in music, including Angela Maria, whom President Vargas called Sapoti and with whom she developed a long-distance friendship. Speaking of Miranda after her death, Angela Maria reported that "no one interpreted the samba with more authority, as if it were her very own. Every Brazilian feels a longing, tears of pain, for this loss."[86]

Carmen Miranda had gained personal success in Brazil in ways that paralleled Vargas's own gains. Female performers of all ages and backgrounds looked to her as a model. She had helped changed the gender dynamics in the radio and recording industries. Able to perform in multiple forums, she highlighted the importance of blackness to Brazilianness. This she did with her voice, her eyes, and her body. There is no doubt that the popular classes adored her. So did the politicians in the Vargas regime. Indeed, Vargas believed that her relationship with Brazilians reflected on him.[87]

Even without Vargas's efforts, Carmen Miranda would have galvanized support from the masses that adored her. The criticism of her performance in the United States had come mostly from the middle-class press, who harbored what Caetano Veloso has aptly described as both pride and shame. Upon her death, there was no doubt that there would be a cult around Carmen Miranda. Her funeral in Rio on August 13, 1955, was the perfect ritual for the beginning of that cult while marking the end of an era.[88]

Carmen Miranda's journey north occurred precisely at the moment when she had made the appropriation of a black musical icon complete. But one cannot forget her childhood among Afro-Brazilians. Her musical partnership with Caymmi had allowed her to discover the Bahiana, to adopt it and tailor it to her own tastes. Indeed, Miranda's personal style and charisma and her sense of humor were often considered as outrageous as her outfits, partly because she was a white woman with money who put on black costumes and promoted black music. No wonder some in the Brazilian elite resented her. Remarkably, it was the popular classes that continued to support her throughout the 1940s and early 1950s.

The Brazilian system allowed Miranda and other women to rise on the coattails of black and *mulato* entertainers and composers, but she also learned to perform within the emerging social and gender codes that assured her financial success. Yet she also served as a conduit through which many unknown musicians could present their talents. Brazilian white racial hegemony, similar to hegemony elsewhere, provided a set of rules that defined the parameters of opportunity, even though Vargas's focus on the nation to the exclusion of race further marginalized the emergence of many black voices. Individual performers and artists implicated in the system must certainly be examined on an individual basis. Carmen Miranda, the musician, performer, entertainer, and satirist, left behind a body of work that demonstrated the complex ways in which blackness is performed and celebrated in Brazil.[89]

CHAPTER SIX

Race and Brazilianness Abroad in the Early Era of Globalization

Brasil!

Mostra a tua cara

Quero ver quem paga

Pra gente ficar assim. Brasil![1]

——————————— Cazuza, "Brasil"

To Brazilians in 1955, the year of Carmen Miranda's death, there was no doubt that Orpheus was a woman and her name was Carmen Miranda. Brazilians changed the plot significantly, substituting the Brazilian nation for Euridice, the United States for Hades, and North American capitalists for the hyenas. This was a patriotic fable that also ended in death and tragedy. Miranda had invested so much time and energy to get from the radio to the casinos to the silver screen in Brazil before going on to Hollywood. While there were oracles along the way, no one could resist the powers of Hades. The oracles foretold the protagonist's death, but when it came to pass, the nation was nonetheless shocked. Carmen Miranda, an adopted daughter of Rio de Janeiro, had moved to the United States, where she became a global icon, only to return in a coffin less than two decades later.

This final chapter examines the role that Carmen Miranda and other popular Brazilian performers played in the promotion of Brazilian popular music outside of Brazil. It also examines the role that Afro-diasporic culture and identity played in performing Brazil abroad. With markets closed off to them in Europe at the height of the national production, Brazilians first traveled to South American countries such as Argentina to export their musical rhythms, before traveling to the United States. Outside of Brazil, Brazilian popular music maintained its connection to its Afro-Brazilian roots, although with time it would also be influenced by other Afro-diasporic traditions such as the rumba, jazz, and other American and international popular traditions.

For the most part, white Brazilian performers became the most important ambassadors of Brazilian popular music in the United States, although Afro-Brazilians had performed in Argentina since the 1920s. Afro-Brazilians had begun to make inroads into the top echelons of radio and stage performers, but few of them would have opportunities to perform in the pre-1950s segregated United States. In the face of segregation, Brazilian performers played a significant role in shaping North America's first mass-media notions of Latinidad, or Latinness—an identity that built upon commonly accepted conceptions of blackness. Carmen Miranda's Africaneity played a central role in the cross-national dialogue.

The Death of Carmen Miranda: Long Live Carmen Miranda!

Prior to her death in Beverly Hills, California, Carmen Miranda had just signed a contract with the Follies Theater to appear in Mexico for two weeks in September 1955. It would have been her first appearance there and an important symbolic moment in crossing over and reaching out to the largest Spanish-speaking audience outside of the United States. She would have been nicely rewarded at $4,500 a week. That performance was not to be.[2]

In the United States, Carmen Miranda had been confronted with her own heritage and her notions of Brazilianness and blackness. Like many performers who traveled to the United States, she had to adjust her attitude about race and about herself to survive in a world that was racially segregated. In the United States, she relied less on verbal understanding in Portuguese to communicate (although witty lyrics remained a part of her repertoire) and more on her body to communicate—what Brazilians already understood as a part of Brazil's Afro-Brazilian musical tradition—that is to say, an expression of Africaneity. North Americans called her performance "Latin" for three reasons: it had come from the region that French intellectuals in the nineteenth century had dubbed "Latin America," and it was performed by "Latin"-looking people—understood as tanned or brown skinned. But the term "Latin" also allowed people in the United States to develop another cultural category that seemed to be neither white nor black. Yet it was precisely because white, mostly female bodies performed dances in a style associated with blackness in both the United States and Brazil that "Latinness" emerged as new way of gazing at the black body. "Latinness," as a hybrid cultural identity, was in direct opposition to both "whiteness" and "blackness," which most Americans still continued to view as mutually exclusive.

In his 1939 review of *The Streets of Paris* in the *New York Post*, Herbert Drake vividly illustrates how Brazilian performers come to represent "Latinness," "Tropicalness," and nonwhiteness with carnival and "Fun! Fun! Fun!" After seeing Miranda perform on Broadway, Drake reported:

> Miss Miranda is dark tan and shining with a personality apparently indigenous to Brazil. *Whatever it is*, she is wonderful to watch but the lady does not appear except once, when she sings a few monotonously fascinating chants, in Portuguese, *perhaps*. All the while she looks fabulously like a tropical Tallulah rampant against a costume-ball background, but very wicked around the eyes. She does serve as a particular symbol of the high-stepping, band-leading speed and glitter of the show.[3] (italics mine)

Carmen Miranda's body became a contested commodity both in Brazil and the United States. Miranda provided the United States with an exotic joie de vivre in the midst and in the aftermath of a dreary war. But Miranda also tested the racial boundaries of the United States, and helped to define Latinidad for a nation that had long ignored its southern neighbors or dismissed them as culturally inferior. In a political and economic world in which communities are defined as "us" and "them," Carmen Miranda was caught among many worlds. This struggle was only resolved on her death when Brazil—not Portugal, where she was born, or the United States, where she became an international star—claimed her body like a sacred relic. Her corpse arrived in Rio on August 13, 1955, embalmed and ready for a national pageantry of mourning and celebration in a ritual that Puerto Rican author Edgardo Rodríguez Juliá has called "the kingdom of conflicting emotions . . . in which the disorganized sense of interior time does not choose between attacking death and denying it, since the deceptive state of the deceased in some sense remains alive and has not yet been relegated to memory."[4]

Carmen Miranda's body had returned to Brazil seven days after her death in Beverly Hills, and the country was still stunned. There was hardly enough time to mourn the absence of a neighbor, much less understand or put finality to such an important personality—not because she had gone to Hollywood, as so many writers and commentators implied, but because, like Francisco Alves, she represented so much for the Cariocas, and by extension for Brazil. Miranda's exaggerated performance also touched Brazil's nationalist nerve, and Lucia Lippi Oliveira has pointed out that Brazilian intellectuals have historically accentuated how Brazil is different (and better) than the United States while coming to grips with their sense of inferiority.[5]

Brazilian Performers Abroad: Issues of Blackness and Patriotism

At the height of the "Golden Age of Radio" in the middle of the 1930s, and with the establishment of national radio, recording, and cinema stars, the impending conflicts in Europe meant that Europe would begin to close its doors to Latin American and other foreign performers. Brazilians were increasingly traveling internationally. Argentine radio, with its center in Buenos Aires, experienced its "Golden Age" at approximately the same time as its Brazilian counterpart, and Buenos Aires became a major destination for many Brazilian performers.

Brazilians in Argentina

In the 1930s, a trip to Buenos Aires to perform on the radio or in one of the local clubs or theaters was considered a great honor and an experience that many desired. Indeed, news of the Brazilians performing in Buenos Aires contributed to the city's mystique, even more enhanced by vanity magazines and other popular publications. "The Land of Gardel," as many musicians called it in honor of the Uruguayan born tango singer Carlos Gardel, was undoubtedly one of the most important cities in South America.[6]

Ironically, Pixinguinha and the Oito Batutes had also preceded the great radio and cinema performers there. On their return from Paris in 1922, Pixinguinha and his band signed a contract to perform at the Empire Theater in Buenos Aires. According to biographer Sérgio Cabral, this was not without controversy, as the Brazilian government refused to grant the band any substantial funding to help underwrite the trip. Even without funding, Pixinguinha and his band served as de facto ambassadors of Brazilian music. The band played a key role in breaking down barriers in a city that, like some establishments in Rio, harbored a host of prejudices against black performers. "The impression one received of the band," wrote the Argentine newspaper *La Nación*, "is pleasant and rare, one would say that one was listening to a beautiful and vibrant tune in an unknown language."[7]

Other musical groups such as Los Guanabarinos, whose Spanish name catered to the *porteño* audience, also graced the stages of the Buenos Aires theaters, playing sambas and *marchinas* of the day. In addition to groups from Brazil, other performers came from much farther abroad, including those from the United States, Mexico, and Europe. The list of idols who passed through Buenos Aires was long: Josephine Baker, Marian Anderson, and the many Brazilians, all attracting audiences to local theaters. Francisco Alves and Mário Reis were among the Brazilians who performed at the Cine Broadway on October 1, 1931. The duo appeared with singer Luprece Miranda, guitar player Arthur Nascimento, the dancer known as Nestor, and Cecilia Zenatti.[8]

By the mid 1930s, Carmen and Aurora Miranda had become regular visitors to the *porteño* cultural scene, more so than Alves or Reis, performing Afro-Brazilian-inspired music for their first international audiences. On July 25, 1936, the Argentine paper *Radiolandia* simply reported, "The Miranda Sisters Have Arrived," with details as to how audiences could hear the most popular female duo from Rio de Janeiro. The report came complete with a picture of the sisters aboard the ship the *Captain Arcona* with radio owner Jaime Yankelevich, Juan Cassio, Rosales Aikman, Mercedes Simone, and the famous speaker César Ladeira.[9] The sisters remained in the news for their entire stay, often appearing in photographs with Argentine entertainers and producers. Carmen Miranda was the invited guest at Radio Belgrano on October 26, 1934, and again from May 23 to June 6, 1935. Carmen later was a featured guest at Radio El Mundo in March 1936.[10]

Although the Argentines would import many types of Brazilian music, the popular Afro-Brazilian sounds were in greatest demand. The terms "popular" and "erudite" were not common in Argentina. Rather, radio announcers used the terms "danceable" and "folkloric" to describe the music, and not necessarily to market programs to any target audience. Brazilians performed in both categories in programs that were usually scheduled for every fifteen minutes. On radio station LRI, for example, *música bailable* (dance music) featured Brazilian tunes.[11]

When Vargas visited Buenos Aires in May 1935, musicians accompanied him and performed in the Rio de la Plata capital.[12] Moreover, the Estado Novo aimed to foster good relationships with the Argentine public and saw music as an apt tool to do so. After 1937, Vargas funded the one-hour radio program *The Brazilian Hour* in Buenos Aires through Radio El Mundo on Thursday and Saturday evenings. Although the Brazilian government fully backed the program politically, the financial support was often slow in coming. The initial idea of supporting Brazilian musicians in Buenos Aires quickly gave way to economic realities. In the end, local musicians substituted for imported ones, including a host of European immigrant musicians who claimed to be familiar with Brazilian music.

Buenos Aires represented an important international space in the Brazilian imagination, one that helped to globalize Brazilian popular music. Prior to her invitation to the United States in late 1939, Carmen Miranda had earned such a following in Rio de la Plata that an offer to return to Buenos Aires was on the table at the time that the invitation to perform in New York materialized.[13] Although the market in Buenos Aires continued to absorb Brazilian singers and performers well into the 1960s, new opportunities in the United States would draw Brazilian performers northward.

Meeting Good Neighbors: Brazilianness and Blackness Across Borders

Brazilian performers traveled to the United States in the late 1930s and the 1940s for two major reasons: economic opportunities and international exposure. Once there, Brazilians not only had to adjust to a new language but also to new social values and to an entertainment industry with different modes of operation. Brazilian performers took their cultural baggage, their ideas about race and nationhood, with them. Indeed, these ideas would be commodified as they "performed Brazil" in front of unfamiliar audiences. The interaction between Brazilian performers and U.S. audiences entailed struggle, dialogue, and stereotyping. The result was a media-produced sense of Latinidad shaped as much by the U.S. "Good Neighbor Policy," a foreign policy agenda from 1933 to 1947, as it was by North American conceptualizations of blackness and whiteness in an era of segregation.

Although some Brazilian performers utilized Latinidad to their advantage, their experiences and options were nonetheless limited.[14] Designed to bring the United States and Latin America closer together, the Good Neighbor Policy was an extension of the gendered colonial rhetoric of empire that authors such as Ella Shohat have analyzed in other parts of the world.[15] Pervading North American geopolitical policies affected how and when Brazilians in the United States constructed their spaces and identities and how they would engage with North American audiences. The earlier 1904 Roosevelt Corollary, which historians view as a reiteration of the 1823 Monroe Doctrine that warned European powers to stay out of the Americas, had already set an ethnocentric and paternalistic tone that encouraged people in the United States to regard all of Latin America as their "backyard."[16]

Although President Franklin Delano Roosevelt crafted a foreign policy agenda aimed at fostering better ties with Latin America, his Good Neighbor Policy cemented images of exotic, albeit fun-loving foreigners, while pursuing interests aimed at opening Latin American markets to U.S. investors. Moreover, performers from Brazil were exotic foreigners who helped entertain American audiences during the war in Europe. Both male and female performers traveled to the United States, but it was the feminine, nonthreatening images of Brazil that gained currency.[17] What could be less threatening in the 1940s, for example, than the ubiquitous image of Carmen Miranda, a white Brazilian woman with fruit on her head, moving her body to enchanting tunes?[18]

During World War II, the Office of Inter-American Affairs, along with important cultural centers such as Hollywood, forged alliances with Brazil and other Latin American countries to galvanize support for the Allies, and American institutions provided employment opportunities unavailable in Brazil, thus encouraging northbound migration. In her article on U.S. immigration policy toward Mexico, Saskia Sassen explains that immigration from underdeveloped countries such as Brazil to developed countries like the United States is not merely an arbitrary activity independent of larger global patterns. The

United States has played a crucial role in the expansion of the world economy, and this in turn has played an important role in what Sassen calls "the mobilization of people into migrations." Performers and other artists constitute a vibrant sector in the flow of human capital.[19]

The restrictive immigration policies in the United States arose during a period in American history where legalized racial segregation was a way of life across the South and de facto segregation was practiced widely in the rest of the country. Thus, it is no surprise that the majority of Brazilians in the United States prior to the 1960s were white. U.S. segregation, based on the "one-drop rule," not only relegated blacks to the position of second-class citizens but also established social codes that would discourage, if not make illegal, the mixing of races in diverse venues, including nightclubs and films. White Brazilians occupied an ambiguous social space during segregation, which could give rise to cultural conflict, particularly since these very performers had worked closely with black musicians in Brazil. Aloysio de Oliveira, director of the Bando da Lua, has explained, for example, how U.S. racial codes affected the composition of his band. Segregation also limited where Afro-Brazilians could socialize.[20]

Brazilian scholar Gilberto Freyre, who had traveled and studied in the United States in the 1920s, best articulated the conflict inherent to this ambiguous space as he wrote about Brazilian cultural identity using the United States as a counterpoint. According to Freyre, his desire to write about Brazil occurred when he was in New York. As Lewis Hanke tells us in *Gilberto Freyre: Vida y obra*, Freyre remembered "with bitterness the disrespectful phrase from two Anglo-Saxon tourists that spoke of the fearful Mongrel aspect of the Brazilian population." Freyre eventually led a new wave of Brazilian scholarship that defended miscegenation, which he believed had created a unique people in the tropics.[21]

In *Casa grande e senzala* (*The masters and the slaves*), Freyre highlighted the importance of Brazil's cultural, sexual, spiritual, psychological, social, and racial mixing and intermingling. A fierce nationalist with an interest in promoting what he called *lusotropicalism*, or the unique Portuguese ability to adapt to the peoples and customs of the tropical regions and by extension the so-called darker races, Freyre's nostalgic and often idealized view of the Brazilian past was influenced by his life and travels in the United States. Freyre's ideas illustrate how Brazil's "imagined identity" was forged as a result of the experiences in the United States during segregation. Indeed, intellectual explanations of Brazil's identity, like national identities everywhere, remain closely connected to the exchange of global capital and the power of the media.[22]

Despite racial and class prejudices, official state-mandated segregation had been antithetical to the Latin American experience in general and the Brazilian experience in particular.[23] At the same time, proto-Latino residents and immigrants (the term "Latino" was not yet in vogue), the majority of whom were of Mexican ancestry, understood the importance of claiming a white racial identity in a nation that treated blacks as second-class citizens.[24] From the 1930s to the 1950s, "Latin" did not necessarily refer to U.S. residents but more often than not to an ambiguous exotic or foreign identity that contrasted with mainstream white Americans. Despite their low numbers, Brazilian performers played a disproportionately large role in shaping the early image of Latinidad and its connection to blackness.[25]

Brazilian Performers in the United States

Carmen and Aurora Miranda, the members of the Banda da Lua, Ary Barroso, Elsie Houston, and other musicians traveled to the United States as mature and seasoned performers, and would help meet a growing demand for exotic entertainment during World War II.[26] According to film historian Allen L. Woll, by 1937 the Hollywood musical had begun to change, after riding a wave of highly successful and extravagant hits that allowed audiences to escape from the doldrums of the Great Depression. Given the rising interest in so-called Latin music, Hollywood's adoption of Latin American themes for many of its musicals seemed logical.[27] Without the Hollywood musical, it is doubtful that Brazilians would have made such an impact on the popular culture of the United States in the 1940s.

At the same time, one cannot deny the charismatic charm of Carmen Miranda. Although American composers wrote the musical numbers that Miranda sang on Broadway, she and the Banda da Lua made the compositions hers by adding Africanisms, mentioning African-derived foods, and injecting Afro-Brazilian-like rhythms into the first Brazilian American musical hybrid (ironically, a rumba), with translating help from Aloysio de Oliveira:

Ai ai ai ai
E o canto do pregoneiro
Que com sua harmonia
Traz alegria
In South American Way

Ai ai ai ai
E o que faz em seu tabuleiro
Vende pra ioiô
In South American Way

E vende vatapá
E vende caruru
E vende mungunzá
Vende umbu

No taboleiro tem
Oi tem tudo tem
E só não tem meu bem
Berenguedém

Ai ai ai ai
Have you ever danced in the tropics?
With that hazy lazy
Like, kind of crazy
Like South American Way
Ai ai ai ai

Have you ever kissed in the moonlight
In the grand and glorious
Gay notorious
South American Way

In the 1940s, "South American Way" provided an accessible and easily digested image of South America, and a niche for Miranda in the North American entertainment industry. Although the song does not mention the Bahiana, most of the tune's images of South America came directly from Dorival Caymmi's "O qué é que a Bahiana tem?" Miranda dressed as the Bahiana and utilized her body, particularly her hips and shoulders, both in *The Streets of Paris* and in her first U.S. movie, *Down Argentine Way* (1940), to perform this tune. She continued to promote Afro-Brazilian traditions across class and racial lines as the embodied representative of a "South American Way."

That Carmen Miranda continued to utilize the Bahiana mask is hardly surprising. In *Down Argentine Way*, she starred with Betty Grable, Charlotte Greenwood, and Don Ameche. Director Irving Cummings gave Miranda a small role in which she performed four songs dressed in some variation of the Bahiana. The songs were indicative of her rapid transformation from "the Queen of Samba" to Hollywood performer of hybrid Latin numbers in which the Afro-Brazilianisms remained fundamental. In addition to "South American Way," Miranda performed the Brazilian composition "Mamãe o quero," a Brazilian *marchinha*; the *embolada* "Bambu bambu"; and "Touradas em Madrid," also a *marchinha*, in a Hollywood setting of Buenos Aires that recalled generic exotic Latin images.[28]

After fourteen successful months in the United States, during which she won over female and male audiences alike, Carmen Miranda returned home to Brazil on July 7, 1940. Cannily dressed in green and yellow, the Brazilian national colors, Miranda was greeted by thousands of fans who led her in a festive parade through the Zona Sul of Rio de Janeiro.[29] Not everyone was happy with her success in the United States, however. The São Paulo paper, *A Folha da Noite*, registered the opinion of many who objected to her particular representation of Brazil: "So that's how Brazil shines in the United States: with a Portuguese woman singing bad-tasting black sambas. It is really like that! And so that's how it should be. Because there really aren't many people in this country who are worth as much as that Carmen, that great and excellent Carmen who left to sing nonsense abroad."[30]

Upper-class Brazilians were particularly concerned with their image abroad, and preferred to emphasize their European, rather than their African, heritage. They understood Miranda's Africaneity; they just did not like it. Carmen Miranda had risen to international attention performing popular music clearly associated with blacks in Brazil. Adding more nationalist fuel to the fire was the fact that Miranda had retained a Portuguese passport, apparently out of respect for her parents.[31]

On her return to the United States in October 1940, Miranda performed in another Broadway production, *Sons O' Fun*, in New York City before moving to Los Angeles, where she embarked on a frenzied schedule that included appearances in films, on the radio, and in nightclubs and theaters. Despite these multiple forums, Miranda became best known both to Americans and Brazilians as a film star. Even though her dialogue was often stilted and her comedic qualities were highlighted, the camera captured the serpentine movements of her body and the energy she exuded, qualities more fully appreciated in her live performances. Most Brazilians (and North Americans), moreover, did not see her in clubs, where her numbers were much more imaginative and spontaneous and where she performed well-known Brazilian rhythms. In these more intimate forums, she was able to perform with fewer restrictions, although she often willingly embraced the expanding sense of Latinidad and performed in Spanish. She delighted in performing with her Brazilian band, since, as she reported to the Brazilian press: "You know very well how Brazilian music becomes Cubanized or Mexicanized when it is performed by American orchestras."[32]

Between 1941 and 1947, Miranda appeared in nine Hollywood films: *That Night in Rio* (1941), *Weekend in Havana* (1941), *Springtime in the Rockies* (1942), *The Gang's All Here* (1943), *Four Jills in a Jeep* (1944), *Greenwich Village* (1944), *Something for the Boys* (1944), *Doll Face* (1945), and *If I'm Lucky* (1946). Though her role as a sensual and exotic personality from South America emerged in all these films, she also subverted U.S. stereotypes when she parodied herself in films such as *Doll Face* (where her character refuses to become "just another Carmen"). In addition, Miranda's comedic exaggeration, coupled with her use of food and outrageous fashion, often allowed her to subvert U.S. stereotypes of Latin Americans through humor.[33] This is particularly evident in *The Gang's All Here*, where, according to Shari Roberts, Miranda "lampoons both U.S.–Latin American trade relations and notions of feminine sexuality . . . through the casting of Miranda as the overseer of countless enormous swaying phallic bananas buoyed up by lines of chorus girls who dance above other girls who have oversized strawberries between their legs."[34]

Miranda succeeded in the United States as a white exporter, or mask, of Afro-Brazilian music at a time when blacks were only beginning to become national stars in Brazil, although the Brazilian provisional middle class allowed some blacks, and particularly *mulatos*, to enter its circles. Segregation and black marginalization in the United States allowed no such flexibility. Dorival Caymmi, the Afro-Brazilian composer who helped Miranda first create her Bahiana and who went on to create hundreds of compositions about Bahia, did not receive an invitation to perform or work in the United States, although other Brazilian white performers such as Ary Barroso did. This is not to say that black Brazilian performers did not perform in the United States, only that given the U.S. codes of segregation, the opportunities afforded to white performers were greater. The list of Brazilian white performers included Carmen's sister Aurora, Ary Barroso, Aloysio de Oliveira and the members of the Bando Da Lua, and many others who continued to perform songs inspired by black Brazilian traditions.

Patrice Pavis convincingly argues that intercultural theater resonates best with audiences when it is highlighted in the body, the personality, and the culture of multiple participants. Miranda was a "hit" precisely because her individualized white "Afro-Brazilianized" body was unlike any body that middle-class white audiences had seen. Despite her attempts to escape the comparisons with her sister, Aurora Miranda performed within similar parameters. At the same time, Carmen had to search for a new stage identity, and it is unclear whether she attained what Pavis has called "the corporeal cultural check-up" that allowed her to fine tune her art and performance. Indeed, in the absence of Brazilian mentors and outside of the organic Brazilian context, many of Miranda's staged performances were "cultural stereotypes" for metatheatrical amusement."[35]

Considering the Africaneity of the Brazilian performances, it is surprising that the African American press paid little attention to Carmen Miranda, let alone Aurora Miranda or any of the other Brazilian performers in the United States. There are two explanations for this. First, African American newspapers such as the *Chicago Defender*, the *New York Amsterdam News*, the *Baltimore Afro-American*, and the *Los Angeles Sentinel* were community-based papers dedicated to promoting black rights and achievement. Thus, when the *Chicago Defender* reviewed RKO's *Flying Down to Rio*, the paper focused on the African American songstress and actress Etta Motten and the "race dancers" who performed in the movie. "Etta Motten's singing makes this film hot," wrote the *Chicago Defender* on March 31, 1934. Three months later the paper reported that "RKO did two things for the race. It gave Etta Motten her big chance as the singer of 'Carioca' and showed that race dancers could not only master Fred Astaire's most intricate steps but also add considerable individuality to them."[36] Six years later, while critics in the white mainstream press focused on the "Brazilian Bombshell" with the release of *Down Argentine Way* in 1941, the *Amsterdam News* focused on the marvels of African American dancers Harold and Fayard Nicholas.[37]

Etta Motten and the troupe of African American dancers play Brazilian characters who steam up the screen with their song and dance, and as one white American character remarked, "no wonder it never gets cold in this country." Long before Carmen Miranda traveled to the United States, Motten had appeared before American audiences dressed as a Bahiana, with a basket of fake fruit on her head.

African American invisibility in the mainstream press also helps to account for the rise in black media devoted to blacks. Even though the song "Carioca" was nominated for an Academy Award in 1934, Etta Motten's performance in the movie was rarely highlighted in the white mainstream press.[38]

The second reason why the African American press did not document the diasporic links between Brazilian performers and black performers has to do with the formation of national communities. Despite marginalization and segregation, African American newspapers often shared similar political philosophy and national frameworks with their white mainstream counterparts, and these frameworks often shaped cultural views of foreign countries. Thus, the *Amsterdam News* described Carmen Miranda as an exotic "tantalizing torrid-voiced singing star of South America," without a hint of solidarity. Yet the white and black press in the United States understood the shared geographical solidarity when performances came to the United States through black bodies such as Katherine Dunham, who brought cultural influences from the Caribbean and South America to American stage and screen. In 1939, Dunham and her dance company began filming Warner Brothers' *Carnival of Rhythm*, a short film written by Stanley Martin and directed by Jean Negulesco, which would be released in 1941. The Brazilian influence was clear, as the film included dance numbers such as "Los Indios" and "Ciudad maravillosa" (both spelled in Spanish), as well as "Batucada" and "Adeus terras." Also inspired by the Brazilian woman from Bahia, Dunham created her choreography for Bahiana in 1939 with the composer Don Alfonso, which premiered at a concert at the University of Cincinnati. She continued to perform her Bahiana routine on stage throughout the 1940s.[39]

More critical attention needs to be given to the cross-diasporic borrowing by black artists, but the possibility that white artists who performed black cultural practices could displace African American musicians did not go unnoticed by the African American press. In November 1940, for example, the *Amsterdam News* asked whether the rise of white musicians in jazz would mean that blacks would not find employment. The paper also questioned why white musicians wanted to learn how to play "the way blacks do." Given the history of black marginalization, the paper's worries were not misplaced.[40]

Beyond Carmen Miranda: Other Brazilian Performers in the United States

When Aurora Miranda arrived in the United States in 1940, she took advantage of the growing opportunities for Latin American entertainers, particularly women, and of the buzz that her sister had created.[41] Because of Carmen's hectic schedule, Aurora often communicated with friends and other contacts including composers and members of the Sociedade Brasileira de Artes Teatrais (SBAT), the major association responsible for copyright in Brazil, to help secure "authentic" Brazilian compositions. On March 19, 1941, for example, Aurora's letter to Almirante, who had been Carmen's close collaborator and friend in Brazil, hinted at the legal problems raised by performing music internationally, and the fact that American companies were requesting copyright permissions for compositions whose origins neither she nor Carmen could verify.[42]

Problems with copyright were notorious, particularly with widely known music of folk or popular origins that had no registered author. The case of the Afro-Brazilian spoken-style *embolada* "Bambu bambu," which Almirante eventually copyrighted, is a case in point. Almirante claimed that he became familiar with the tune around 1924, but that in late December 1939, he received a contract from Wallace Downey, Carmen Miranda's representative in Brazil, to verify his authorship of the piece. Almirante had copyrighted the music in question based on a recording that he had made, but he later received news that Donga and J. Tomaz claimed that they were the true authors of "Bambu Bambu" and would sue him for signing an illegal contract.[43]

Early on in their careers in the United States, Carmen and Aurora Miranda continued promoting, recording, and celebrating popular Afro-Brazilian tunes that they had learned in Brazil before they would adopt and record other Latin American and Caribbean rhythms, and English numbers as well. While Carmen's exclusive movie contract limited her appearances, Aurora's performances ranged from radio appearances, to nightclub acts, to appearances in more established concert venues such as the Inter-American House–sponsored event that took place at Carnegie Hall. The performance at Carnegie Hall featured Aurora, along with other concert and popular performers from Latin America, including the Cuban popular singer Estelita, the lyrical singer Carolina Segrera, and the Chilean baritone Carlo Morelli.[44]

In New York, Aurora Miranda made a name for herself in 1942 with *Earl Carrol's Vanities* Broadway show, followed by an appearance in another review, *The Downtowners*. *Earl Carrol's Vanities* had scheduled appearances in Los Angeles, Cleveland, and even Mexico City. Aurora also recorded songs in Portuguese with Decca records: "A jardineira," "Cidade maravilhosa," "Aurora," "Pastorinhas," "Meu limão," "Meu limoneiro," and "Seu condutor"—songs based on popular Brazilian rhythms and utilizing the voice of popular characters. She also appeared in commercials for Decca, all with the Bando da Lua.[45]

In 1944, Aurora Miranda took a small role in the Warner Brother's film *The Conspirators*, playing a sultry nightclub performer in Portugal. Typical of World War II–era films, *The Conspirators* centered on the figure of Vincent Van Der Lyn, a Dutch freedom fighter in World War II who is forced to flee to neutral Lisbon to escape the Nazis. In Lisbon, Der Lyn comes into contact with a group of men plotting against the Nazis, led by Ricardo Quintanilla, who knows that one among them is spying for the Nazis, and needs Van Der Lyn to help identify the traitor. Aurora's performance helped bring the ambience of Lisbon's nightlife alive for cinema audiences.

Aurora followed this experience with the 1944 film noir *The Phantom Lady*, in which she played a theater performer who happens to wear the same hat as the female protagonist, the "phantom lady." Aurora's character in the film, Estela Monteiro, the star of the theatrical revue *Chica Boom Boom*, performed what North American audiences would come to consider a Latin number sung in Portuguese, although its roots could not necessarily be traced back to Brazil. These types of compositions aimed to add a certain Latin American flavor to the productions, albeit deeply influenced by the Afro-diasporic tradition that was recognizable and decidedly upbeat, although not necessarily comedic.[46]

In an interview with *P.M. Weekly News* in October 1941, Aurora Miranda highlighted the differences between her and her sister because she was afraid that people would call her "just another Carmen Miranda."[47] She repeated these concerns to Earl Wilson of the *New York Post* almost three years later, when her English had improved and she was beginning to develop a reputation among English-speaking audiences. "One way that I am different," she remarked, "is that I don't dance. I only have the rhythm with my body." She continued: "I am called Aurora because I was born at 6 A.M. in the morning—my father saw the sun coming up in the summer. He said we call her Aurora. . . . I don't go to any voice teacher, and I don't know anything about moosk [*sic*], but all the popular singers in Brazil don't know anything about moosk [*sic*]. . . . Hollywood wants me to wear the Bahiana, the headdress and be like Carmen, but I must be deefrant [*sic*]."[48] To separate her stage image even further from her sister, she often went by the name Aurora, without the Miranda, as the credits of film *The Phantom Lady* indicate. Decca Records catalogs also indicate that Aurora used the pseudonym "Aurora Mendoza" when she recorded with the Bando da Lua.[49]

Despite Aurora's claims, her stage image was remarkably similar to the Bahiana. In Joseph Stanley's musical *Brazil*, for example, Aurora teams up with Mexican performer Tito Guizar, Virginia Bruce, and others to create a musical that, according to the press book poster that spelled out the word "BRAZIL," was:

Bursting with melody!
Romance in a Latin Manner,
Aflame with spectacle
Zenith of entertainment thrills
Illuminated with stars!
Lavish with laughter and luscious senoritas.[50]

In one scene, Aurora performs a solo within a large chorus number dressed in colorful attire and a modest head wrap made out of cloth, although not nearly as flamboyant as the headgear associated with Carmen's Bahiana. On her own, Aurora did not escape the critical comparisons to her sister, and as one critic reported in the Brazilian film magazine *Cena Muda*, she was "less sophisticated than Carmen."[51] Ironically, in the United States, neither the Mirandas nor the U.S. publicity made reference to their Afro-Brazilian influences. Both, nonetheless, continued to pay tribute to their Afro-Brazilian foundations in their performances but became exotic Latin icons in the U.S. media.

In 1944, Aurora Miranda branched out on her own and made history in the animation industry in the United States when she went to work for Walt Disney in *The Three Caballeros*. Aurora and her Mexican costars, Dora Luz and Carmen Molina, would have the distinction of being the first live actors to appear in a new genre of animated films in which human actors interacted with animated cartoon characters. Walt Disney wanted Aurora for the role in the Brazil segment and had not considered Carmen. Still, Aurora would play a Bahiana and continue the Carioca tradition of mythologizing Bahia as a magical place of music and merriment, quite removed from social and political reality.[52]

The Three Caballeros, nonetheless, exemplifies the cross-national masking prevalent in many Brazilian performances in the United States. All of the tunes performed in the "Bahia section" are clearly inspired by Afro-Brazilian rhythms. Aurora also dressed like the Bahiana to sing Ary Barroso's "Os Quindins de Iáia" (Iáia's coconut cakes), selling her wares on the street. Her body, and particularly her hips, moves to the rhythm until the entire animated city is shaking and bouncing to the contagious beat as she sings in Portuguese. Audiences get an animated view of Bahia, a place where the roads shake with rhythms. Although Bahia is one of Brazil's most African cities, no black actors appear in the film number. Aurora and the men from the Bando da Lua who appear in the scene with her are all tanned, although not too dark.[53]

Race and Nationhood: Other Brazilian Performers

Carmen and Aurora Miranda were undoubtedly the most important Brazilian performers in the United States in the 1940s, giving credence to the idea of Brazilian performance as gendered, and American audiences readily accepted and received sensualized female Latin American images. At the same time, Brazilian men such as Ary Barroso and the male members of the Bando da Lua played important parts in constructing images of Brazil abroad. The experiences of other white Brazilians such as Henrique Britto and Laurindo de Almeida shed light on the complexities and multilayered interaction inherent to cross-national exchange.

Britto had been a member of the pioneering popular Carioca band the Bando de Tangarás, comprised of musical luminaries such as Almirante, Noel Rosa, Lamartine Babo, and Braguinha. With the disintegration of the band in 1932, Britto left Brazil to play in the Brazilian national band (led by Romeu Silva) at the Olympics in Los Angeles in July and August of that year. When the band was forced to return home because of lack of funds, Britto, a guitar player, stayed on for a year and played in various nightclubs.[54]

Britto's story of enhanced opportunity in the United States parallels that of guitarist Laurindo de Almeida, who left Brazil in 1946 as a result of a moralistic anticrime platform at the end of Getúlio Vargas's Estado Novo in 1945. Vargas's successor, Eurico Gaspar Dutra, instituted a number of repressive measures, which included revoking the Communist Party's legal standing and intervening in labor unions. The government also launched an attack on immorality and began to crack down on prostitution, vagrancy, and gambling. The focus on gambling meant the closing of all casinos, and thus the end to the employment they provided hundreds of musicians and performers throughout the country, but particularly in Rio de Janeiro.

Scrambling to find new employment, many Brazilian musicians left the country just as international demand for Latin American performers, particularly in the United States, seemed to be rising. Almeida headed north.[55] Almeida, who is considered by many to be a pioneer of Brazilian jazz cross-pollination because of his finger-style playing, offered American audiences and musicians a new way of performing. Not surprisingly, he was invited to perform with a number of North American musicians, including Stan Kenton in Los Angeles in the 1950s and John Lewis. After 1950, he worked on a number of film scores for Twentieth Century Fox, including *Rawhide* (1951).[56]

Both Britto's and Almeida's stories illustrate the complex relation between the social and economic reality of Brazil that influenced their decisions to leave. Like the Mirandas, they were able to perform in the United States because of the expertise they had acquired in Brazil from being around Afro-Brazilian music and culture. Thus, in many ways Brazilian musicians who left Brazil were afforded opportunities because they were able to perform Brazilian culture—based on and inspired by Afro-Brazilian cultural influences—in the United States.

The case of Ary Barroso, author of "Aquarela do Brasil" and perhaps one of Brazil's most well known popular composers, underscores the complex relationship between Brazil and the United States. Barroso moved to the United States to work for Walt Disney on a number of projects, but also ended up working for the now defunct Republic films, in addition to collaborating on a number of different projects, including a Broadway musical adaptation of Bertita Harding's *The Amazon Throne*.[57]

In a letter to his wife back in Brazil dated January 15, 1944, Barroso claimed: "I am as popular here as I am in Brazil with one exception: here my name is admired, respected."[58]

Like many other Brazilian musicians, Barroso's success abroad was tied to his celebration of Brazil and popular Brazilian culture that make specific references to the country's African legacy. In "Aquarela do Brasil," first performed for Hollywood by Aloysio de Oliveira in the 1943 Disney movie *Saludos Amigos*, Barroso makes direct reference to the figure of the *mãe preta* (the black mother), the Congo king, and the joyous *mulato*.[59]

That producers such as Disney and many others adhered to a given "Latin typecasting" is undeniable. The majority of film critics were either ignorant of the African influence on Brazilian culture or chose to ignore it. Of all the Latin-themed films of the 1930s, the only film to actually include black actors was *Flying Down to Rio* (1932), which was produced before the goals of the Good Neighbor Policy were articulated. At the same time, Disney allowed for the participation of Brazilians in creating many Latin icons, including the yellow and green parrot Zé Carioca, modeled after the Carioca *malandro*, and the hybrid dance the "Uncle Samba." Furthermore, given the opportunities available, Brazilians such as Aloysio de Oliveira and Carmen and Aurora Miranda acknowledged their agency in an unprecedented period of cross-cultural collaborations. They were not forced to work and live in segregated areas, yet they were not able to choose and cultivate their own images.

Even an important artist like Orson Welles was not able to release images that went against existing social norms. As a cultural ambassador to Latin America, Welles had made controversial films that documented the life of the black underclass in Brazil. One film documented the black presence in Brazilian carnival, while another showed the plight of fishermen in the Northeast. Neither of them was released until 1992 in a video called *Its All True*.[60] The fact that Welles's work was censured illustrates the limits of individual agency in the United States even for whites, particularly when one's views clash with prevailing geopolitical and commercial interests.

Many Brazilian travelers to Los Angeles raved about how well Brazilians were being treated there, supporting the notion that Latin Americans had "conquered" Hollywood. On the other hand, some in the North American press (like their Brazilian counterparts) approached the new "Latin" presence critically, and not necessarily on racial grounds. On January 28, 1940, Lucile Neville indicated that "any story with a plot about revolutions, tamale workers or the love of a marimba player for a beauteous senorita sounds fine to producers just now. But Hollywood can make a tremendous mistake, according to the comparatively few Latin-understanding movie people here."[61] Neville was well aware of the sensitivity and responses of the Latin American press to U.S. ethnocentrism and stereotyping. Nonetheless, she saw progress being made as directors and producers were beginning to ask for advice on South American cultures.

It is no coincidence that most of the Brazilian performers who made their way to the United States prior to the 1960s were white. What a conundrum for white performers who had lived in Brazil and had collaborated with black singers, songwriters, and musicians and in many cases relied on the promotion of black Brazilian tunes, practices, and icons. Carmen Miranda's home in Beverly Hills became what some called the "unofficial Brazilian embassy," a place where Brazilians of all races often gathered to avoid the institutionalized racism in bars, clubs, and restaurants that barred blacks from fraternizing with whites. In Helena Solberg's documentary *Carmen Miranda: Bananas Is My Business*, the Nicholas brothers, two African American performers who knew and worked with Miranda, explain how public social policy turned Miranda's private space into a multicultural haven. Ironically, performers such as Carmen Miranda had to confront the inequalities inherent to their own social and cultural backgrounds as they faced racism and ethnocentrism in the United States.

A Note on Black Brazilian Performers in the United States

Although white performers such as Carmen and Aurora Miranda, Ary Barroso, Aloysio de Oliveira, and others were able to take advantage of the opportunities to perform and contribute to the emerging sense of Latinidad, many of them were uncomfortable with U.S. racial codes and the etiquette surrounding segregation. Carmen Miranda found ways to make her home a sanctuary where all of her friends of diverse backgrounds could mingle. Oliveira was forced to change the composition of the Bando da Lua because one of his white members was married to a black Brazilian woman, and he refused to travel with her to the United States. In his memoir *De Banda a Lua*, Oliveira also expressed his anxiety over the visit of his childhood Afro-Brazilian friend Haroldo Barbosa.[62] White Brazilian performers thus understood their relative privilege compared to their nonwhite Brazilian counterparts.

On the other hand, the experiences of nonwhite Brazilian performers who traveled or immigrated to the United States before desegregation provide us with a different window on to issues of cross-national racial identities.

Afro-Brazilian Sinval Silva's visit to Carmen Miranda in 1951 is an interesting case to consider. In Brazil, Silva had worked as Miranda's chauffeur and had written and composed many tunes for her, including the classic "Adeus batucada," before he went on to become a performer in his own right. In his biography *Carmen: A vida de Carmen Miranda a brasileira mais famosa do século XX*, Ruy Castro reports that during Silva's visit, Miranda had asked him to drive her automobile while she sat in the front seat. Apparently, she had forgotten that a white woman did not sit in the front seat with a black man, a faux pas that was quickly pointed out to her by a passing motorist.[63]

In Silva's discussions of his experience in the United States, he never registered a complaint or noted any ill treatment. Indeed, on his return to Rio he reported to the Brazilian press that his visit with Miranda had been an absolute success and that he himself had performed in a number of venues in Los Angeles. It is difficult to verify whether Silva actually performed in the United States and whether he performed in segregated clubs. Like Barroso and many other immigrants before and after him, Silva spoke about the United States in glowing terms as a means to legitimize and cast a positive light on Miranda's and his experiences abroad.

This tendency is echoed by the pioneering black singer Carmen Costa, who provides additional insights about the experience of black Brazilians in the United States.[64] Although she was an Afro-Brazilian performer, Costa traveled to the United States because of her marriage to a white American. In 1945, Costa married the American Hans van Koehler and one year later moved with him to New Jersey. Even though, according to one version, he abandoned her in the United States, she would continue to live in New York and Rio for the next three decades before returning to Brazil permanently in the 1970s. While on the East Coast of the United States, she performed Brazilian, Spanish, and American standards. Her most acclaimed performance was an appearance at New York City's Triboro Theater, a forum for many other performers, including African Americans and Puerto Ricans. She also performed with Lionel Hampton and Dizzy Gillespie, two important African American musicians, and in the 1960s she participated in the bossa nova–jazz exchanges in New York City. Like immigrants the world over, Costa also had to work at jobs that she did not quite anticipate. Ironically, she landed a job at an RCA record factory pressing records. Like Silva, however, in her interviews with the press and with the interviewers at the Museum of Image and Sound in Rio, she highlighted her positive experiences, her hard work, and her ability to persevere in the United States.[65]

Costa arrived in the United States the same year as Farnésio Dutra da Silva, better known as Dick Farney, a name that he chose because its sounded more American. Farney, who had an impressive musical education, gained an international reputation in Rio as the crooner for the Carlos Machado Orchestra and for performing at the Cassino da Urca in Rio. Like Carmen Miranda and unlike Carmen Costa, when he arrived in New York he was already well connected. He performed with a host of black and white musicians and entertainers, including Nat "King" Cole, and even performed American standards in English abroad. In 1947, he landed a recording contract with RCA and a lucrative performing contract at the Peacock Alley Bar at the Waldorf Astoria Hotel in New York City ten years later. Talent aside, such opportunities were hardly within the grasp of an immigrant woman without contacts, let alone a black woman like Costa.[66]

Of all the Brazilian performers in the United States between 1930 and 1960, Elsie Houston's life was perhaps the most tragic (she committed suicide in 1943) and at the same time best represents the conflicting cross-national identity of Brazilians who are "neither white nor black," to quote the title of Carl Degler's now classic 1971 book. A trained lyrical singer with important musical and business connections, Houston was, nonetheless, interested in performing Brazilian haute culture as well as Afro-Brazilian and Afro–Latin American popular and folk traditions. She was equally at ease singing opera and performing what would come to be called in the United States "voodoo numbers." Houston's father, an expatriate American living in Brazil, was related to the Sam Houston family of Texas. She was married to the French surrealist poet Benjamin Péret, and like him became interested in Brazilian folkloric music, eventually publishing the book *Chants populaires du Brésil* in France and several other essays.

According to the *New York Times*, Houston, who performed regularly at New York's Rainbow Room, had become a mandatory act for any concert featuring South American music. At the same time, the American press made frequent reference to her dark skin and her "voodoo dances." While Olin Down wrote of her "voodoo incantations" in the *New York Times*, Grace Turner's May 1940 article on food recipes from Brazil that featured Houston began with a description of Houston's exotic looks: "Dark, slim to the point of thinness, vivid in every motion and the quick soft undertones of her Latin American speech, Elsie Houston, the internationally known Brazilian singer, is an exotic creature who you do not naturally associate with the household kitchen. . . . Everything about Houston is colorful."[67]

Houston's exotic looks fascinated North Americans, no doubt enhanced her "voodoo performances," and certainly kept her in the press. Like the Miranda sisters, Houston was obliged to adjust her performances to the North American gaze. In Brazil, her avant-garde performances and her research in African and indigenous folk culture, which had been a part of the growing debates and investigations of the modernist intellectuals and music aficionados such as Mário de Andrade, were transformed into performances that she herself called "voodoo dances." In 1940, when she compared Brazilian music to North American music with pride, she was being patriotic to combat a sense of inferiority, similar to what Caetano Veloso has called Brazil's cultural pride and shame.[68] Houston goes on to describe Portuguese, African, and indigenous music in Brazil in essentialized terms typical of Mário de Andrade, Gilbero Freyre, Raul Bopp, and the many other modernist writers of the 1920s and 1930s, but she also utilized American terms to dialogue with the American audiences.

Houston's story exemplifies the difficulty of creating a space in a foreign land, and highlights the ways in which immigrants, white and nonwhite, often are reduced to a one-dimensional identity. How could segregated North Americans make room for an upper-class Brazilian of mixed racial ancestry who grew up speaking French and performed in French nightclubs and who was equally at home performing concert music and folk or popular forms? Houston grew up in privileged environments in Rio and Europe in which her skin color may not have played a restricting role. In the absence of a Brazilian community on the East Coast, she lived among the small French émigré community. Her life in the United States must be understood as an individual experience, and her choices must be placed into their proper historical context.

Further work needs to be conducted to examine how Houston's life in the United States contributed to her suicide. It is worth pointing out, however, that less-privileged performers such as Silva and Costa assert that they took advantage of their varied opportunities in the United States before returning home to Brazil. Indeed, they looked back on their experience in the United States as an important "conquest." Yet their lives should also be carefully contextualized according to the choices available to them. At the same time, it is important to recognize that national identities continue to play defining roles in the experiences of immigrants of diverse backgrounds.

Conclusion

The American entertainment industry is a multibillion dollar business that has an enormous impact on perceptions throughout the Western Hemisphere. Film and musical producers have always been fascinated with the exotic. Unfortunately, more often than not this interest has not been a healthy thirst to learn about the "other," but rather it has led to the appropriation and transformation of the foreign culture into static images for entertainment purposes. In many cases, even when foreign people are present, they serve as an exotic backdrop to the central plot. In other cases, performers participate in their own representations. In her essay on gender and empire, Ella Shohat has illustrated how Hollywood filmmakers often feminize foreign cultures to sanction the Western need for intervention and/or dominance. In the case of Brazilian actors, however, this view must also be supplemented by an analysis that recognizes the agency of well-established performers who not only took these images "to the bank," so to speak, but also often subverted or creatively engaged them on and off stage.[69]

By the 1950s, the Latin American popular music boom in the United States initiated by Carmen Miranda and the Bando da Lua in 1939 was beginning to subside. Meanwhile, television, which was quickly becoming an important forum for the mass distribution of entertainment, would give Miranda new life and an opportunity to once again adapt her act to a new milieu. Indeed, she would die the day after recording a performance on the Jimmy Durante television show in front of an eager audience in 1955. Brazilians were instrumental in preparing American audiences for the more diverse "Latin" performers of the 1950s, including the *I Love Lucy* show that starred Lucille Ball and the Cuban orchestra leader Desi Arnaz, her husband both in real life and on the television show. It is no coincidence that in the third episode of the show, on October 22, 1951, Lucy wears the Bahiana outfit, replete with fruit on her head, in an episode in which she tried to rekindle her romance with her Cuban husband.

Transnational residence, nonetheless, urges us to redefine immigration in terms of multiple crossings and loyalties across national borders and forces us to examine how concepts such as blackness and whiteness travel cross-nationally. The experience of nonwhite performers adds another level of conceptualization and forces us to reexamine the meaning of racial and social codes across national boundaries.

The performance of blackness constituted a critical aspect of Brazil's music at home. Therefore it is not surprising that it also played an important role abroad. Carmen Miranda's success in the United States was possible both because she was a white woman and because she performed recognizable black music. But Miranda was not only black on stage. Her life in Brazil, despite her privilege, taught her a distinct mode of interracial interaction, and she later faced difficulty adjusting to North American social mores and practices. According to the

Nicholas brothers, Miranda rarely socialized outside of her home. Her household, with the constant coming and going of friends and family members, also provided Miranda with a security blanket against the ethnocentrism in the United States at the time.[70]

Brazilian performers abroad were forced to create, forge, or otherwise navigate new and old identities within the North American imagination, an imagination nourished by imperialistic notions of manifest destiny, political and economic interests, and popular culture. Performers have helped contextualize issues of race, nationhood, and Latinidad and its relationship to blackness. The experiences of black Brazilians emphasize the fact that Latinness and blackness where hardly mutually exclusive. Moreover, evidence suggests that Latinness in the United States was constructed by transforming understood codes of blackness for white foreign bodies.

Afro-Brazilian Performers and the Legacy of Music of the Vargas Era

This work could easily have been called "A Historical Ethnography of the Golden Age of Brazilian Popular Music in the Time of Getúlio Vargas." It was under President Vargas's watch that the urban rhythms of Rio de Janeiro were propagated through the emerging mass media. It was also with the help of many of Vargas's policies that Brazilian popular music went global. As we have also seen, issues of race, class, gender, and the quest for authentic popular celebration emerged as a result of the modernist generation that catapulted Vargas into the presidency in 1930. The modernists also sustained this cultural outlook and orientation through the Ministry of Education and Culture as well as other institutions. Blackness played a critical if not central role in the Brazilian discourse on nationhood. One generation after abolition, the Brazilian system succeeded in celebrating its black legacy even while marginalizing it from the most important positions in radio and cinema and other important national forums that represented Brazil and Brazilianness in general and Brazilian popular music in particular. At the same time, whites recognized and celebrated "their" (national) blackness on the major stages of Brazilian popular music.

Chapters 1 through 3 highlighted the importance of Afro-Brazilian pioneers and blackness to the foundation of the Brazilian popular music sound, aesthetic, and content. In chapter 1, I emphasized the role of Afro-Brazilian pioneers in the decades after abolition and the construction of the black mask that would come to represent Brazilian performance. I also pointed out how French intellectuals played an important role in the internationalization of Brazilian popular music. Chapter 2 showed how Afro-Brazilians joined together in collective forums to celebrate their individual and neighborhood identities as well as their nation. I noted that Afro-Brazilians were better represented in popular, more democratic forums, where membership was not restricted by stated and understood social codes. Chapter 3 emphasized the exclusion of black Brazilians from the technological advances of radio and cinema, while blackness and Afro-Brazilian cultural traditions and influences remained crucial to the promotion of Brazilianness in these forums. In many ways, the "*mulato* escape hatch" continued to provide a bridge between blacks and whites and was essential for the smooth functioning of what I have called the provisional middle class. The temporary condition of respectability and acceptability was essential in an environment where the elite, the intellectuals, and the poor and disenfranchised shared the intimate spaces where the production of performances took place.

Chapters 4 and 5 utilized the lives of Francisco Alves and Carmen Miranda, two of Brazil's most revered white icons, as springboards into the social history of Brazilian popular music. Both stars came from humble beginnings and collaborated with a host of other performers, instrumentalists, and composers who had played important roles in the history of Brazilian popular music. Like other white performers, they grew up with Afro-Brazilian musical and aesthetic influences, worked and traveled with Afro-Brazilians, and collaborated on a number of seminal projects for the theater, the radio, and the cinema.

In the early 1930s, Alves, the "King of the Voice," had become one of the most successful male singers, while Miranda made a name for herself as the female "Queen of Samba." Although they became part of an elite circle of performers who could earn a living from their craft, they relied almost exclusively on Afro-Brazilian idioms from the lower classes, which helped to revolutionize Brazil's national music tastes. Their lives, performances, and relationships to other popular musicians, particularly black Brazilians, have shed light on the complex relations of race, class, and gender as well as the relationship between nationhood and Afro-diasporic cultures.

Important moments of popular music performance represent critical watersheds in Brazil's cultural history. Yet as we saw in chapter 6, it was mostly female performers, and particularly Carmen Miranda and her Africaneity, that took Brazilian music global. My analysis of Brazilian performers abroad reveals the connection between patriotism and Africaneity and helps us fully explain Elsie Houston's pride when she said that musically, Brazil had progressed more than the United States because of its perspective and inclusion of its black music into its national repertoire. Indeed, Afro-Brazilian traditions, memories, and contributions have survived in the recorded performances of many radio programs, in records, and in films, despite the marginalization of Afro-Brazilians.

Frantz Fanon's classic *Black Skin, White Masks* highlights the struggle of black people in a white world. "White face, black mask" in Brazil illustrates the cultural and social schizophrenia of the early twentieth century. Yet it also highlights the centrality of blackness to the Brazilian national ethos. Appropriation and authenticity often worked together on the same stage and in one performance. Blackness became a mask, a mechanism through and by which Brazilians could celebrate "authentic" national culture. That white or almost white performers came to represent the nation and celebrate blackness has as much to do with white privilege and the depth of Brazilian discrimination as it has to do with what some scholars have called Brazil's inherited inferiority complex. White performers such as Carmen Miranda and Francisco Alves, who had grown up in poor neighborhoods and who lived in the midst of musicians, composers, and other performers, maintained a level of legitimacy even as they left their neighborhoods and secured their position in the middle class. Throughout the 1930s, other performers maintained their links with popular music through collaborations with talented musicians from the popular classes and through extolling the virtues and aesthetics of popular revelry, including samba, carnival, and the social reality of the common folk. Other white musicians and performers partnered with Afro-Brazilians and helped to bring popular Brazilian music to the masses and to the nation.

In economic terms, poor white musicians and performers did not necessarily fare better than their black counterparts. In addition, many *mulato* and *mestiço* performers ranked among the most important radio personalities. Indeed, the idea of the "provisional middle class" aptly describes the ambiguous, often temporary space in which Brazilian musicians of all classes and races cohabitated. These music circles also allowed Afro-Brazilian performers to gain national recognition, although the majority of those who became "stars" were *mulatos* such as Orlando Silva, Sílvio Caldas, Araci de Almeida, Dorival Caymmi, and Angela Maria.[1] Black performers from Pixinguinha, Donga, and Ismael Silva to Carmen Costa and Grande Otelo nonetheless left their marks on the nation. But Carmen Miranda and Francisco Alves were in a league of their own. They were among the few who were able to make a living from performing in the middle-class forums. At the same time, they captured the hearts and emotions of Brazilians of all walks of life, just as Vargas captured their minds and moved them politically through a critical stage of modernization. Brazilians had deposited, or projected, their desires and aspirations onto these national performers. The funerals of both Alves and Miranda, in 1952 and 1955, respectively, indicated just how important they had become to Brazilians. Thousands of Brazilians were in attendance to mourn the nation's loss, but Dionysus, the Greek god of celebration, and Exú, the African orisha known as a trickster, were not totally absent.

Any attempt to reconstruct the dynamics of the early social history of Brazilian popular music must underscore the importance of Brazilian popular music to Brazilian life in general; the central importance of Rio de Janeiro, the capital of the nation in the first half of the twentieth century; and the role of performers in the consolidation of national culture. Brazilians in the 1950s and 1960s understood the importance of the 1930s and of the icons that decade produced. As these idols passed away, Brazilians reclaimed them and highlighted their importance through public funerals and wakes and other ceremonies. As the Puerto Rican writer Edgardo Rodrígues Juliá so beautifully explained, "the wake is the kingdom of conflicting emotions, the space in which the disorganized interior time does not decide whether to give into death or deny it."[2] Moreover, the rituals that celebrate a deceased's memory have the ironic capacity of breaking the chronological relationship between life and memory. At the end of the 1930s, Carmen and Aurora Miranda had left Brazil for the United States. Mário Reis had retired early. Francisco Alves continued on, although his title as "the King of the Voice" soon transformed into "the Elder of the Old Guard." Memories of Afro-Brazilians have lived on.

The Legacy of the Golden Performers

Four years after Carmen Miranda's death, João Gilberto, a twenty-seven-year-old Bahian singer-songwriter, recorded *Chega de saudade*, one of the hallmarks of a new, slick, and innovative way of singing samba, known as bossa nova. The bossa nova, a vibrant new modern wave that emerged from the middle classes of the Zona Sul of Rio de Janeiro in the mid 1950s, although still connected to the Afro-diasporic traditions of Brazil, revolutionized Brazilian musical performance, injecting the popular musical tradition with an intimate and subdued sense of lyricism. Bossa nova was popular music's answer to the agitation of a new generation flourishing in the midst of what Thomas Skidmore has called "experiments in democracy."[3] The music also marked the rise of President Juscelino Kubitschek de Oliveira.[4]

In a new political era with a new social and political consciousness, many of the middle-class white bossa nova stars would be largely responsible for recognizing and resurrecting the marginalized Afro-Brazilian musical talents who had been eclipsed by the radio and recording artists. For many, Brazil continued to be the nation that had successfully blended elements of "primitive cultures" with European elements, producing a magical union like no other place on earth. Yet it is clear, as Elsie Houston noted, that "the most rich musical influence was without doubt the black. Our marvelous variety of syncopated, nervous, sensual, spirited and sensual rhythms, we owe to blacks, as well as its free quality and its sense of invention."[5] Bossa nova musicians such as João Gilberto, Tom Jobim, and Vinicius de Morais often confirmed this.

Like Elsie Houston, well-known interpreters from the Vargas era such as Carmen Miranda, Francisco Alves, Aurora Miranda, Mário Reis, and many others explicitly and implicitly acknowledged the contribution of Africans and Afro-Brazilians to Brazilian popular music in general and to their personal repertoires in particular. Indeed, the musical production of the Vargas era was decidedly Afro-Brazilian, regardless of the racial background of the popular interpreters and performers. Throughout this work, we have seen this in the lyrics, in the instrumentation, and in the examples of dance performances, as well as in the reliance on Afro-Brazilian musicians and composers for the creation of sambas, *marchas, emboabas, batuques, lundus, modinhas,* and the many other musical forms and genres.

It would be overreaching to argue that Brazilian music was African. Afrocentricity in the Brazilian context, as in any American context, implies a given level of transformation or cultural adaptation. In the introduction to his book on Brazilian popular music, for example, Ricardo Cravo Albin, founder of the Museum of Image and Sound in Rio de Janeiro, celebrates the mythical cultural unity of Brazilian Indians, enslaved Africans and their Portuguese colonizers as well as each one's contribution to a *mestiço* musical tradition.[6] While such characterizations of the mixed nature of Brazilian popular music attest to a symbolic truth, they have ignored the unequal social dynamics that marginalized and commodified blacks and their cultural products and often prohibited blacks from reaping the benefits from their labor.

A Final Word on Culture and Politics

Despite the celebration of racial and cultural miscegenation that characterized sectors of Brazilian culture, the multiple legacies of the diverse Africans and their descendants marked Brazilian popular music in ways that Europeans and Native peoples have not. Thus, Gilberto Freyre's assertion of the centrality of the African experience to Brazilian life rings true, particularly in regard to popular music. Gilberto Gil, musician and minister of culture in Luiz Inácio "Lula" da Silva's Worker's Party administration, has insightfully remarked on the shortcoming of Freyre's original observation: "The problem is that in the first decades of the twentieth century, miscegenation received a whimsical reading in Brazil: A myth of the Portuguese gentle nature was constructed and projected using facts. This myth affirmed the lack of prejudice and discrimination in our country and we know that is not true."[7]

Curiously, in the political and social climate of Brazil from the late 1920s to the early 1950s, Africaneity emerged not as an identity but as a cultural heritage to which whites as well as blacks had access and could "own." With reason, Pan-Africanism, which began as a cross-national collaborative project at the beginning of the twentieth century, had little impact on Brazil—even after the emergence of important Brazilian Pan-Africanists such as Abdias do Nascimento.[8]

People of African descent may have responded to similar national and local contexts in similar ways, but their relative access to power—including media, education, and capital—and their visibility on the global stage determined their contributions to Pan-Africanism, that is to say, the extent to which they connected their struggles beyond their national borders. Ironically, for most of the twentieth century, Afro-Brazilians were unable to connect to cross-national black alliances because of lack of access to global markets, language barriers, and dictatorship and censorship that stymied civil participation.

In his book *The Practice of Diaspora: Literature, Translation, and the Rise of Black Internationalism*, Brent Edwards argues that the only way to contemplate transnational black discourses is "by attending to the ways that discourses of internationalism travel, the ways they are translated, disseminated, reformulated, and debated in transnational contexts marked by difference."[9] Yet performance in a *mestiço* environment provided additional challenges to understanding how blackness travels. As we have seen, in Brazil performers of all ethnicities often utilized the mask of blackness. For others, the mask served as a glue that bound together a fragmented identity. When Brazilian blackness traveled to the United States, it was in the form of white or whitened, mostly female bodies, which contributed to the forging of a Latin aesthetics.

The intersections of ideas of blackness and performers need further exploration. I am interested in African Americans in Brazil and Brazilians in the United States, but this comparison already illustrates a power relation: the mere notion of black Brazilians performing in the United States during segregation, for example, means that we are speaking of a very small number of people. Few African American performers actually made their way to the Brazilian stages, and many of those who did in the Roaring Twenties went by way of Paris. One such performer who traveled that route was Josephine Baker.[10]

The Brazilian group Bohemios Brasileiros opened Baker's show by playing some of Baker's numbers and mixing in Brazilian songs, although they were booed off the stage. Brazilians nonetheless responded warmly to Baker in ways similar to her audiences in Paris. In the popular press, Baker was presented as either "the French *mulata*" or "the American *mulata francesa*." Her blackness was celebrated as an expression of freedom and sensuality, as an international global phenomenon and not necessarily as part of any type of Pan-African solidarity. The Brazilian press compared Baker with Brazil's reigning queen of the musical revue, Aracy Cortes. On this occasion Cortes performed Brazilian numbers for Baker at the Confeteria Colombo in downtown Rio.[11]

Baker spoke warmly of Brazilians and of her reception in Brazil, and returned to Brazil more than a decade after Carmen Miranda and the Bando da Lua had already made their way to the United States and samba had taken the country by storm. By this time Brazilian rhythms had already entered into the global market—and Baker, as consumer and performer, promised to carry and perform Brazilian music wherever she went. To this, Carmen Miranda responded that she was happy that Baker loved Brazilian music but that Brazil did not need any other ambassadors since samba was already quite well known globally.

Gender considerations notwithstanding, the issue of "owner-ship" raises a number of compelling questions. Who can legitimately represent black idioms from Brazil? The black American performer? Or the white Brazilian who grew up among Afro-Brazilians? Baker's and Miranda's performances must be carefully placed into the proper historical context of the 1920s and 1930s, when African Americans regarded "Brazil" as a racial paradise of a sort. W. E. B. DuBois praised not only Brazil's racial interaction, for example, but reported in the magazine *Crisis* that Brazil was "fusing into one light mulatto race," and that there was no color or social bar to advancement. Others, such as E. R. James, also compared Brazil favorably, as in his *Chicago Defender* article of June 14, 1921. At one point, Brazil was considered a destination for the possible migration of industrious African Americans.[12]

American music in general and African-American idioms in par-ticular must be seen as a global commodity promoted and consumed by Brazilians, but few Brazilians actually had contacts or deep famil-iarity with African Americans in the 1930s and 1940s. Not until the creation of the Teatro Experimental do Negro (TEN) did black Brazil-ians pursue a conscious diasporic plan that promoted Pan-Africanism. Indeed, Nascimento would use African American history, heroes, and idioms to forge a diasporic consciousness. He would seek out African American performers visiting Brazil, such as Katherine Dunham, but he also established long-distance relations with others, such as Langston Hughes, so that he could pursue his own Brazilian agenda of raising black consciousness.

Still, the power relations among blacks should be noted. Brazil's blackness was national, and African American blackness became globally normative through a series of processes that had to do both with the denial of blackness in Brazil and American access to the international capitalist means of communication. Here it is important to add commentary on Brazilians in the United States. North Americans and Europeans were relatively more mobile and had more opportunities to travel than Brazilians. African American and black European ideas and music and cultural productions also circulated internationally with greater frequency than their Brazilian counterparts. Furthermore, while North Americans, black and white, could organize ways of performing in Brazil, the opposite was hardly within the realm of the possible for Brazilians. This was particularly true for black Brazilians, not only because of segregation in the United States but also because of the overwhelming poverty and lack of opportunities for nonwhite Brazilians. This did not mean that black Brazilian idioms did not circulate within the broad American milieu. On the contrary, white Brazilians such as Carmen Miranda served as ambassadors of popular Brazilian idioms and often assumed the voice of the "*nega*" or the "*mulata*." While Miranda performed in blackface in Brazil, however, she did not do so in the United States.

Miranda's performance presents us with an interesting conundrum. We cannot forget that segregation in the United States deterred black Brazilians from performing there and that African Americans had access to fewer opportunities than their white counterparts. In fact, most Brazilian cultural idioms before the 1950s entered the United States through the white-controlled mass media and not through black forums, although African American performers such as Katherine Dunham used their unique training and access to promote diasporic connections.

Cross-National Performance: Blackness and Transnationality

Bossa nova brought another group of white performers to the United States, adding on another layer of Brazilian-American cross-pollination of African influences, this time with the evolved jazz of the 1950s. These cross-national connections have continued with capoeira and break dancing, hip hop and *pagode*. Today institutionalized segregation has long passed, and blacks and white performers in the United States are free to cross racial, color, and class divides in a more complicated globalized world of radio, cinema, television, and the Internet.

In the last decade, many of Brazil's intellectuals, leaders, and activists have emerged as leaders and spokespersons in a new Pan-Africanist movement, thanks in part to political and cultural collaborations with people in the United States. Globally renowned popular musicians such as Caetano Veloso and Gilbert Gil have continued to highlight Brazilians' problematic racial legacy, while still pointing to Brazil's unique heritage and potential for peoples of all backgrounds to celebrate the black Brazilian past.

Gil and Veloso's 1992 song "Haiti," for example, is a denunciation of racism and social inequality while highlighting the complexity of race in Brazil. While "Haiti" also constituted a protest against the murder of 111 prisoners in a penitentiary system in São Paulo, Gil's 1984 record *Raça Humana* contained the single "Mão de limpeza," which pierced the silence about race, labor, and stereotypes and the hypocrisy of the white elite that invented an inferiority sense of blackness.[13]

More recently, Gil's 2002 reggae album *Kaya Ngan Daya* (in the tradition of a number of other artists, including Cidade Negra) serves as an example of the multiple ways that traditions continue to cross-fertilize one another. In a concert in Burlington, Vermont, sponsored by the local environmentalist movement there in 2000, Gil spoke of the importance of Bob Marley to his life and to the cause of social justice before singing four of Marley's songs. In 2002, Gil honored Marley in *Kaya Ngan Daya*, although many did not appreciate or understand the importance of the cross-fertilization. Dori Caymmi, son of Dorival Caymmi, for example, remarked to *O Globo* that "reggae was unbearable and it is incomprehensible why Gil would like reggae."[14]

As the minister of culture in the first Workers' Party government in 2003, Gilberto Gil, who is from Bahia, also represents an important tendency in Brazilian black consciousness and performance to recognize with patriotic zeal the *mestiço* nature of Brazilian culture. In English, Gil would probably say that he is "black," and he celebrates openly his Bahian roots, but Gil has insisted on his hybridity. In Portuguese, Gil has referred to himself as an *afromestiço*, which he claims gives an accurate representation of his racial identity (black) and his cultural identity (*mestiço*). This claim connects him to women such as Elsie Houston and nationalists such as Gilberto Freyre and to many of the performers studied in this work. By claiming the term—that is to say, the mask of the *mestiço*, albeit an *afromestiço*—Gil affirms his blackness while situating himself within the inclusive and predominant myth of Brazil as a country of *mestiços*, where miscegenation and cultural syncretism have been fundamental to national formation. This idea was accepted by the Worker's Party and was central to its platform throughout the 2002 electoral campaign.[15] In this way, performers such as Carmen Miranda could be called white *mestiços*.

For Gil, the internal diversity within Brazil proves that Brazilians are, in fact, a *mestiço* people who have created a country that is essentially syncretic. Like many Brazilians, Gil agrees with Claude Levi Strauss, who indicated there are many Brazils, and Gil wanted his ministry to respect, appreciate, and celebrate each one without necessarily giving in to the market demands of globalization. Gil's pride in that diversity, particularly when he compares it to his restricted view of the United States, imbues Brazil with special qualities—a new world within a new world.

The minister has insisted on the need to understand and embrace miscegenation and syncretism as fundamental forces of the Brazilian reality:

When I emphasize the essential *mestiço* and syncretic character of my people and of my culture, I do not want to say that this has not occurred in other places in the world. Of course it has, and it will always occur. But, we have to understand three fundamental aspects of our historical and cultural configuration: first, the high level of miscegenation that marked Brazil. This was and continues to be a fact historically worthy of note. Second, the fact that very diverse cultures mixed on a deep level. Our culture, with all of its internal differences is totally syncretic. From its beginning, since the Portuguese colonizers were not able to impose a rigid dividing line between the dominant culture and the culture of those dominated. Third, the fact that in addition to being *mestiços*, we see ourselves and recognize ourselves as such. Contrary to what has happened in the United States, where a person is either black or white, we look at our skin and recognize many different shades of color. Brazilians, unlike North Americans, want to assume all of their ancestors.[16]

Gil's discourse is a call for a recognition of blackness and *mestiço*-ness, like Latinidad, as complementary concepts and identities.[17] The early dynamics of "white face, black mask" in the minister of culture's view was thus the first step in the formulation of a *mestiço* identity that would allow everyone to celebrate politically, economically, and socially the mixed cultural identity of all Brazilians. "White face, black mask" aptly symbolizes the cultural and social dichotomy of the early development of Brazilian popular culture. As Brazilians have accepted more "black faces" as national and global representatives, a legitimate language of a *mestiço* Brazil has also emerged. Attempts to regard *mestiços* and blacks as mutually exclusive misunderstand the cultural and social continuum in Brazil. The social history of Brazilian popular music demonstrates the difficulty of determining where blackness ends and whiteness begins.

Notes

INTRODUCTION. Setting the Stage

1. "Brazilian Music on the Air," *New York Times*, November 10, 1940, 158.
2. bell hooks, *Black Looks: Race and Representation* (Boston: South End Press, 1992), 117.
3. Carl Degler, *Neither Black Nor White: Slavery and Race Relations in Brazil and the United States* (New York: MacMillan, 1971).
4. See Stuart Hall, "The Local and the Global: Globalization and Identity," in *Culture, Globalization and the World System*, ed. A. King (London: McMillan, 1991), 19–39.
5. Caetano Veloso and Gilberto Gil, "Haiti" from the album Tropicália II (1993).

6. Oneyda Alvarenga, *Música popular brasileña* (Mexico City: Fondo de Cultura Económica, 1947), 20–21. See also John Storm Roberts, *Black Music of Two Worlds: African, Caribbean, Latin and African-American Traditions*, 2nd ed. (New York: Schirmer Books, 1998), 74; and Mariza Lira, "História social da música popular carioca," *Revista da Música Popular*, no. 4 (January 1955): 10–11.

7. Patrice Pavis, ed., *The Intercultural Performance Reader* (London: Routledge, 1996), introduction.

8. American and Brazilian scholars have compared and contrasted race and race relations in a host of disciplines. For a review of the major comparative historical works on slavery and race relations in the United States and Brazil, see chapter 1 of Darién J. Davis, *Avoiding the Dark: Race, Nation and National Culture in Modern Brazil* (Aldershot, England: Ashgate International/Center for Research in Ethnic Studies, 2000). In my review, "Two New Books on Race," *Radical History Review* (Fall 1999), I try to dispel the myth that miscegenation was only present in Brazil and absent in the United States.

9. F. James Davis, *Who Is Black? One Nation's Definition* (University Park: Pennsylvania State University Press, 1997), 29.

10. José Ligeiro Coelho, "Carmen Miranda: An Afro-Brazilian Paradox" (Ph.D. diss., New York University, 1998). See, for example, Darién J. Davis, "To Be or Not to Be Brazilian: Carmen Miranda's Quest for Fame and 'Authenticity' in the United States," in *Strange Pilgrimages: Latin Americans Abroad*, ed. Ingrid E. Fey and Karen Racine (Wilmington, Del.: Scholarly Resources, 2000), 233–248; and Samuel Araújo, "Acoustic Labor in the Timing of Everyday Life: A Critical Contribution to the History of Samba in Rio de Janeiro" (Ph.D. diss., University of Illinois at Urbana-Champaign, 1992).

11. Judith Williams, "Uma Mulata, Sim!: Araci Cortes, 'the Mulatta' of the *Teatro de Revista*," *Women and Performance: A Journal of Feminist Theory* 16, no. 1 (March 2006): 7–26; Micol Seigel, "The Point of Comparison: Transnational Racial Construction, Brazil and the United States" (Ph.D. diss., New York University, 2001).

12. Susan Gubar, *Racechanges: White Skin, Black Face in American Culture* (New York: Oxford University Press, 1997); Eric Lott, *Love and Theft: Blackface Minstrelsy and the American Working Class* (New York: Oxford University Press, 1993); Alicia Arrizón, *Latina Performances: Traversing the Stage* (Bloomington: Indiana University Press, 1999). See Carlota Caulfield and Darién J. Davis, eds., *A Companion to U.S. Latino Literatures* (Rochester, N.Y.: Boydell and Brewer, 2007).

13. João Gilberto Lucas Coelho, "Breves anotações sobre a constituição de 1934," in *Constituição e constituinte*, ed. Maria Rosa Abreu (Brasília: Editora UnB, 1987), 27. National education was still an embarrassment, because of its blatant disregard for the understanding of the Afro-Brazilian reality.

14. *Constituições Brasileiras* (São Paulo: Sugestões Literárias S.A., 1978), 447. Amendment 3 later added that any civil servant could be dismissed for participation in subversive activities of a social or political nature (December 18, 1935).

15. Thomas Skidmore, "Racial Ideas and Social Policy in Brazil, 1870–1940," in *The Idea of Race in Latin America, 1870–1940*, ed. Richard Graham (Austin: University of Texas Press, 1990), 7–36.

16. Charles R, Boxer, "The Colour Question in the Portuguese Empire, 1415–1825," *Proceedings of the British Academy* 47 (1961): 113–138. See also C. R. Boxer, *Race Relations in the Portuguese Colonial Empire, 1415–1825* (London: Oxford University Press, 1963).

17. Ricardo Cravo Albin, *O livro de ouro da MPB* (Rio de Janeiro: Edouro, 2004), 10.

18. Gergóire de Villanova, "Elsie Houston e a cultura afro-brasiliera," in *Elsie Houston* (São Paulo: Projeto Negras Memórias, Memórias Negras, 2003), 27–31.

19. See Michael George Hanchard, *Orpheus and Power: The Movimento Negro of Rio de Janeiro and São Paulo, Brazil, 1945–1988* (Princeton, N.J.: Princeton University Press, 1994).

CHAPTER ONE. Afro–Brazilian Pioneers, Blackness, and the Roots of Brazilian Popular Music

1. George Reid Andrews, *Afro–Latin America* (Oxford: Oxford University Press), 5.
2. Stuart Hall, "Notes on Deconstructing the Popular," in *People's History and Socialist Theory*, ed. R. Samuel (London: Routledge and Kegan Paul, 1981), 227–240.
3. John Charles Chasteen, "The Prehistory of Samba; Carnival Dancing in Rio de Janeiro, 1840–1917," *Journal of Latin American Studies* 28 (1990): 29–47.
4. For a discussion of the Bahian roots of the samba, see Nei Lopes, *O negro no Rio de Janeiro e sua tradição musical* (Rio de Janeiro: Pallas, 1992); Roberto Moura, *Tia Ciata e a pequena África no Rio de Janeiro* (Rio de Janeiro: Funarte, 1983); José Ramos Tinhorão, *Pequena história da música popular: Da modinha ao tropicália* (São Paulo: Art, 1986); and Ary Vasconcelos, *Raízes da MPB* (Brasília: Martins/MEC, 1977). Rafael José de Menezes Bastos discusses these claims in "The 'Origin of Samba' as the Invention of Brazil (Why Do Songs Have Music?)," *British Journal of Ethnomusicology* 8 (1999): 67–96.
5. Donga, interview, tape recording, Museu da Imagem e do Som (MIS), Rio de Janeiro, April 16, 1969.
6. "Ciata, uma tia que foi a mãe do samba," *História do Samba* no. 1 (São Paulo, 1997): 13; Interview Pixinguinha, tape recording, MIS, May 22, 1968.
7. For an analysis of police practices in Rio at the turn of the century, see Thomas Halloway, *Policing Rio de Janeiro: Repression and Resistance in a Nineteenth Century City* (Stanford, Calif.: Stanford University Press, 1993).
8. "A voz do morro," translation mine. The original lyrics are: "Eu sou o samba / A voz do morro sou eu mesmo sim senhor / Quero mostrar ao mundo que tenho valor / Eu sou o rei do terreiro / Eu sou o samba / Sou natural daqui do Rio de Janeiro / Sou eu quem levo a alegria / Para milhões de corações brasileiros."
9. Daniel E. Walker, *No More No More: Slavery and Cultural Resistance in*

Havana and New Orleans (Minneapolis: University of Minnesota Press, 2004).

10. See http://www.pixinguinha.com.br; MIS Interview, *Pixinguinha*, tape recording, October 6, 1966; and Sérgio Cabral, *Pixinguinha: Vida e obra* (Rio de Janeiro: Lumiar Editora, 1997), 13–32.

11. Maria Lira, *Chiquinha Gonzaga: Grande compositora popular brasileira* (Rio de Janeiro: Funarte, 1978), 49–67.

12. Tinhorão, *Pequena história da música popular*, 118–119. The song was written or at least dedicated to the carnival group Rosa de Ouro (Golden Rose), which is mentioned by name in the second stanza.

13. The first stanza of the song in Portuguese: "O abre alas / Que eu quero passar / Eu sou da Lira / Não posso negar." "Lira" refers to singing and merriment and also to the bohemian lifestyle.

14. Benjamin Costallat, "A nota," *Jornal do Brasil*, February 3, 1935, reprinted in Lira, *Chiquinha Gonzaga*, 127.

15. For a discussion of miscegenation and the emergence of the *mestiço*, see Hermano Vianna, *O mistério do samba* (Rio de Janeiro: José Zahar Editor/UFRJ, 1995), 63–74.

16. Edigar de Alencar, *Nosso sinhô do samba* (Rio de Janeiro: Civilização Brasileira, 1968), 102–103.

17. Cabral, *Pixinguinha*, 154–155.

18. Vinícius de Moraes, "Mestre Ismael Silva," *Revista da Música Popular Extra* (Rio de Janeiro, n.d.): 4–5.

19. Jairo Severiano and Zuza Homem de Mello, *A Canção no tempo: 85 anos de músicas brasileiras* (São Paulo: Editora 34, 1997), 53–54. See Ismael Silva, recorded interview, by the Museum of Image and Sound, July 16, 1969, in *Pioneiros do samba* (Rio de Janeiro: MIS, 2002), 178–179.

20. Angenor de Oliveira (Cartola), recorded interview, MIS, March 3, 1967, Rio de Janeiro.

21. Abel Cardoso Jr., *Carmen Miranda: A cantora do Brasil* (Rio de Janeiro, 1978), 241; Abel Cardoso Jr., *Francisco Alves: As mil canções do rei da voz* (Curitiba, Brazil: Revivendo, 1998), 179, 235, 239, 250.

22. Oliveira, interview.

23. Francisco Alves, working for Odeon, recorded three as a solo performance, having previously recorded Cartola's "Que infeliz sou" in 1929

and a duet with Mário Reis, "Perdão meu bem," in 1932. Carmen Miranda recorded "Tenho um novo amor" in May 1932 on the RCA Victor label. Sílvio Caldas also recorded Cartola's "Na foresta" with RCA Victor, although he wrote the music to the song. On the same label, Araci de Almeida later recorded "Não quero mais."

24. Heitor dos Prazeres, recorded interview, MIS, 1966; Alba Lirio and Heitor dos Prazeres Filho, *Heitor dos Prazeres: Sua arte e seu tempo* (Rio de Janeiro: ND Comunicação, 2003), 39–44.

25. Prazeres, interview; Lirio and Prazeres Filho, *Heitor dos Prazeres*, 39–44.

26. Aurora Miranda, recorded interview, May 18, 1967.

27. From the *Ultima hora*, November 14, 1975, reprinted in *Na Cadênicia do Samba*, 46.

28. Ronald W. Walters, *Pan-Africanisms in the African Diaspora* (Detroit: Wayne State University Press, 1993), 326.

29. John Henrik Clarke, "Marcus Garvey: The Harlem Years," *Transition* no. 46 (1974): 15.

30. Oswald Spengler, *The Decline of the West*, trans. Charles Francis Atkinson (New York: A. A. Knopf, 1926–1928).

31. Edmund David Cronon, *Black Moses: The Story of Marcus Garvey and the United Negro Improvement Association* (Madison: University of Wisconsin Press, 1955), 63.

32. For an excellent social history of the *choro*, see Tamara Elena Livingston-Isenhour and Thomas George Carcas Garcia, *Choro: A Social History of a Brazilian Popular Music* (Bloomington: Indiana University Press, 2005).

33. Cabral, *Pixinguinha*, 143.

34. Ingebor Harer, "Ragtime," in *African American Music: An Introduction*, ed. Mellonee V. Burnim and Portia K. Maultsby (New York: Routledge, 2006), 127–143.

35. Rebee Garofalo, "The Music Industry," in Burnim and Maultsby, *African American Music*, 393–430.

36. Alvarenga, *Música popular brasileña*.

37. Bernard Gendron, *Between Montmartre and the Mudd Club: Popular Music and the Avant-garde* (Chicago: University of Chicago Press), 93.

38. For a history of the De Chocolat's role in the popular theater, see Orlando de Barros, *Corações de Chocolat: A historia da companhia negra*

de revistas, 1926–1927 (Rio de Janeiro: Livre Expressão, 2005).

39. See Hermínio Bello de Cravalho, *O canto do Pajé: Villa-Lobos e a música popular brasileira* (Rio de Janeiro: Espaço e Tempo, 1988).

40. Cabral, *Pixinguinha*, 71; Donga, interview.

41. Donga, interview.

42. On this point, Pixinguinha disagrees with his partner, Donga, claiming that the presentations in Paris were just like the ones in Brazil and that they played only Brazilian music to distinguish themselves from the many musicians from the United States and the Caribbean. See Cabral, *Pixinguinha*, 79. The fact that they performed to lyrics in French, however, already indicates that they adjusted their performance.

43. Included here are the first two stanzas of the samba. The full composition appears in Cabral, *Pixinguinha*, 77–78.

44. Donga, interview.

45. Cabral, *Pixinguinha*, 71–85. See *Le Journal* (Paris) September 7 and 8, 1922.

46. Carmen Miranda's response to Baker's performance was reported in the *Diário da Noite* on May 23, 1939, and reprinted in Cardoso, *Carmen Miranda*, 209. Roberto Ruiz, *Araci Cortes: Linda flor* (Rio de Janeiro: Funarte, 1984), 209.

47. Pixinguinha, tape recording, MIS, Rio de Janeiro, October 6, 1966.

48. Charles Baudelaire "The Painter of Modern Life," in *Baudelaire: Selected Writings on Art and Artists*, trans. P. E. Chavert (New York: Cambridge University Press, 1972).

49. Gendron, *Between Montmartre and the Mudd Club*, 93.

50. Daniella Thomas, "The Boeuf Chronicles," http://www.brazzil.com/daniv.texts/Le_Boeuf, accessed February 5, 2004.

51. Darius Milhaud, "A música brasileira," *Ariel* no. 7 (April 1924): 264.

52. Darius Milhaud, *Saudades do Brasil* (Paris: Editions Max Eschig, 1922); Darius Milhaud, *Dans les rues de Rio* (Paris: Editions Max Eschig, 1995).

53. Quoted in Thomas, "Boeuf Chronicles."

54. Darius Milhaud, *Notes Without Music* (New York: Knopf, 1953). See also Daniella Thomas on Brazil, http://daniv.blogspot.com/archives/2003_02_01_daniv_archive.html.

55. *Vem mulata ter comigo*
    Vamos ver o Carnaval
    Eu quero gozar contigo
    Esta festa sem rival.

    Vem cá, vem cá, vem cá
    meu bem.
    Como eu não há
    ninguém.

    Pula, pula, perereca
    E segura esta boneca [repeat]
    Vem cá, vem cá, vem cá [repeat]
    Olá

    Segura o cabrito [repeat]
    O boi é bem manso [repeat]
    Mulata cutuba [repeat]
    Agüenta o balanço [repeat]

56. Mário de Andrade, *Dicionário musical brasiliero* (São Paulo: *Editora Itatiaia*, 1984), 501.

57. See George Bernanos, *Le Brésil: des homes sont venus* (Monaco: Documents d'art, 1952).

58. Borges Pereira and João Batista, *Cor, profissão e mobilidade*: O negro e o rádio de São Paulo (São Paulo: Edusp, 2001), 192, 213.

CHAPTER TWO. Afro-Brazilians and the Early Popular Music Forums of Rio de Janeiro

1. Sérgio Cabral, "Getúlio Vargas and Brazilian Popular Music," in *Ensaios de opinião* (Rio de Janeiro: Editora Inúbia, 1975), 36–41.

2. Cabral, "Getúlio Vargas," 38.

3. Heitor Villa-Lobos, *A música nacionalista no governo Getúlio Vargas* (Rio de Janeiro: D.I.P., 1941), 1.

4. Villa-Lobos, *Música nacionalista*, 40.

5. See Isabel Cristina Dias, "Elsie Houston (1902–1945) cantora e pesqui-sadora brasileira" (Master's thesis, UNESP, São Paulo campus, 2000).

6. Coelho, "Carmen Miranda," 5.

7. Sérgio Cabral, *No tempo de Ari Barroso* (Rio de Janeiro: Lumiar Editora), 183. Before the 1930s, it was difficult to record percussion instruments, since the existing technology using wax was not able to adequately capture the vibrations. The electric recording systems made recording big bands possible, and most radio stations had their own orchestras. Rádio Nacional would later resolve this challenge by redistributing the rhythm to the other instruments.

8. John Edwards Phillip, *The African Heritage of White America*, in *Africanisms in American Culture*, ed. Joseph E. Holloway (Bloomington: Indiana University Press, 1990), 225–239; Melville J. Herskovits, "What Has Africa Given America?" *New Republic* 84, no. 1083 (1935): 9–94.

9. Brasil Gerson, *História das ruas do Rio de Janeiro*, 5th ed. (Rio de Janeiro: Lacerda Editora, 2000), 1–4.

10. Marly Motta, *Rio: Cidade-capital* (Rio de Janeiro: JZE, 2004), 11.

11. *Delegacia Especial de Segurança Política e Social* (DESPS), 1944–1962, Arquivo Nacional (AN). Rio de Janeiro.

12. See Ruy Guerra and Chico Buarque de Holanda, *Opera do malandro* (1986).

13. Joe Carioca was the Disney character, modeled after the *malandro*, who explores Brazil with Donald Duck. See Walt Disney's *The Three Caballeros* (1944), for example.

14. Roberto da Matta, *A casa é a rua: Espaço, cidadania, mulher e morte no Brasil* (São Paulo: Brasiliense), 1985.

15. While Rio's musicians hailed from all over the city, the neighborhoods of Madureira, Realengo, Niteroi, and Santa Cruz are overrepresented in the data, although this information must also be viewed with caution since musicians often registered their information only with street addresses and neighborhood.

16. Authorities also kept files on orchestra leaders. In contrast to the instrumentalists, orchestra leaders were well-educated, tended to earn more money, and lived in more middle-class neighborhoods, although this was not universal. They identified overwhelming as white.

17. See Walter Benjamin, *Illuminations*. Ed. and trans. Hannah Arendt (London: H. Zohn, 1973).

18. IBGE, *Anuário estatístico do Brasil* (Rio de Janeiro: IBGE, 1936), 36; IBGE, *Anuário estatístico do Brasil* (Rio de Janeiro: IBGE, 1946), 35.

19. IBGE, *Anuário estatístico do Brasil* (1936), 36.

20. IBGE, *Anuário estatístico do Brasil* (Rio de Janeiro: IBGE, 1949), 30–31.

21. Moura, *Tia Ciata*, 2.

22. For historical and contemporary memoirs and poetry about Lapa, see Isabel Lustosa, org., *Lapa do desterro e do desvario: Uma antologia* (Rio de Janeiro: Casa da Palavra, 2001).

23. IBGE, *Anuário estatístico do Brasil* (1936), 36.

24. Andrade, *Dicionário musical brasileiro*, 307. The *marcha*, according to Mário de Andrade, represented a genre of composition characterized by a binary rhythm and following the stanza-refrain-stanza-refrain pattern typical of military compositions. This style suited group dynamics and was quickly adopted and popularized by the carnival *blocos*.

25. Lamartine Babo and Irmãos Valença, "O teu cabelo não nega" (1931). The opening stanza begins: "O teu cabelo não nega / Mulata / Porque és mulata na cor / Mas como a cor não paga / Mulata / Mulata eu quero teu amor."

26. Oneyda Avarenga, *Música popular brasileña* (Mexico and Buenos Aires: Fondo de Cultura Económica, 1947), 19–20.

27. Sidney W. Mintz and Richard Price, *The Birth of African-American Culture: An Anthropological Perspective*, 2nd ed. (Boston: Beacon Press, 1992), ix.

28. IBGE, *Anuário estatístico do Brasil* (Rio de Janeiro: IBGE, 1939), 802.

29. IBGE, *Anuário estatístico do Brasil* (1939), 802, 806.

30. IBGE, *Anuário estatístico do Brasil* (1939), 802, 806.

31. The history and development of the samba schools is well documented by a host of researchers, including Sérgio Cabral, *As escolas de samba do Rio de Janeiro* (Rio de Janeiro: Lumiar, 1996), and Haroldo Costa, *Na candência do samba* (Rio de Janeiro: Novas Direções, 2000).

32. Many, such as the Banda da Ipanema, Copacabana, and Bola Preta, have traditions that go back decades.

33. Alison Raphael, "From Popular Culture to Microenterprise: The History

of the Brazilian Samba Schools," *Latin American Music Review* 11, no. 1 (June 1990): 73–83.

34. Costa, *Na cadência do samba*, 59. The term "samba school" only came into vogue in the late 1920s.

35. See the extensive biography by Carlos Didier, *Orestes Barbosa: Repórter, cronista e poeta* (São Paulo: Agir, 2006).

36. *A Crítica* (January 1929); *Correio da Noite* (1935); Janeiro 1982 (commemorative publication on the history of samba); Costa, *Na cadência do samba*, 94.

37. Maria Isaura Pereira de Queiroz, *Carnaval brasileiro: O vivido e o mito* (São Paulo: Editora Brasiliense, 1992), 71.

38. Whether Bastos referred to himself as *mestiço* is difficult to ascertain. Most biographies claim that he was born to a Portuguese small business owner and a seamstress (no race given).

39. Cabral, *As escolas de samba*, 77–82. Other names included Para o Ano Sai Melhor (So That the New Year Is Better), Vai Como Pode (Come as You Can), Depois Eu Digo (I Will Tell You Later), and fique firme (Stay Strong). As late as 1937, names such as Cada Ano Sou Melhor (Every Year I'm Better) dotted the carnival landscape and still in 1946 groups such as Vou Se Quiser (I'll Go if I Want To), Fique Firm (Stay Strong), and Filhos do Deserto (Children of the Dessert) participated in carnival.

40. Cabral, *As escolas de samba*, 379–381.

41. Herivelto Martins and Grande Othelo, "Praça Onze" (1942), digital recording, Musical Archives, Instituto Moreira Salles, Rio de Janeiro.

42. Moura, *Tia Ciata*, 61–63; Francisco Guimarães, *Na roda do samba* (Rio de Janeiro: MEC-Funarte, 1987), 7; Hermano Vianna, *The Mystery of Samba: Popular Music and National Identity in Brazil*, trans. John Charles Chasteen (Chapel Hill: University of North Carolina Press, 1998), introduction.

43. IBGE, *Anuário estatístico do Brasil* (1936), 204.

44. See, for example, Edmundo Romanelli's revues *Alô alô Madureira*, Manuscript Division, Biblioteca Nacional, Teatro Censura. The censors removed words related to the male sexual organ, and more innocently the mere mention that the character Mulher (Woman) is accused of

having a lover.

45. Cardoso, *Carmen Miranda*, 18–26; *Alô alô Madureira*, Mansucript Division, Biblioteca Nacional, Rio de Janeiro.

46. IBGE, *Anuário estatístico do Brasil* (1936), 36, 205.

47. Evelyn Furquim Werneck Lima, *Arquitetura do espetáculo* (Rio de Janeiro: UFRJ Editora, 2000), 306.

48. Dorival Caymmi, recorded interview, MIS, November 24, 1966.

49. Jamelão, live performance, March 14, 2003, Teatro Leblon.

50. DESPS, Arquivo Nacional, Rio de Janeiro.

51. Sílvio Caldas, recorded interview, MIS, June 4, 1968.

52. Gerson, *História das ruas do Rio*, 300; "Cassino da Urca" folder, Funarte library and archives, Rio de Janeiro.

53. For a list of other guests, see Carlos Machado, *Memórias sem maquiagem* (Livraria Cultura Editora, 1978). The humorist Manuel Pêra is the father of contemporary actresses Maríla and Sandra Pêra.

54. Machado, *Memórias*, 131.

55. Machado, *Memórias*, 100–101.

56. Quintandinha brochure and guide, Petrópolis, Rio de Janeiro, printed circa 2000.

57. Quintandinha brochure and guide, Petrópolis, Rio de Janeiro, printed circa 2000.

58. Lisa Shaw, *The Social History of the Brazilian Samba* (Brookfield, Vt.: Ashgate, 1999), 183.

CHAPTER THREE. Race, Class, and Technology in the Promotion of the Popular Brazilian Sound

1. Lucia Lippi Oliveira, "Identidade e alteridade no Brasil . . ." in *Decantando a república:* Inventário histórico e político da canção moderna brasileira Vol. 2 *Retrato em branco e preto da nação brasileira* (Rio de Janeiro: Editora Nova Fronteira), 97; Caetano Veloso, "Caricature and Conqueror, Pride and Shame," *New York Times*, October 20, 1991, sec. H, 34 and 51.

2. The songs were digitized by the Instituto Moreira Salles. "Malandro" (1929) was written by Francisco Alves and Freire Junior, although Ismael

Silva has claimed to be the author on various occasions. De Chocolat wrote "Mulata," which praises her beauty over others in Brazil, in 1929. Eduardo Souto's "Eu quero uma mulher bem preta" (1929) was written in homage to Josephine Baker, who had captivated Brazilians with her performances in Rio that year. See also A. R. de Jesus, "Rio chic" (1929/1930), and J. Calazans, "Meu Brasil (1929 or 1930).

3. Francisco Alves, "A vadiagem" (1929): "A vadiagem eu dexei / Não quero mais saber / arranjei outra vida / Porque deste modo / Não se pode mais viver."

4. Cláudia Neiva de Matos, *Acertei no milhar: Malandragem e samba no tempo de Getúlio* (Rio de Janeiro: Paz e Terra, 1982), 158–159. On this topic, see Cabral, *Getúlio Vargas*, 40. Wilson Batista and Ataulfo Alves's samba "O bonde São Januário" is frequently cited to indicate the extent to which the regime often changed lyrics and meaning. The original, which apparently focused on antisocial behavior, was changed to promote work when it was finally recorded in 1940.

5. Originally recorded in 1941, the lyrics are partially reproduced in Silvana Goulart, *Sob a verdade oficial: Ideologia, propaganda e censura no Estado Novo* (São Paulo: Editora Marco Zero, 1990), 21.

6. Recorded in 1941, reprinted in Alencar, *O carnaval carioca através da música* (Rio de Janeiro: Freitas Bastos, 1965), 286. "Eu hoje sou feliz, / E posso aconselhar; / Quem faz o que eu já fiz / Só pode melhorar . . . / E quem diz que o trabalho / Não dá camisa a ninguém / Não tem razão. Não tem. Não tem"

7. Martins Castelo, "O samba e o conceito de trabalho," *Cultura e Política* 2, no. 22 (1942): 174; Goulart, *Sob a verdade oficial*, 23.

8. Written and composed by Ary Barboso and Kid Pepe with the Victor band Diabo do Céu.

9. Heloísa Paulo, *Estado Novo e propaganda em Portugal e no Brasil* (São Paulo: Livraria Minerva, 1994), 65.

10. Wanderley Guilherme dos Santos, "Malandro? Qual malandro?" in *Decantando a república: Inventário histórico e político da canção popular moderna brasileira*, vol. 3 (Rio de Janeiro: Editora Nova Fronteira), 21–38. For a good explanation of the *jeitinho*, see Antonio Luciano de Andrade Tosta, "American Dream: Jeitinho Brasileiro: On the Crossroads of

Cultural Identities in Brazilian-American Literature," chapter 8 in Caulfield and Davis, *Companion to U.S. Latino Literatures.*

11. Almeida Azevedo, "A nossa música popular," *A voz do rádio* 1, no. 1 (March 28, 1935): 13.

12. Cardoso, *Carmen Miranda*, 26–27; Severiano and Mello, *Canção no tempo*, 177–186.

13. Ruth de Souza interview in Ricardo Gaspar Müller, org., *Dionysios: Teatro Experimental do Negro* (Rio de Janeiro: Funarte, 1988), 123.

14. "Voltei a cantar," *Carioca* (Rio de Janeiro), August 19, 1939, 39–40.

15. Miranda, interview.

16. Stella Caymmi, *Dorival Caymmi: O mar e o tempo* (São Paulo: Editora 34, 2001), 159.

17. Bryan McCann, *Hello, Hello Brazil: Popular Music in the Making of Modern Brazil* (Durham, N.C.: Duke University Press, 2004), 22.

18. Cited in Lia Calabre, *A era do rádio* (Rio de Janeiro: Jorge Zahar Editor), 27–28.

19. *A história do samba* (São Paulo: Globo Editora, 2001), 184–185.

20. Jairo Severiano and Zuza Homem de Mello, *A canção no tempo: 85 anos de músicas brasileiras* Vol. 1: *1901–1957* (São Paulo: Editora 34, 1997), 93; *Anuário estatístico do Brasil* Ano V (IBGE 1939/1940), 1121. McCann echoes the importance of Casé in *Hello, Hello Brazil*, 49–51.

21. "Contract signed by Amadeu Silva," *A Casa Edison e seutempo*, org. Humberto Franceschi, CD-ROM "Direitos autorais." The CD-ROM contains more than two hundred contracts of a similar nature between musicians and Fred Figner, owner and manager of Odeon.

22. Severiano and Mello, *A canção no tempo*, 50.

23. See the major magazines such as *Careta* for ads from radio companies such as Victor or Westinghouse with companies in Rio, São Paulo, and Buenos Aires.

24. Humberto M. Franceshi, *A Casa Edison e seu tempo* (Rio de Janeiro: Petrobrás, 2002), 195–203.

25. IBGE, *Anuário estatístico do Brasil* (Rio de Janeiro: IBGE, 1939/1940), 1122.

26. Cardoso, *Francisco Alves*, 22.

27. João Batista Borges Pereira, *Cor, profissão e mobilidade: O negro e o rádio*

de São Paulo, 2nd ed. (São Paulo: edUSP, 2001), 112.

28. Cabral, *Pixinguinha*, 154–155.
29. Caymmi, *Dorival Caymmi*, 116.
30. Caymmi, *Dorival Caymmi*, 123–124.
31. Severiano and Mello, *A canção no tempo*, 93; "Rádio Nacional," pamphlet, March 30, 1929, Archives of Rádio Nacional, Praça Mauá, Rio de Janeiro.
32. MIS, "Coleção Pre-8: Rádio Nacional," unpublished pamphlet on Rádio Nacional, September 1996.
33. The band was comprised of many pioneers, including Almirante, playing *pandeiro* and singing; Noel Rosa on guitar; Henrique Britto on guitar; João de Barro, better known as Braguinha, voice and guitar; and Alvinho, voice and guitar.
34. Franceschi, *A Casa Edison e seu tempo*, 197.
35. Norma Tapajós, interview, home of Norma Tapajós, Botafogo, Rio de Janeiro, February 10, 2003.
36. *Rádio Nacional: 20 anos de liderança e serviço do Brasil, 1936–1956* (commemorative pamphlet published in 1956).
37. Borges Pereira, *Cor*, 110–111, 211.
38. Interview published in *O Malho*, August 31, 1929, and reproduced in Cardoso, *Franciso Alves*, 25–26.
39. Quoted in Alan Pomerance, *Repeal of the Blues: How Black Entertainers Influenced Civil Rights* (New York: Citadel Press, 1991), 136.
40. Sílvio Caldas, recorded interview, June 4, 1968, MIS, 1968.
41. Caldas, interview.
42. Carlos Didier and João Máximo, *Noel Rosa: Uma biografia* (Brasília: Editora da Universidade de Brasília, 1990), 228; Cardoso, *Francisco Alves*, 27.
43. Jonas Vieira, *Orlando Silva: O cantor das multidões*, 2nd ed. (Rio de Janeiro: Funarte, 1997), 20–22.
44. Vieira, *Orlando Silva*, 11, 53.
45. Vieira, *Orlando Silva*, 129.
46. Interview about Noel Rosa with various friends, including Araci de Almeida, tape recording, Museum of Image and Sound, May 4, 1967; Severiano and Mello, *A canção no tempo*, 147; David Nasser, *Parceiro da*

glória: 45 anos da música popular brasileira (Rio de Janeiro: Livraria José Olympio, 1983), 69–70.

47. Cartola, interview. See also José Novaes, *Nélson Cavaquinho: Luto e melancolia na música popular brasileira* (Rio de Janeiro: Editora Intertexto e Oficina do Autor Editora, 2004).

48. Walter Benjamin, "The Work of Art in the Age of Mechanical Reproduction," in *Illuminations*, 217–252.

49. This ingenuity and use of the film to represent popular tastes can be seen in the *chanchadas*, for example. See Robert Stam, "Carmen Miranda, Grande Otelo and the Chanchada," in *Tropical Multiculturalism: A Comparative History of Race in Brazilian Cinema and Culture* (Durham, N.C.: Duke University Press, 1997), 79–105.

50. Pixinguinha, MIS, tape recording, October 6, 1966.

51. Cabral, *Pixinguinha*, 44–46, 121; Interview, Pixinguinha, MIS, tape recording, October 6, 1966.

52. Cardoso, *Carmen Miranda*, 20–23.

53. Al Jolson, *The Jazz Singer* (1927). Many musicians found employment as dubbers or providing Portuguese voices to foreign films. Braguinha, who, along with Noel Rosa, had been one of the original founders of the Banda dos Tangarás, worked on the sound for *Snow White and the Seven Dwarfs* in Portuguese (*Blanca da Neve*). Dalva de Oliveira lent her voice to the main character Blanca da Neve, and Carlos Galhardo was the voice of the prince in a musical revue that opened up in Cinêlandia on May 9, 1938.

54. Ademar Gonzaga, *Alô alô carnaval* (1936). See poster ad owned by Centro Cultural Banco do Brasil. The film was shown at the Centro Cultural Banco do Brasil, Rio de Janeiro, in the spring of 2003.

55. Gonzaga, *Alô alô carnaval*. In one of the numbers, men dance and girate to the voice of one of the singers using feminine mannerisms that could easily be mistaken for camp or drag.

56. Jaime Costa, recorded interview, MIS, September 28, 1979.

57. Gonzaga, *Alô alô carnaval*; Severiano and Mello, *A canção no tempo*, 138.

58. Edigar de Alencar, *O carnaval carioca através da música* (Rio de Janeiro: Freitas Bastos, 1965), 245. Stam has treated the theme of race and

representation in *Tropical Multiculturalism*. For a historical analysis of the film industry in Brazil, see Randall Johnson, *The film Industry in Brazil: Culture and State* (Pittsburgh: University of Pittsburgh Press, 1987).

59. Marcel Camus, *Orfeu Negro* (1959).

60. "História adminsitrativa: Divisão de Polícia Política e Social, 1944–1962," introduction to unpublished catalog of Arquivo Público do Estado do Rio de Janeiro

61. Vieira, *Orlando Silva*, 67.

62. Miranda, interview.

63. Luís Antônio Giron, *Mário Reis: O fino do samba* (São Paulo: Editora 34, 2003), 112; Lúcio Rangel and Maria Lúcia Rangel, *Sambistas e chorões: Aspectos e figuras da música popular brasileira* (Rio de Janeiro: Francisco Aves Editora, 1962), 61

64. Severiano and Mello, *A canção no tempo*, 100.

65. See John Nist, *The Modernist Movement in Brazil: A Literary Study* (Austin: University of Texas Press, 1967). In *Avoiding the Dark*, I argue that these intellectuals maintained a strong relationship with the Vargas regime and helped institutionalize a racial-national paradigm of Brazilianness. For an analysis of race and ethnicity that takes into account immigrant populations, see Jeffrey Lesser, *Negotiating National Identity: Immigrants, Minorities, and the Struggle for Ethnicity in Brazil* (Durham, N.C.: Duke University Press, 1999).

CHAPTER FOUR. Race, Class, and the Making of "the King"

1. Peter Guralnick, *The Last Train to Memphis: The Rise of Elvis Presley* (London: Abacus, 1994), 28.

2. See front pages of *O Dia*, September 28, 1952, and *Jornal do Brasil*, September 28, 1952.

3. Elmo Lins, "Chico Alves: Luto, herança e desespero," *Manchete* no. 25 (October 11, 1952), cover and 10, 21–24.

4. "A Lapa," in Isabel Lustosa org. *Lapa do desterro e do desvario: Uma antologia* (Rio de Janeiro: Casa da Palavra, 2001), 88.

5. *Lapa do desterro e do desvario*, 116–117.
6. Madame Satã, *Memórias de Madame Satã* (Rio de Janeiro: Lidador, 1972), 17.
7. Nasser, *Parceiro da glória*, 247–252.
8. Nasser, *Parceiro da glória*, 262.
9. Nasser, *Parceiro da glória*, 262–267; Vicente Celestino, recorded interview, MIS, Rio de Janeiro, April 19, 1967. The impact of Celestino on Brazilian music is laid out in a permanent exhibit at the Vicente Celestino Museum in the town of Conservatória in the state of Rio de Janeiro.
10. Salvyano Cavalcanti de Paiva, *Viva o rebolado: Vida e morte do teatro de revista brasileiro* (Rio de Janeiro: Nova Fronteira, 1991), 213–214.
11. See *Jornal do Brasil*, September 30, 1952, cover, and *Diário Carioca*, September 28, 1952, cover; Alencar, *Nosso sinhô do samba*, 101; "Chico Alves," *Diário da noite*, September 29, 1952, folder "Francisco Alves," Sala Mozart Araújo, Library of the Bank of Brazil Cultural Center, Rio de Janeiro.
12. This was clear in recordings such as "Fala meu louro" (Speak my parrot, 1921) and "Eu sou brasileiro" (I am Brazilian, 1927).
13. Reprinted in Cardoso, *Franciso Alves*, 163. The first stanza begins with a reference to Baker:

    > *Eu quero uma mulher bem preta*
    > *Vem pra cá a Josephine*
    > *Perturbará a nossa vida*
    > *Não deu sorte na Argentina*
    > *Que não tem gente sabida*
    > *Eu quero uma pretinha*
    > *Vem nua, vem nua*
    > *Que seja cheirosinha*
    > *Vem nua, vem nua*

14. "Última adeus ao Rei da Voz," *Noite ilustrada*, October 7, 1952, 4–5, 31–34. See photos from *O Cruzeiro*, October 11, 1952, 16.
15. "Ultima adeus ao Rei da Voz," 4–5, 31–34.
16. Interview about Noel Rosa with various friends, including Araci de Almeida; Severiano and Mello, *A canção no tempo*, 147; Nasser, *Parceiro*

da gloria, 69–70.

17. Ruiz, *Araci Cortes*, 189–222.

18. Ruiz, *Araci Cortes*, 207, 250–272.

19. Máximo and Didier, *Noel Rosa*, 103.

20. Severiano and Mello, *A canção no tempo*, 91–94, 101.

21. Nasser, *Parceiro da glória*, 247–252; Cardoso, *Francisco Alves*, 21.

22. Giron, *Mário Reis*, 75.

23. See the historical background of Rio's América Football Club on the team's Web site, www.america-rj.com.br.

24. Quote cited in Luís Antônio Giron, "Compositor por força maior," Caderno Fim de semana, *Gazeta Mercantil*, November 6, 1991, 1; Sérgio Cabral, "Há 50 anos um estilo de cantar foi inventado: O estilo Mário Reis," *Jornal do Brasil*,(Caderno B) January 18, 1973, 1.

25. Alencar, *Nosso sinhô do samba*, 102–103.

26. Alencar, *Nosso sinhô do samba*, 1–3, 103–104; Giron, *Mário Reis*, 62.

27. Enegé, "Discografia completa de Mário Reis," *Revista da música popular brasileira* no. 7 (May–June 1955); Alencar, *Nosso sinhô do samba*, 95.

28. Alencar, *Nosso sinhô do samba*, 165–173.

29. David Nasser, *Chico Viola* (Rio de Janeiro: Edições O Cruzeiro, S.A., 1966), 117.

30. "Morreu a cigarra da cidade," *A Notícia*, August 5, 1930; "Morreu o popular compositor Sinhô," *O Jornal*, August 5, 1930; and several other articles from August 5, 1930, are reprinted in Alencar, *Nosso sinhô do samba*, 144–148

31. "A primeiras audições de nossa madrinha," *A voz do rádio* 1, no. 4 (April 11, 1935): 6. For a representative description of Reis, see *Diário de notícias*, November 11, 1931, 5, where Reis is described as "the Gardel of Rio."

32. Scholars are indebted to the pioneering work of Florestan Fernandes on blacks in Brazilian society. For more recent work, see Reid Andrews, *Blacks and Whites in São Paulo, 1888–1988* (Madison: University of Wisconsin Press, 1991); and Darién Davis, *Afro-Brasileiros Hoje* (São Paulo: Summus, 2000).

33. Caymmi, interview.

34. "Noel Rosa," *A modinha* (Bahia) 3, no. 68 (May 1937): 1.

35. Máximo and Didier, *Noel Rosa*, 219.

36. Máximo and Didier, *Noel Rosa*, 219–224.

37. *Diário carioca*, May 6, 1937, n.p.

38. *Diário carioca*, May 6, 1937, n.p.

39. Aloysio de Oliveira, *De banda pra lua* (Rio de Janeiro: Record, 1983), 40.

40. Oliveira, *De banda pra lua*, 48–49.

41. Giron, *Mário Reis*, 243.

42. "Ele criou o modo brasileiro de cantar," *Jornal do Brasil*, October 1981, 1.

43. Sala Mozart Araújo, A 097 14810. See also "Mário Reis," *Manchete*, October 17, 1981, 130.

44. Máximo and Didier, *Noel Rosa*, 228.

45. Máximo and Didier, *Noel Rosa*, 228; Cardoso, *Francisco Alves*, 27.

46. Vieira, *Orlando Silva*, 129.

47. Vieira, *Orlando Silva*, 133.

48. *O Dia*, August 8, 1978, 11.

49. See articles and interviews with Sérgio Cabral, Clara Nunes, Carlos Galhardo, Emilinha Borba, Marlene, Paulo Tapajós, Nelson Gonçalves, and others throughout *O Globo*, August 8, 1978. Similar articles appeared on the same day in *Última hora* and *Tribuna da imprensa*.

50. Sérgio Bettencourt column, *Última hora*, August 10, 1978, n.p.

51. Lúcio Rangel, "Araci de Almeida responde," *Revista da música popular* 1, no. 1 (1954): 18.

52. Giron, *Mário Reis*, 196.

53. Rangel and Rangel, *Sambistas e chorões*, 61; Nasser, *Parceiro da glória*, 240–246; Sérgio Cabral, "Uma tarde com Mario Reis," *Diário de notícias*, Rio de Janeiro, April 24, 1974, n.p.

54. "Se você jurar," Sheet Music P5939, Sala Mozart Araújo.

55. Ataulfo Alves, recorded interview, November 17, 1966, MIS, Rio de Janeiro.

56. *A história do samba*, Vol. II (São Paulo: Globo Editora, 1997), 202; Silva, interview; Elsa Soares, *Do cóccix até o pescoço* (Mainga Discos, 2002), track 6.

57. *A história do samba*, Vol. II, 202.

58. Severiano and Mello, *A canção no tempo*, 53–54; *Pioneiros do samba* (Rio de Janeiro: MIS, 2002), 178–179.

59. See *Diário de notícias*, September 30, 1952; *A Manhã*, September 28, 1952.

60. Norma Tapajós, interview.

61. Cardoso, *Franciso Alves*, 171, 458.

62. For a good history of *Tropicália*, see Chris Dunn, *Brutality's Garden: Tropicália and the Emergence of a Brazilian Counter-Culture* (Chapel Hill: University of North Carolina Press, 2001). The era of the music festivals is superbly treated in Zuza Homem de Mello, *A era dos festivais: uma parábola* (São Paulo: Editora 34, 2003).

63. Clipping from *Amiga*, October 21, 1981.

64. Wallace Stevens, "The Idea of Order at Key West," in *The Palm at the End of the Mind*, ed. *Holly Stevens* (New York Vintage Books, 1972), 97–99.

CHAPTER FIVE. Africaneity, Performance, and the Women
of Brazilian Popular Music

1. The quote is taken from Dulce Damasceno de Brito, *O ABC de Carmen Miranda* (São Paulo: Companhia Editora Nacional, 1986), 79.

2. Coelho, "Carmen Miranda," 12.

3. Paul Gilroy utilizes the term "Africaneity" in his "Sounds Authentic: Black Music, Ethnicity, and the Challenge of a 'Changing' Same," *Black Music Research Journal* 11, no. 2 (Autumn 1991): 111–136.

4. "Morre Carmen Costa, da marchinha 'Cachaça,'" *Folha Ilustrada*, April 26, 2007, 1.

5. *Love and Theft*, 38–88.

6. Lira, *Chiquinha Gonzaga*, 49–67. See also Nancy Saporta Sternbach et al, "Feminisms in Latin America: From Bogotá to San Bernardo," *Signs* 17, no. 2 (Winter 1992): 393–434.

7. Costallat, "Nota," 127.

8. Ruiz, *Araci Cortes*, 208–209.

9. Aracy Cortes, recorded interview, Museum of Image and Sound (Lapa),

Rio de Janeiro, November 3, 1967.

10. Máximo and Didier, *Noel Rosa*, 322–325.

11. McCann, *Hello, Hello Brazil*, 198–201.

12. McCann, *Hello, Hello Brazil*, 198–201.

13. *Delegacia Especial de Segurança Política e Social* (DESPS).

14. See the beginning of the introduction to this book for Houston's exact words.

15. Gilroy, "Sounds Authentic," 111–136.

16. Edward Thorpe, *Black Dance* (Woodstock, N.Y.: Overlook Press), 13; Gilroy, "Sounds Authentic," 111–136.

17. Zita Allen, "What Is Black Dance?" http://www.pbs.org/wnet/freetodance/behind/behind_blackdance3.html, accessed December 12, 2006.

18. See Alvarenga, *Música Popular Brasileña*. Also cited in Roberts, *Black Music of Two Worlds*, 74.

19. Joubert de Carvalho, recorded interview, MIS, Rio de Janeiro May 10, 1972.

20. Carvalho, interview; "Joubert de Carvalho," *Nova historia da música popular brasileira* (São Paulo: Editora Abril, 1977), 4–12; "Hyenas," *Última hora* (Rio) August 8, 1955, 5.

21. IBGE, *Anuário estatístico do Brasil* (1939/1940), 1308.

22. Cardoso, *Carmen Miranda*, 17–18.

23. Miranda, interview.

24. Cabral, *No tempo do Ari Barroso*, 105.

25. See the series of excerpts from a number of newspapers, including *O Paiz* and the *Diário de Notícias* from 1930, quoted in Cardoso, *Carmen Miranda*, 65–68.

26. Cabral, *No tempo do Ari Barroso*, 105, 218–237.

27. Oliveira, *De banda pra lua*, 17, 20.

28. Mário de Moraes, *Recordações de Ary Barroso: Último depoimento*, 2nd ed. (Rio de Janeiro: Funarte, 2003), 46; Cardoso, *Carmen Miranda*, 246; Cabral, *No tempo do Ari Barroso*, 146.

29. Moraes, "Recordações de Ary Barroso," 106; photograph in *O Diário da Noite*, August 13, 1955, 4; Cabral, *No tempo de Ari Barroso*, 215–218, 237; "Perdeu o Brasil a Maior Intérprete da Sua Música Popular," *O Globo*, October 6, 1955, 6. See Caetano Veloso, "Carmen Mirandadada," in

Brazilian Popular Music and Globalization, ed. Christopher Perrone and Christopher Dunn (Gainesville: University Press of Florida, 2001).

30. Nasser, *Parceiro da glória*, 306–308. Carmen Miranda later recorded "Tabuleiro da Baiana" in the typical style that paid homage to Bahia, as did Aurora's "Os quindins de Iaiá," which appeared in *The Three Caballeros*.

31. Ary Barroso, "Aquarela do Brasil," (1939), HMB027 Museu da Imagem e do Som, Rio de Janeiro.

32. Barroso, "Aquarela do Brasil," English translation from Claus Schreiner, 113–114.

33. Norma Tapajós, interview.

34. The family lived at Rua Joaquim Silva number 53 in Lapa, close to the theater and musical centers, and then on the Travessa do Comércio between Praça 15 and the Rua do Ouvidor.

35. Cardoso, *Carmen Miranda*, 21. The Portuguese version of the biography was used for this information. See Martha Gil-Montero, *A pequena notável* (Rio de Janeiro: Editora Record, 1989), 30–43; Moura, *Tia Ciata*, 2, 18–20; and Guimarães, *Na roda do samba*, 7.

36. Franceshi, *A Casa Edison e seu tempo*, 17–27.

37. Cardoso, *Carmen Miranda*, 21–25; Abel Cardoso Jr., interview by author, tape recording, Sorocaba, São Paulo, April 15, 2003. See interview with Abel Cardoso Jr. in Marcos Vinícius Parizatto, *Aurora: A notável irmã de Carmen* (SBT, 2002).

38. Cardoso, *Carmen Miranda*, 247; Alencar, *O carnaval carioca através da música*, 246.

39. *Música popular brasileira: Assis Valente* (São Paulo: Edição Victor Civita, 1970), 7.

40. Orlando de Barros, *Custódio Mesquita: Um compositor romântico no tempo de Vargas (1930–1945)*, (Rio de Janeiro: Funarte/EdUERJ), 76, 411. For Orlando de Barros, the 1936 Odeon recording copies the concept and organization of Mesquita's original, more sentimental fox-trot, transforming it into a lively *marcha* and changing the voice from male to female.

41. Cardoso, *Carmen Miranda*, 400.

Nós somos as cantoras do rádio,
levamos a vida a cantar
De noite embalamos teu sono
De manhã nós vamos te acordar
Nós somos as cantoras do rádio,
Nossas canções cruzando o espaço azul
Vão reunindo num grande abraço corações de Norte a Sul

Canto pelos espaços afora
Vou semeando cantigas, dando alegria a quem chora
(bum, bum, bum, bum, bum, bum)
Canto, pois sei que a minha canção
Vai dissipar a tristeza que mora no teu coração

Canto para te ver mais contente
Pois a ventura dos outros é alegria da gente
(bum, bum, bum, bum, bum, bum)
Canto e sou feliz só assim
Agora peço que cantes um pouquinho para mim

42. Pavis, *Intercultural Performance Reader*, introduction.
43. Coelho, "Carmen Miranda."
44. Alencar, *O carnaval carioca através da música*, 246.
45. Miranda, interview. There are two other later recorded interviews with Aurora Miranda in which she discusses the same issues but with considerably less accuracy and details.
46. Miranda, interview.
47. Mário Lago, *Na rolança do tempo* (Rio de Janeiro: Civilização Brasileira, 1976), 223; Caymmi, *Dorival Caymmi*, 112–113.
48. See reportage with photo of Aurora and Carmen on the beach in Copacabana in *A Voz do rádio* 1, no. 3 (April 11, 1935).
49. Marcos Vinícius Parizatto, *Aurora: A notável irmã de Carmen* (SBT, 2002).
50. Martha Gil-Montero, *Brazilian Bombshell: The Biography of Carmen Miranda* (New York: Donald I. Fine, 1989), 33.
51. Andrade, *Dicionário musical brasileiro*, 53.

52. Sinval Silva, recorded interview, January 20, 1967, MIS; Senhora da Silva, interview, Rio de Janeiro, April 15, 1996; Cardoso, *Carmen Miranda*, 390.

53. Sinval Silva, "Detailed Explanation of His Recorded Music," MIS, file Sinval Silva, S/D; Andrade, *Dicionário muscial brasileiro*, 52–53.

54. "E Samba de Sinval," *O Jornal* (Vida Moderna section), March 25, 1972, 1; "Sinval Silva: A volta do compositor de Carmen Miranda," *O Globo* (Rio) July 3, 1973, n.p.

55. "Morreu ontem Carmen Miranda," *Correio da Manhã*, August 6, 1955, Primeiro Caderno, 5.

56. "A morte trouxe Carmen de volta," *Manchete*, August 20, 1955, 23; Cardoso, *Carmen Miranda*, 225.

57. *Historia do samba*, vol. 14, 269.

58. João Carlos Rodrigues, *O negro brasileiro e o cinema* (Rio de Janeiro: Pallas, 2001), 86. See photograph and report on Angela Maria in *Amiga*, February 8, 1972.

59. *História do samba*, vol. 14, 261, 274.

60. José Ramos Tinhorão, *História social da música popular brasileira* (Lisboa: Editorial Caminho, 1990), 207.

61. Sigmund Freud, "Jokes and Their Relation to the Unconscious," in *The Standard Edition to the Complete Works of Sigmund Freud*, vol. 8 (London: Hogarth Press and the Institute of Psycho-Analysis, 1960), 221.

62. Miranda encouraged celebration in songs such as "Disso é que eu gosto," September 6, 1940, recording.

63. See, for example, J. C. Flugel, "Humor and Laughter," *Handbook of Social Psychology* 2 (1954): 709–716. See also Freud, "Jokes and Their Relation to the Unconscious," 200.

64. Brito, *O ABC de Carmen Miranda*, 11.

65. "Carmen Miranda: The Brazilian fireball," (SH114), Sussex, England: World Record Club, side 1, track no. 5.

66. "Carmen Miranda" (Curitiba: Revivendo Musicas Comercio de Discos, 1990?); "Eu Gosto da Minha Terra," recorded March 1930, track 8.

67. Arlindo Marques and Roberto Roberti, "Nova Descoberta," released in 1935; Joubert de Carvalho, "Terra Morena," released in 1936.

68. Quoted in Cardoso, *Carmen Miranda*, 101, 177–178.

69. Alencar, *O carnaval carioca através da música*, 246.

70. Alencar, *O carnaval carioca através da música*, 246

71. "Carmen Miranda: The Brazilian Recordings," by Augusto Vassuer-Marques and Porto Luis Peixoto (West Sussex: Harlequin, 1993), song no. 19. "Sai da toca Brasil" was written by Joubert de Carvalho (recorded in 1938).

72. The original recording of May 2, 1939, can be found on the remastered disc "Carmen Miranda: The Brazilian Recordings," song no. 10. "Preto e branco" was also recorded by Aracy Cortes in 1930.

73. The original Portuguese lyrics to "O nêgo no samba" are:

> *Samba de nêgo*
> *quebra os quadris*
> *Samba de nêgo*
> *tem parati*
> *Samba de nêgo, oi, oi*
> *sempre na ponta*
> *Samba de nêgo, meu bem*
> *me deixa tonta*
>
> *Num samba, branco se escangaia*
> *Num samba, nêgo bom se espaia*
> *Num samba, branco não tem jeito, meu bem*
> *Num samba, nêgo nasce feito*

74. Written and composed by Ary Barboso and Kid Pepe with the Victor Band "Diabo do céu"; recorded in 1935.

75. The first stanza begins: "Mulatinho Bamba / ô mulato mulatinho bamba / como desacata quando samba. The last stanza: Por causa deste mulatinho / eu fico na janela / o dia inteirinho / Quando ele passa na calçada / parece o Clark Gable / em 'Acorrentada.'"

76. Waldemar M. Da Silva, 1937.

77. Sinval Silva, 1937.

78. Arlindo Marques Jr. and Roberti Roberts, 1935.

79. Almir Chediak, *Songbook: Dorival Caymmi* (Rio de Janeiro: Lumiar Editora, 1994), 48. The original recording can be found on the remastered

disc "Carmen Miranda: The Brazilian Recordings."

80. Helena Solberg, *Carmen Miranda: Bananas Is My Business* (1995).

81. Cardoso, *Carmen Miranda*, 39. See "Morreu Carmen Miranda," *O Dia* (Rio de Janeiro), August 6, 1955, 1; "Carmen Miranda ficará al lado de Chico Alves," August 6–7, 1955.

82. *Música popular brasileira: Assis Valente*, 2nd ed. (São Paulo, 1977), 2–7.

83. *Música popular brasileira: Assis Valente*, 8.

84. Caymmi, *Dorival Caymmi*, 368.

85. "No tabuleiro da Baiana" by Ary Barroso (1936), "Baiana do tabuleiro" by André Filho (1937), "Quando eu penso na Bahia" (When I think about Bahia) by Ary e Luiz Peixoto (1937), "Nas cadeiras da Baiana" (On a Bahiana's hips) by Portelo Juno and Léo Cardoso (1938), and "Na Bahia" (In Bahia) by Herivelto Martins and Humberto Porto (1938).

86. Column of interviews in *A Última Hora* (Rio) on the day after Carmen's death, August 8, 1955, 1.

87. Gil-Montero, *Brazilian Bombshell*, 70; Ana Rita Mendonça, *Carmen Miranda foi a Washington* (Rio and São Paulo: Editora Record, 1999), 117–121.

88. See Veloso, "Caricature and Conqueror"; Mendonça, *Carmen Miranda foi a Washington*, 117.

89. Ruy Castro, *Carmen: A vida de Carmen Miranda a brasileira mais famosa do século XX* (São Paulo: Companhia das Letras, 2005), 169; Cardoso, *Carmen Miranda*, 438; Cortes, interview.

CHAPTER SIX. Race and Brazilianness Abroad in the Early Era of Globalization

1. Loosely translated: "Brasil!, Show your face / I want to see who will pay / For us to remain this way / Brasil!"

2. Front page, *A Noite*, August 8, 1955.

3. Hubert Drake, "The Theatres," *New York Post*, June 30, 1939.

4. Translation mine. Edgardo Rodríguez Juliá, *El entierro de Cortijo*, 3rd ed. (Rio Piedras: Ediciones Huracán, 1985). Adapted loosely from Juliá's words: "el espacio donde el desordenando tiempo interior no se decide

entre atacar la muerte o negarla, ello por la engañosa estadía de ese muerto que aun no se ha convertido en recuerdo."

5. Oliveira, "Identidade e alteridade no Brasil," 97; Veloso, "Carmen Miranda."

6. In the mid 1930s, Uruguay boasted one of the most extensive radio-diffusion networks comprised of sixteen radio stations of which Radio Carve was the most important: Carve, Westinghouse, Espectador, Radio Sport, Monte Carlo, Fada Radio, La Voz de Radio, Radio Uruguay, Edison Broadcasting, Rádio Nacional, Radio Aguila, Radio Artigas, Centenário Broadcasting, Radio Fenix, Tribuna Sonora, and La Estación Feminina del Uruguay. As in Brazil and Argentina, the print press was closely associated with radio stations.

7. Cabral, *Pixinguinha*, 89. See *La Nación* (December 1922).

8. Miranda, interview.

9. "Llegaron Las Hermanas Miranda," *Radiolandia*, July 25, 1936, no. 436, n.p.

10. "C. M and Aurora with Tomás Simari-el actor de las mil voces . . ." (Radio Belgrano), *Radiolandia*, August 22, 1936, no. 440, n.p.

11. *Sintonía* carried the radio programs at the end of the magazine, organized by radio station; *Radiolandia* programs were organized by date.

12. MDB 9/4/5 Buenos Aires "Ofícios" April–July 1936, Arquivo do Itamaraty, Rio de Janeiro.

13. Mário Reis, interview with the *Diário da Noite*, November 11, 1931, n.p.

14. Sander L. Gilman, *Difference and Pathology: Stereotypes of Sexuality, Race, and Madness* (Ithaca, N.Y.: Cornell University Press, 1985).

15. Ella Shohat, "Gender and the Culture of Empire: Towards a Feminist Ethnography of the Cinema," *Quarterly Review of film and Video* 13 (1990): 45–84.

16. The Roosevelt Corollary, 1904, http://www.latinamericanstudies.org/ us-relations/roosevelt-corollary.htm, accessed January 6, 2006; George W. Crichfield, *American Supremacy: The Rise and Progress of the Latin American Republics and Their Relations to the United States under the Monroe Doctrine* (New York: Brentano's, 1908); Bryce Wood, *The Making of the Good Neighbor Policy* (New York: Columbia University Press, 1961), 130; Donald W. Roland, org., *History of the Office of the*

Coordinator of Inter-American Affairs (Washington D.C.: U.S. Government Printing Office, 1947).

17. Alberto Sandoval-Sanchez, *José Can You See? Latinos On and Off Broadway* (Madison: University of Wisconsin Press, 1999), 24–31.

18. Julianne Burton, "Don Juanito Duck and the Imperial Patriarchal Unconscious: Disney Studios, the Good Neighbor Policy and the Packaging of Latin America," in *Nationalisms and Sexualities,* ed. Andrew Parker et al. (New York: Routledge, 1992o, 21–41; Laura Mulvey, *Visual and Other Pleasures (*Bloomington: Indiana University Press, 1989), 19.

19. Saskia Sassen, "U.S. Immigration Policy toward Mexico in a Global Economy," *Journal of International Affairs* 43, no. 2 (1990): 369–381.

20. Oliveira, *De banda para a lua,* 85; Thomas Skidmore, *Black into White: Race and Nationality in Brazilian Thought* (Durham, N.C.: Duke University Press, 1993).

21. Lewis Hanke, *Gilberto Freyre: Vida y obra. Bibliografía antología (*New York: Instituto de las Españas en los Estados Unidos, 1939); Gilberto Freyre, "O homem brasileiro: Formação étnica e cultural," in *Estudo de problemas brasileiros* (Recife, Brazil: Universidade Federal de Pernambuco, 1971), 167–178.

22. Gilberto Freyre, *Casa-grande & senzala: Formação da família brasileira sob o regime de economia patriarchal,* 2 vols. (1933; Recife, Brazil: Imprensa Oficial, 1966–1970).

23. Frank Tannenbaum, *Slave and Citizen: The Negro in the Americas* (New York: Vintage Books, 1946); Stanley Elkins, *Slavery: A Problem in American Institutional and Intellectual Life* (Chicago: University of Chicago Press, 1959).

24. For a brief historical assessment of the U.S. census, see David Hendricks and Amy Patterson, "Genealogy Notes: The 1930 Census in Perspective" 34, no. 2 (Summer 2002), at http://www.archives.gov/publications/prologue/2002/summer/1930-census-perspective.html, accessed August 15, 2006.

25. Bureau of the Census, Social and Economic Statistics Administration, U.S. Department of Commerce, *15th Census of the U.S. 1930 Population*, Vol. 2 *General Report* (Washington D.C.: U.S. Department of Commerce, 1933), 350; Darién J. Davis, "The Brazilian-Americans:

Demography and Identity of An Emerging Latino Minority," *Latino Review of Books* (Spring/Fall 1997): 8–15.

26. George Black, *The Good Neighbor* (New York: Pantheon Books, 1988), 60–71.

27. Allen L. Woll, *The Hollywood Musical Goes to War* (Chicago: Nelson-Hall, 1983), 105–109; Sérgio Augusto, "Hollywood Looks at Brazil: From Carmen Miranda to *Moonraker*," in *Brazilian Cinema*, expanded ed., ed. Randal Johnson and Robert Stam (New York: Columbia University Press, 1995), 351–361.

28. "*Down Argentine Way* with Betty Grable at the Roxy," *New York Times*, October 18, 1940.

29. "Rio Hails Carmen Miranda," *New York Times*, July 11, 1949. See *O Globo*, July 7, 1940, 2.

30. Quoted in Cardoso, *Carmen Miranda*, 163; "É assim que o Brasil brilha?" *Folha da Noite*, January 30, 1940, 3. See also *Careta*, September 28, 1940.

31. Gil-Montero, *Brazilian Bombshell*, 215–216; Vincent Terrace, *Radio Programs, 1924–1984: A Catalog of Over 1800 Shows* (Jefferson, N.C.: McFarland, 1999), 242.

32. Quoted in Cardoso, *Carmen Miranda*, 195–196, from Alex Viany in *O Cruzeiro*, November 13, 1948.

33. Shari Roberts, "The Lady in the Tutti-Frutti Hat: Carmen Miranda, a Spectacle of Ethnicity," *Cinema Journal* 32, no. 3 (Spring 1993): 15.

34. Roberts, "Lady in the Tutti-Frutti Hat," 15.

35. Pavis, *Intercultural Performance Reader*, introduction.

36. "Etta Motten's Singing Makes This Film Hot: Flying Down to Rio Is Picture Featuring Star," *Chicago Defender*, March 31, 1934; "Fred Astaire Tells Race Dancers to Be Original," *Chicago Defender*, February 2, 1935.

37. "Nicholas Duo Awarded Long film Contract," *New York Amsterdam News*, November 23, 1940. See also http://www.brightlightsfilm.com/26/flying.html.

38. Thornton Freeland, *Flying Down to Rio* (1933). See the article on the film in *Variety*: "*Flying Down to Rio*," January 1, 1934, http://www.variety.com/review/VE1117790993.html?categoryid=31&cs=1&p=0.

39. B. Harpe, "Tribute to Katherine Dunham—Obituary," *Dancing Times*

96, no. 1153 (September 2006): 71. See the photograph of Dunham as the Bahiana in the *New Amsterdam "Star" News*, June 21, 1941. A. Kraut, "Between Primitivism and Diaspora: The Dance Performances of Josephine Baker, Zora Neale Hurston, and Katherine Dunham," *Theatre Journal* 55, no. 3 (October 2003): 433–450. See also the excellent Web site on Dunham at http://lcweb2.1oc.gov/cocoon/ihas/html/dunham/dunham-home.html.

40. Dan Burley, "Does Blackout Loom for Negro Bands," *New York Amsterdam News*, November 23, 1940.

41. See interviews in Helena Solberg, *Carmen Miranda: Bananas Is My Business* (New York: Noon Pictures, 1996).

42. Aurora Miranda, "Letter to Almirante," March 19, 1941, MIS Archives (Praça Tiradentes), Rio de Janeiro.

43. Daniela Thomas, "Untangling the Web of 'Bambo do Bambu,'" January 29, 2003, http://daniv.blogspot.com/archives/2003_01_01_daniv_archive.html, accessed October 2, 2006.

44. "Music Fiesta Held at Carnegie Hall," *New York Times*, October 29, 1941; "Screen News Here and in Hollywood," *New York Times*, May 7, 1941.

45. Oliveira, *De banda para lua*, 117. See also Decca Records catalog; Walter Teixeira Alves, "A Discografia de Aurora Miranda," unpublished catalog, 1976.

46. *Phantom Lady* (1944).

47. "Sister Carmen Is a Big Star So Aurora Omits the 'Miranda,'" *P.M. Weekly News*, October 12, 1941, n.p., in Folder "Aurora Miranda," Division of Theatre, New York Public Library, Lincoln Center, New York City.

48. Earl Wilson, "Hokay, Go Home Keed, They Said to Aurora but Aurora, Carmen Miranda's Sister, Showed Hollywood Up," *New York Post*, October 13, 1941, in Folder "Aurora Miranda," Division of Theatre, New York Public Library, Lincoln Center.

49. See Michel Ruppli, Decca Records catalog, Vol. 1, Eastern and Southern Sessions, 1934–1942, 154, 159; "Sister Carmen Is a Big Star So Aurora Omits the 'Miranda.'"

50. Press Book 1944, Microfilm Reel #143, New York Public Library, Lincoln Center.

51. Quoted in Cabral, *No tempo de Ari Barroso*, 230. The posters declared

that Brazil was a "Pan-American Musical Serenade to Romana" and that it was "packed with exquisitely beautiful girls from the four corners of the Americas."

52. "Of Local Origin," *New York Times*, May 30, 1944, 25; Thomas Pryor, "By Way of Report: Fox to Experiment with 'The Fighting Lady— Aurora Miranda Kisses the Air,'" *New York Times*, September 24, 1944, X3; "The Screen," *New York Times*, November 20, 1944, 25.

53. *Os quindins de Iaiá / Cumé, cumé, cumé?*
    Os quindins de Iaiá / Cumé, cumé, cumé?
    Os quindins de Iaiá / Cumé?

    Cumé que faz chorar / Os zóinho de Iaiá
    Cumé, cumé, cumé? / Os zóinho de Iaiá
    Cumé, cumé, cumé? / Os zóinho de Iaiá
    Cumé?

    Cumé que faz penar / O jeitão de Iaiá
    Me dá, me dá / Uma dor
    Me dá, me dá / Que não sei
    Se é, se é / Se é ou não amor
    Só sei que Iaiá tem umas coisas
    Que as outras mulher não tem
    O que é?
    Os quindins de Iaiá / Os quindins de Iaiá
    Os quindins de Iaiá / Os quindins de Iaiá

    Tem tanta coisa de valor / Nesse mundo de Nosso Senhor
    Tem a flor da meia-noite / Escondida no terreiro
    Tem música e beleza / Na voz do boiadeiro
    A prata da lua cheia / No leque dos coqueiros
    O sorriso das crianças / A toada dos vaqueiros
    Mas juro por Virgem Maria / Que nada disso pode matar . . .
    O quê? / Os quindins de Iaiá

54. Didier and Máximo, *Noel Rosa*, 218.

55. Didier and Máximo, *Noel Rosa*, 218.

56. "Obituaries," *Guardian Online*, August 8, 1995. Almeida died on July

26, 1995. See www.laurindoalmeida.com.
57. Cabral, *No tempo de Ari Barroso.*
58. Cabral, *No tempo de Ari Barroso*, 209–213.
59. Norman Ferguson and Wilfred Jackson, *Saludos Amigos* (RKO, 1942). Barroso's original Portuguese composition was translated and adapted for this film by Aloysio de Oliveira and S. K. Russell. The original Portuguese lyrics are:

> *Brasil*
> *Meu Brasil brasileiro*
> *Meu mulato insoneiro*
> *Vou cantarte nos meus versos*
> *Ô Brasil, samba que dá*
> *Bamboleio, que faz gingá*
> *Ô Brasil, do meu amor*
> *Terra do Nosso Senhor*
> *Brasil!*
> *Brasil!*
> *Pra mim . . .*
> *Pra mim . . .*
> *Ô abre a cortina do passado*
> *Tira a mãe preta do serrado*
> *Bota o Rei Congo no congado*
> *Brasil!*
> *Brasil!*
> *Pra mim . . .*
> *Pra mim . . .*
> *Deixa, cantar de novo o trovador*
> *À merencória luz da lua*
> *Toda a canção do meu amor . . .*
> *Quero ver essa dona caminhando*
> *Pelos salões arrastando*
> *O seu vestido rendado*
> *Brasil!*
> *Brasil!*
> *Prá mim . . .*

Prá mim . . .
Meu Brasil brasileiro
Meu mulato insoneiro
Vou cantar-te nos meus versos
Ô Brasil, samba que dá
Bamboleio, que faz gingá
Ô Brasil, do meu amor
Terra do Nosso Senhor
Brasil!
Brasil!
Pra mim . . .
Pra mim . . .
Ô esse coqueiro que dá coco
E onde amarro a minha rede
Nas noites claras de luar
Brasil!
Brasil!
Pra mim . . .
Pra mim . . .
Ô oi essas fontes murmurantes
Oi onde eu mato a minha sede
E onde a lua vem brincar
Oi esse Brasil lindo e trigueiro
É o meu Brasil brasileiro
Terra de samba e pandeiro
Brasil!
Brasil!
Pra mim . . .
Pra mim . . .

60. Robert Levine, *The Brazilian Photographs of Genevieve Naylor, 1940–1942* (Durham, N.C.: Duke University Press, 1998).
61. Lucile Neville, "Now That Hollywood Has Discovered Latin America, Anything Can Happen," *Washington Post*, January 28, 1940, A1.
62. Oliveira, *De banda a lua*, 109.
63. Castro, *Carmen*, 486–487.

64. For additional comments on black Brazilian women in the United States, see Maria Angela de Jesus, *Ruth de Souza: Estrela negra* (São Paulo, 2004), 107.

65. Tom Cordoso, "Carmen Costa, de arrumadeira a diva do canto colloquial," Agenda do Samba & Choro Jornal do valor Econômico http://www.samba-choro.com.br/s-c/tribuna/samba-choro.0207/0287.html, accessed March 3, 2005; Carmen Costa, recorded interview, MIS, August 23, 1972.

66. Kees Shoof, "Brazil's Most American Crooner: (Review) Dick Farney No Palco CD," http://musicabrasileira.org/reviewsinterviews/dfpalco.html, accessed September 15, 2004.

67. Olin Down, "Composers' Group in Concert Here: Elsie Houston Soloist," *New York Times*, March 11, 1940; Grace Turner, "Good-Will Recipes from Rio," *Los Angeles Times*, April 20, 1941; Jack Gould, "News and Gossip of the Night Clubs," *New York Times*, March 6, 1938.

68. Veloso, "Caricature and Conqueror, Pride and Shame."

69. Shohat, "Gender and the Culture of Empire," 45–84.

70. Solberg, *Carmen Miranda*.

CONCLUSION. Afro-Brazilian Performers and the Legacy of Music of the Vargas Era

1. "Ele criou o modo brasileiro de cantar," 1.

2. *El entierro de Cortijo* (Ediciones Huracán, 1985), 11.

3. Thomas Skidmore, *Politics in Brazil, 1930–1964: An Experiment in Democracy* (New York: Oxford University Press, 1967). For an excellent history of bossa nova, see Ruy Castro, *Chega de saudade: A historia e as histórias da bossa nova*, 2nd ed. (São Paulo: Compendia das Letras, 1990).

4. Museu da Imagem e do Som, *500 anos da musical popular brasileira* (Rio de Janeiro: MIS Editor, 2001), 120–124.

5. Villanova, "Elsie Houston."

6. Alvin, *O livro de ouro de MPB*, 10–11.

7. Gilberto Gil speech at the inauguration of the new president of the Palmares Cultural Foundation, February 11, 2003; reprinted on the

Ministry of Culture Web site www.cultura.gov.br., accessed April 20, 2003.

8. Walters, *Pan-Africanism in the African Diaspora*, 326.

9. Brent Hayes Edwards, *The Practice of Diaspora: Literature, Translation, and the Rise of Black Internationalism* (Cambridge, Mass.: Harvard University Press, 2003), 7.

10. Notes from JFG Notebook, Arquivo Nacional 4.1.411, "O Hino Nacional No 'Show' da Jospehine Deu 'Cana,'" *O Jornal* 24–8-69, Box P 6 CAD 3.

11. Williams, "Uma mulata," 7–26.

12. See *Crisis*, April 1914, 286–287.

13. Gilberto Gil, "A mão da limpeza," *Raça Humana* (WEA, 1984), track 6.

14. "Eleitos do xiita Dori Caymmi," *O Globo*, April 23, 2003, Segundo Caderno, 1 and 3.

15. Sandra Almada, "Lula, lá e agora, José?" *Raça* 7, no. 66: 58–63.

16. Gilberto Gil speech at the inauguration of the new president of the Palmares Cultural Foundation. Gil's comparison to the United States, often reiterated by other Brazilians, reflects a one-dimensional view that does not recognize the United States' own historical sensitivity to differences in skin color. These differences were often recorded in the censuses. Moreover, over the last twenty years, the issue of either black or white has changed, in part due to intermarriage and the growth and influx of Latin Americans, Asians, and people from the Middle East. In the 2000 U.S. census, there was also a category for biracial.

17. This is not to say that Gil is consistent or even adamant about this terminology. Explaining his musical preferences on his Web site, he remarks: "Depois do samba e do baião o que mais gusto e do reggae. Coisa de neguinho. Neguinho gosta de batuque não tem jeito." (After the samba and the baião what I like most is reggae. It's a black thing. Blacks like the beat. There's no two ways about it).

Brazilian Musical Terms

Baião. A musical and dance form thought to have originated in the northeast. This contemporary urban form, dominated by the accordion, was championed by Luiz Gonzaga.

Bamba. An authority of popular musical traditions such as samba. Also, a popular musician of Rio de Janeiro; a samba musician.

Batuque. A rhythm of Afro-Brazilian origin, usually played with percussion music. Can also refer to a performance or jam session, but almost always associated with music of Afro-Brazilian origin.

Bossa Nova. A style of urbanized samba-song that originated in Rio de Janeiro. Most scholars consider the release of João Gilberto's "Chega de saudade" in 1958 as the official beginning of bossa nova.

Cavaquinho. A small four-stringed instrument played with the fingers, probably of Portuguese origin.

Choro. A genre created by Brazilian musicians combining and experimenting with various elements of the waltz, the schottisch, the polka, and the minuet, with various African beats and rhythms. According to some folklorists, the term comes from a type of dance performed by enslaved Africans on the plantation.

Cuica. A type of percussion instrument in the form of a small drum. In the interior of the drum there is a small narrow protruding sticklike fixture made of leather in contact with the membrane of drum. Music is made by pulling the stick, creating friction that produces a vibrating sound.

Embolada. A form of comedic or satirical poetical spoken musical form. The performer usually is able to enunciate the music at a rapid pace and may even improvise.

Festas juninas. Brazil's winter festivals celebrated with music and dance throughout Brazil during the month of June. The major festival, the Feast of Saint John the Baptist, is on June 24.

Lundu. This is considered one of the first modern Afro-Brazilian musical and dance forms. The *lundu* was a fusion of European and African elements. Scholars have traced its origins to the eighteenth century.

Marcha marchinha. Tunes developed from the beat of military bands and elaborated for marching crowds during the carnival season. The *marcha-rancho* developed from wind instruments.

Maxixe. Originating from musicians or bands in the middle of the nineteenth century, the term was used to describe an accelerated musical style. Some have argued that it was originally an accelerated form of dancing the Brazilian combination of the tango and polka. Also known also as the Brazilian tango.

Pandeiro. A percussion instrument that consists of a wooden circular-shaped structure covered (although sometimes not) by a membrane of animal skin. Small circular metal plates encase the perimeter. The equivalent of the tambourine in English.

Pastoras. Choral or backup singers in groups. Championed by Heitor dos Prazeres.

Pontos de umbanda. Drumbeats associated with the sacred music of the Afro-

Brazilian religion Umbanda.

Roda. A circle created for group dances or performing arts such as capoeira. Dancers may dance together in the circle, or *roda*, but very often a couple or an individual performs within the circle as members of the circle look on.

Samba. The basic and foundational genre of Brazilian popular music. Originally from Rio de Janeiro but influenced heavily by Bahian rhythms. The word originates from the word "*semba*," apparently an Angolan word that denotes the in-and-out movement of the navel.

Sambista. A musician who plays samba music.

Seresteiro. A person who sings the soft serenade music. Similar to the English word "serenader."

Surdo. The big circular drums associated with the samba school.

Toadas. A short lyrical song usually with a romantic or comedic theme.

Bibliography

Archives and Special Collections

Arquivo da Rádio Nacional, Rio de Janeiro
Arquivo do Itamaraty, Rio de Janeiro
Arquivo Nacional (AN), Rio de Janeiro
Arquivo Público do Estado do Rio de Janeiro
Biblioteca Nacional (BN), Seção de Música, Ministério da Cultura, Rio de Janeiro
Biblioteca Nacional, Buenos Aires, Argentina
Biblioteca Nacional, Seção de Manuscritos, Rio de Janeiro
Bibliothèque de la ville de Paris, Paris
Centro de Pesquisa e Documentação (CPDOC), Fundação Getúlio Vargas, Rio de Janeiro

Instituto Cultural Cravo Albin, Rio de Janeiro
Instituto Moreira Salles, Digital Music Library
Library of Congress, Washington, D.C.
Museu da Imagem e do Som (MIS), Lapa, Rio de Janeiro
Museu da Imagem e do Som (MIS), Praça Tiradentes, Rio de Janeiro
Museu Histórico do Estado de Rio de Janeiro, Rio de Janeiro, New York
    Public Library, Lincoln Center, New York City
Sala Araújo Mozart, Biblioteca do Centro Cultural Banco do Brasil, Rio de
    Janeiro
Schomburg Center, New York Public Library
Secretaria do Património Histórico e Artístico Nacional, Ministério da Cul-
    tura, Rio de Janeiro

Personal Archives

Abel Cardoso, Sorocaba, São Paulo
Norma Tapajós, Botafogo, Rio de Janeiro

Interviews from Museu da Imagem e do Som (MIS), Rio de Janeiro

Alencar, Edigar de. October 29, 1975.
Almirante (Henrique Foréis Domingues). April 11, 1967.
Alves, Ataulfo. November 17, 1966.
Batista, Linda. November 19, 1970.
Braguinha (João de Barro). June 4, 1968.
Caldas, Sílvio. June 4, 1968.
Cartola (Angenor de Oliveira). March 3, 1967.
Carvalho, Joubert de. May 10, 1972.
Caymmi, Dorival. November 24, 1966.
Celestino, Vicente. May 19, 1967.
Cortes, Araci. November 3, 1967.
Costa, Carmen. August 23, 1972.
De Souza, Ruth. Recorded interview, July 16, 1990, Rio de Janeiro.

Donga (Ernesto Joaquim Maria dos Santos). April 16, 1969.

Gnatalli, Radamés. October 28, 1985.

Heitor dos Prazeres. September 1, 1966.

Jamelão. July 26, 1972.

Lago, Mário. February 17, 1992.

Martins, Herivelto. November 25, 1968.

Miranda, Aurora. May 18, 1967.

Oliveira, Dalva de. May 14, 1970.

Pixinguinha. October 6, 1966.

Pixinguinha. May 22, 1968.

Silva, Orlando. December 11, 1968.

Silva, Sinval. January 20, 1967.

Tapajós, Paulo. May 4, 1967.

Personal Interviews

Albin, Ricardo Cravo. Tape recording, residence in Urca, Rio de Janeirol. December 2003.

Cardoso, Abel, Jr. Tape recording, residence in Sorocaba, São Paulo. March 2003.

Carvalho, Carmen (Carmen Miranda's niece). Tape recording, residence in Copacabana, Rio de Janeiro. March 3, 2003.

Dona Silva, wife of Sinval Silva. Tape Recording, residence in Rio de Janeiro, March 16, 1996.

Stuart, Tony. Recorded telephone interview, August 18, 2004.

Tapajós, Norma. Tape recording, residence in Botafogo, Rio de Janeiro, April 15, 2003.

Latin American Serials

BRAZIL

Careta

A crítica

Cruzeiro do sul
Diário carioca
Diário da noite
Diário de noticias
Folha de São Paulo
Fon fon
Gazeta mercantil
Jornal do Brasil
A manhã
A Modinha (Bahia)
Noite ilustrada
A Notícia
O Dia
O Estado de São Paulo
O Globo
O Jornal
O Malho
Revista da música popular
Tribuna da imprensa
Última hora
Vamos leer
A voz do rádio

ARGENTINE AND URUGUAY
Cine, Radio e Atualidad
El Diario (Buenos Aires)
Radiolandia
Sintonia

U.S. Newspapers and Periodicals

The Chicago Defender
Cosmopolitan
The Crisis

Life
Los Angeles Times
Milwaukee Journals
The New Amsterdam News
New York Post
New York Times
Popular Science
Washington Post

Films and Broadway Revues

Berkeley, Busby. *The Gang's All Here*, 1943.
Camus, Marcel. *Orfeu Negro*, 1959.
Crosland, Alan. *The Jazz Singer*, 1927.
Cummings, Irving. *Down Argentine Way*, 1940.
———. *Spring Time in the Rockies*, 1942.
———. *That Night in Rio*, 1941.
Disney, Walt. *Saludos Amigos*, 1943.
———. *The Three Caballeros*, 1944.
Freeland, Thornton. *Flying Down to Rio*, 1933.
Gonzaga, Ademar. *Alô alô carnaval*, 1936.
Green, Alfred E. *Copacabana*, 1947.
Guerra, Ruy. *Opera do malandro*, 1986.
Lang, Walter. *Weekend in Havana*, 1941.
Marshall, George. *Scared Stiff*, 1953.
Seiler, Lewis. *Doll Face*, 1945.
Seiter, William A. *Four Jills in a Jeep*, 1944.
Siodmak, Robert. *Phantom Lady*, 1944.
Solberg, Helena. *Carmen Miranda: Bananas Is My Business*, 1995.

Published Sources

Abreu, Maria Rosa. ed. *Constituição e constituinte*. Brasília: Editora UnB, 1987.

Abreu, Maurício de A. *Evolução urbana do Rio de Janeiro*, 3rd ed. Rio de Janeiro: Iplanrio, 1977.

Albin, Ricardo Cravo. *O livro de ouro da MPB*. Rio de Janeiro: Ediouro, 2004.

Alencar, Edigar de. *O carnaval carioca através da música*. Rio de Janeiro: Freitas Bastos, 1965.

———. *Nosso sinhô do samba*. Rio de Janeiro: Civilização Brasileira, 1968.

Alvarenga, Oneyda. *Música popular brasileña*. Mexico City: Fondo de Cultura Económica, 1947.

Anderson, Benedict. *Imagined Communities: Reflections on the Origins and Spread of Nationalism*. London: Verso, 1983.

Andrade, Mário de. *Dicionário musical brasileiro*. São Pualo: Editora Itatiaia, 1984.

Andrews, Reid. *Blacks and Whites in São Paulo, 1888–1988*. Madison: University of Wisconsin Press, 1991.

Araújo, Mozart. "Mário Reis, sambista ou bacheral?" *Carioca* 28 (May 2, 1935): 41.

Araújo, Samuel. "Acoustic Labor in the Timing of Everyday Life: A Critical Contribution to the History of Samba in Rio de Janeiro." Ph.D. diss., University of Illinois, 1992.

Arrizón, Alicia. *Latina Performances: Traversing the Stage*. Bloomington: Indiana University Press, 1999.

Avarenga, Oneyda. *Música popular brasileña*. Buenos Aires: Fondo de Cultura Económica, 1947.

Azevedo, Almeida. "A nossa música popular." *A Voz do rádio* 1 (March 28, 1935): 13.

Barbosa, Francisco de Assis. *Testamento de Mário de Andrade e outras reportagens*. Rio de Janeiro: Ministério da Educação e Cultura, Serviço de Documentação, 1954.

Barbosa, Valdinha, and Anne Marie Devoa. *Radamés Gnatalli: O eterno experimentador*. Rio de Janeiro: Funarte, 1985.

Barros, Orlando de. *Corações de Chocolat: A história da companhia negra de revistas (1926–1927)*. Rio de Janeiro: Livre Expressão, 2005.

———. *Custódio Mesquita: Um compositor romântico no tempo de Vargas (1930–1945)*. Rio de Janeiro: Funarte/EdUERJ, 2001.

Bastos, Rafael José de Menezes. "The 'Origin of Samba' as the Invention of Brazil (Why Do Songs Have Music?)." *British Journal of Ethnomusicology* 8 (1999): 67–96.

Baudelaire, Charles. "The Painter of Modern Life." In *Baudelaire: Selected Writings on Art and Artists*. Trans. P. E. Chaver. New York: Cambridge University Press, 1972.

Bello de Carvalho, Hermínio. *O canto do pajé: Villa-Lobos e a música popular brasileira*. Rio de Janeiro: Espaço e tempo, 1988.

Benjamin, Walter. *Illuminations*. Ed. and trans. Hannah Arendt. London: H. Zohn, 1973.

Bernanos, Georges. *Le Brésil: des homes sont vénus*. Monaco: Documents d'art, Monaco, 1952.

Bessara, Bernadete. *Brazilian Immigrants in the United States: Cultural Imperialism and Social Class*. New York: LFB Scholarly Publishing, 2004.

Black, George. *The Good Neighbor*. New York: Pantheon Books, 1988.

Bopp, Raul. *Antología poética*. Rio de Janeiro: Editora Leitura, S.A., 1947.

Borges Pereira, João Batista. *Cor, profissão e mobilidade: O negro e o rádio de São Paulo*. São Paulo: Edusp, 2001.

Bressane, Julio. *O mandarim*. Rio de Janeiro: Sagres, 1995.

Bureau of the Census, Social and Economic Statistics Administration, U.S. Department of Commerce. *15th Census of the U.S. 1930 Population*, Vol. 2, *General Report*. Washington D.C.: U.S. Department of Commerce, 1933.

Burnim, Merllonee V., and Portia K. Maultsby, eds. *African American Music: An Introduction*. New York: Routledge, 2006.

Burton, Julianne. "Don Juanito Duck and the Imperial Patriarchal Unconscious: Disney Studios, the Good Neighbor Policy and the Packaging of Latin America." In *Nationalisms and Sexualities*, ed. Andrew Parker et al. New York: Routledge, 1992.

Butler, Judith. *Gender Trouble: Feminism and the Subversion of Identity*. New York: Routledge, 1999.

Cabral, Sérgio. "Getúlio Vargas and Brazilian Popular Music." In *Ensaios de opinião*. Rio de Janeiro: Editora Inúbia, 1975.

———. "Há 50 anos um estilo de cantar foi inventado: O estilo Mário Reis," *Jornal do Brasil* (Caderno B) (January 18, 1973): 1.

———. *No tempo de Ari Barroso*. Rio de Janeiro: Lumiar Editora, 1990.

———. *Pixinguinha: Vida e obra*. Rio de Janeiro: Lumiar Editora, 1997.

Calabre, Lia. *A era do rádio*. Rio de Janeiro: Jorge Zahar Editor, 2002.

Cardoso, Abel, Jr. *Carmen Miranda: A cantora do Brasil*. São Paulo, The Author, 1978.

———. *Francisco Alves: As mil canções do rei da voz*. Curitiba, Brasil: Revivendo, 1998.

Carretero, Andrés. *Vida cotidiana en Buenos Aires*, Part 3. Buenos Aires: Planeta, 2001.

Castro, Ruy. *Carmen: A vida de Carmen Miranda a brasileira mais famosa do século XX*. São Paulo: Companhia das Letras, 2005.

Caulfield, Carlota, and Darién J. Davis, eds. *A Companion to U.S. Latino Literatures*. Rochester, N.Y.: Boydell and Brewer, 2007.

Caymmi, Stella. *Dorival Caymmi: O mar e o tempo*. São Paulo: Editora 34, 2001.

Chasteen, John Charles. "The Prehistory of Samba: Carnival Dancing in Rio de Janeiro, 1840–1917." *Journal of Latin American Studies* 28: 29–47.

Coelho, José Ligiero. "Carmen Miranda: An Afro-Brazilian Paradox." Ph.D. diss., New York University, 1998.

Consejería de cultura y patrimonio de Extremadura. *La gráfica política del 98*. Cáceres, Spain: Centro Extremeño de Estudios y Cooperación con Iberoamérica, 1998.

Constituições brasileiras. São Paulo: Sugestões Literárias S.A., 1978.

Costa, Haroldo. *Na cadência do samba*. Rio de Janeiro: Novas Direções, 2000.

Crichfield, George W. *American Supremacy: The Rise and Progress of the Latin American Republics and Their Relations to the United States Under the Monroe Doctrine*. New York: Brentano's, 1908.

Damasceno de Brito, Dulce. *O ABC de Carmen Miranda*. São Paulo: Companhia Editora Nacional, 1986.

Da Matta, Roberto. *A casa & a rua: Espaço, cidadania, mulher e morte no*

Brasil. São Paulo: Brasiliense, 1985.

Daniels, Roger. *Guarding the Golden Door: American Immigration Policy and Immigrants since 1882*. New York: Hill and Wang, 2004.

Davis, Darién. *Afro-brasileiros hoje*. London: MRG, 2000.

———. *Avoiding the Dark: Race and the Forging of National Culture in Modern Brazil*. Aldershot: Ashgate International, 2000.

———. "The Brazilian-Americans: Demography and Identity of an Emerging Latino Minority." *Latino Review of Books* (Spring/Fall 1997): 8–15.

———. "To Be or Not to Be Brazilian: Carmen Miranda's Quest For Fame and 'Authenticity' in the United States." In *Strange Pilgrimages: Exile, Travel, and National Identity in Latin America, 1800–1990s*, ed. Ingrid E. Fey and Karen Racine. Wilmington, Del.: Scholarly Resources, 2000.

Davis, F. James. *Who Is Black? One Nation's Definition*. University Park: Pennsylvania State University Press, 1997.

De Alencar, Edigar. *Nosso sinhô do samba*. Rio de Janeiro: Civilização Brasileira, 1968.

De Andrade, Mário. *Dicionário musical brasileiro*. São Paulo: Ministério da Cultura, 1989.

———. *Ensaios sobre a música brasileira*. São Paulo: Martins, 1962.

———. *O movimento modernista*. Rio de Janeiro, 1942.

Decantando a República: Inventário histórico e político da canção popular moderna brasileira. Berenice Cavalcante et al. (Orgs.) Vol. 3. *A cidade não mora mais em mim*. Rio De Janeiro: Editora Nova Fronteira.

Degler, Carl. *Neither Black nor White: Slavery and Race Relations in Brazil and the United States*. New York: MacMillan, 1971.

De Holanda, Nestor. *Memórias do Café Nice: Subterrâneos da música popular brasileira e da vida boêmia de Rio de Janeiro*. Rio de Janeiro: Conquista, 1969.

De Jesus, Maria Angela. *Ruth de Souza: Estrela negra*. São Paulo: Imprensa Oficial de São Paulo, 2004.

De Paiva, Salvyano Cavalcanti. *Viva o rebolado: Vida e morte do teatro de revista brasileira*. Rio de Janeiro: Nova Fronteira, 1991.

Derridá, Jaques. *Positions*. Chicago: University of Chicago Press, 1972.

Didier, Carlos. *Orestes Barbosa: Repórter, cronista e poeta*. São Paulo: Agir, 2006.

Didier, Carlos, and João Máximo. *Noel Rosa: Uma biografia*. Brasilia: Editora UNB., 1990.

Domingues, Henrique Foréis. *No tempo de Noel Rosa*. Rio de Janeiro: Livraria Franciso Alves, 1962.

Dunn, Christopher, and Charles A. Perrone, eds. *Brazilian Popular Music and Globalization*. Gainesville: University Press of Florida, 2001.

Edwards, Brent Hayes. *The Practice of Diaspora: Literature, Translation, and the Rise of Black Internationalism*. Cambridge, Mass.: Harvard University Press, 2003.

Efegê, Jota. *Maxixe: Dança excomungada*. Rio de Janeiro: Conquista: 1974.

Elkins, Stanley. *Slavery: A Problem in American Institutional and Intellectual Life*. Chicago: University of Chicago Press, 1959.

Enegê, "Discografia completa de Mário Reis," *Revista da música popular brasileira* no. 7 (May–June 1955), 38-39.

Fanon, Frantz. *Black Skin, White Masks*. New York: Grove Press, 1994.

Fernades, Florestan. *O negro na sociedade brasileira*. New York: Columbia University Press, 1969.

Franceshi, Humberto M. *A Casa Edison e seu tempo*. (Text and CD Roms) Rio de Janeiro: Petrobras, 2002.

Freud, Sigmund. *On Sexuality: Pelican Freud Library 7*. Harmondsworth: Pelican, 1977.

———. *The Standard Edition to the Complete Works of Sigmund Freud*, vol. 8. London: Hogarth Press and the Institute of Psycho-Analysis, 1960.

Freyre, Gilberto. *Casa-grande & senzala: Formação da família brasileira sob o regime de economia patriarcal*. 2 vols. Recife, Brazil: Imprensa Oficial, 1966–1970.

———. "O homem brasileiro: Formação étnica e cultural." In *Estudo de problemas brasileiros*, 167–178. Recife, Brazil: Universidade Federal de Pernambuco, 1971.

Gallo, Ricardo. *La radio: Ese mundo tan sonoro*. Vol. 2. Buenos Aires: Ediciones Corregidor, 2001.

Garrod, Charles. *Decca Los Angeles Master Numbers*. Vols. 1–3. Zephyrhills, Fla.: Joyce Record Club, 1992.

Gaspar, Ricardo, org. *Teatro experimental do negro*. Rio de Janeiro: Funarte, 1988.

Gendron, Bernard. *Between Montmartre and the Mudd Club: Popular Music and the Avant-garde*. Chicago: University of Chicago Press, 2002.

Geraldo Pereira. São Paulo: Editora Globo S.A., 1997.

Gerson, Brasil. *História das ruas do Rio*. Rio de Janeiro: Lacerda Ed., 2000.

Gilman, Sander L. *Difference and Pathology: Stereotypes of Sexuality, Race, and Madness*. Ithaca, N.Y.: Cornell University Press, 1985.

Gil-Montero, Martha. *The Brazilian Bombshell: The Biography of Carmen Miranda*. New York: Donald I. Fine, 1989.

———. *A pequena notável*. Rio de Janeiro: Editora Record, 1989.

Gilroy, Paul. "Sounds Authentic: Black Music, Ethnicity, and the Challenge of a 'Changing' Same." *Black Music Research Journal* 11, no. 2 (Autumn 1991): 111–136.

Giron, Luís Antônio. "Compositor por força maior." Caderno fim de Semana, *Gazeta Mercantil*, November 6, 1991, 1.

———. *Mario Reis: O fino do samba*. São Paulo: Editora 34, 2003.

Gould, Jack. "News and Gossip of the Night Clubs." *New York Times*, March 6, 1938, 150.

Gubar, Susan. *Racechanges: White Skin, Black Face in American Culture*. New York: Oxford University Press, 1997.

Guimarães, Francisco. *Na roda do samba*. Rio de Janeiro: MEC-Funarte, 1987.

Guralnick, Peter. *The Last Train to Memphis: The Rise of Elvis Presley*. London: Abacus, 2004.

Hall, Stuart. "The Local and the Global: Globalization and Identity." In *Culture, Globalization and the World System*, ed. A. King, 19-39. London: McMillan, 1991.

Halloway, Thomas. *Policing Rio de Janeiro: Repression and Resistance in a Nineteenth Century City*. Stanford, Calif.: Stanford University Press, 1993.

Hanchard, Michael George. *Orpheus and Power: The Movimento Negro of Rio de Janeiro and São Paulo, Brazil, 1945–1988*. Princeton, N.J.: Princeton University Press, 1994.

Hanke, Lewis. *Gilberto Freyre: Vida y obra. Bibliografía antología*. New York: Instituto de las Españas en los Estados Unidos, 1939.

Hirsch, Foster. *The Boys from Syracuse: The Shuberts' Theatrical Empire*. Carbondale: Southern Illinois University Press, 1998.

História da música popular brasileira: Assis Valente. 2nd ed. São Paulo: Abril Cultura, 1977.

História do samba. Vols. 10-11 and 14. São Paulo: Globo Editora, 2001.

Holloway, Joseph, ed. *Africanisms in American Culture.* Bloomington: Indiana University Press, 1990.

hooks, bell. *Black Looks: Race and Representation.* Boston: South End Press, 1992.

IBGE. *Anuário estatístico do Brasil.* Rio de Janeiro: IBGE, 1936.

——. *Anuário estatístico do Brasil.* Rio de Janeiro: IBGE, 1939/1940.

——. *Anuário estatístico do Brasil.* Rio de Janeiro: IBGE, 1946.

——. *Anuário estatístico do Brasil.* Rio de Janeiro: IBGE, 1949.

——. *Anuário estatístico do Brasil.* Rio de Janeiro: IBGE, 1953.

Johnson, Randall. *The Film Industry in Brazil: Culture and State.* Pittsburgh: University of Pittsburgh Press, 1987.

Johnson, Randall, and Robert Stam, eds. *Brazilian Cinema,* exp. ed. New York: Columbia University Press, 1995.

Lago, Mário. *Na rolança do tempo.* Rio de Janeiro: Civilização Brasileira, 1976.

Lesser, Jeffrey. *Negotiating National Identity: Immigrants, Minorities, and the Struggle for Ethnicity in Brazil.* Durham, N.C.: Duke University Press, 1999.

Levine, Robert. *The Brazilian Photographs of Genevieve Naylor, 1940–1942.* Durham, N.C.: Duke University Press, 1998.

——. *Getúlio Vargas: Father of the Poor.* Oxford: Oxford University Press, 1996.

Lins, Elmo. "Chico Alves: Luto, herança e desespero," *Manchete* no. 25 (October 11, 1952): cover and 10, 21–24.

Livingston-Isenhour, Tamara Elena, and Thomas George Carcas Garcia. *Choro: A Social History of a Brazilian Popular Music.* Bloomington: Indiana University Press, 2005.

Lopes, Nei. *O negro no Rio de Janeiro e sua tradição musical.* Rio de Janeiro: Pallas, 1992.

Lott, Eric. *Love and Theft: Blackface, Minstrelsy and the American Working Class.* New York: Oxford University Press, 1993.

Lustosa, Isabel. *Lapa do desterro e do desvario: Uma antologia.* Rio de Janeiro:

Casa da Palavra, 2001.

Machado, Carlos. *Memórias sem maquiagem*. Livraria Cultura Editora, 1978.

MacLachlan, Colin. *A History of Modern Brazil: The Past Against the Future*. Wilmington, Del.: Scholarly Resouces, 2003.

Margolis, Maxine. *Little Brazil: An Ethnography of Brazilian Immigrants in New York City*. Princeton, N.J.: Princeton University Press, 1994.

McCann, Bryan. *Hello, Hello Brazil: Popular Music in the Making of Modern Brazil*. Durham, N.C.: Duke University Press, 2004.

McMann, Frank D. *The Brazil-American Alliance, 1937–1945*. Princeton, N.J.: Princetown University Press, 1973.

Mendonça, Ana Rita. *Carmen Miranda foi a Washinsgton*. Rio and São Paulo: Editora Record, 1999.

Milhaud, Darius. *Dans les rues de Rio*. Paris: Editions Max Eschig, 1995.

———. "A música brasileira." *Ariel* no. 7 (April 1924): 264.

———. *Notes without Music*. New York: Knopf, 1953.

———. *Saudades do Brasil*. Paris: Editions Max Eschig, 1922.

Moraes, Mário de. *Recordações de Ary Barroso: Último depoimento*. Rio de Janeiro: Funarte, 2003.

Moura, Roberto. *Tia Ciata e a pequena África no Rio de Janeiro*. Rio de Janeiro: Funarte, 1983.

Mulvey, Laura. *Visual and Other Pleasures*. Bloomington: Indiana University Press, 1989.

Museu da Imagem e do Som. *500 anos da música popular brasileira*. Rio de Janeiro: MIS Editora, 2001.

Nasser, David. *Chico Viola*. Rio de Janeiro: Edições O Cruzeiro, S.A., 1966.

———. *Parceiro da glória: 45 anos da música popular brasileira*. Rio de Janeiro: Livraria José Olympio, 1983.

Nist, John. *The Modernist Movement in Brazil: A Literary Study*. Austin: University of Texas Press, 1967.

O mundo dos auditórios. Rio de Janeiro: Rio Grafico Editora, 1973.

Oliveira, Aloysio de. *De banda para a lua*. Rio de Janeiro: Editora Record, 1981.

Ong Hing, Bill. *Defining America through Immigration Policy*. Philadelphia: Temple University Press, 2004.

Parizatto, Marcos Vinícius. *Aurora: A notável irmã de Carmen*. SBT, 2002.

Paulo, Heloisa. *Estado novo e propaganda em Portugal e no Brasil*. São Paulo: Livraria Minerva, 1994.

Pavis, Patrice, ed. *The Intercultural Performance Reader*. London: Routledge, 1996.

Pereira de Queiroz, Maria Isaura. *Carnaval brasileiro: O vivido e o mito*. São Paulo, 1992.

Prazeres Filho, Heitor dos. *Heitor dos Prazeres: Sua arte e seu tempo*. Rio de Janeiro: ND Comunicação, 2003.

"Rádio Nacional." Archives of Rádio Nacional, Praça Mauá. Rio de Janeiro (March 30, 1929).

Rangel, Lúcio, and Maria Lúcia Rangel. *Sambistas e chorões: Aspectos e figuras da música popular brasileira*. Rio de Janeiro: Editora Francisco Alves, 1962.

Raphael, Alison. "From Popular Culture to Micro-enterprise: The History of the Brazilian Samba Schools." *Latin American Music Review* 11, no. 1 (June 1990): 73–83.

Ricardo, Cassiano. *Martim Cererê*. São Paulo: Revista de Tribunais, 1928.

Roberts, John Storm. *Black Music of Two Worlds: African, Caribbean, Latin and African-American Traditions*. 2nd ed. New York: Schirmer Books, 1998.

———. *The Impact of Latin American Music on the United States*. 2nd ed. New York: Oxford University Press, 1999.

Rock, David. *Argentina 1516–1987: From Spanish Colonization to Alfonsín*. Berkeley and Los Angeles: University of California Press, 1987.

Rodríquez Juliá, Edgardo. *El entierro de Cortijo*. Puerto Rico: Ediciones Huracán, 1985.

Roland, Donald W., org. *History of the Office of the Coordinator of Inter-American Affairs*. Washington, D.C.: United States Government Printing Office, 1947.

Romanelli, Edmundo. [Review of] *Alô alô Madureira*. Manuscript Division, Biblioteca Nacional, Teatro Censura.

The Roosevelt Corollary, 1904. http://www.latinamericanstudies.org/us-relations/roosevelt-corollary.htm., accessed January 6, 2006.

Ruiz, Roberto. *Araci Cortes: Linda flor*. Rio de Janeiro: Funarte, 1984.

Sandoval-Sanchez, Alberto. *José Can You See?: Latinos On and Off Broadway*.

Madison: University of Wisconsin Press, 1999.

Sassen, Saskia. "U.S. Immigration Policy Toward Mexico in a Global Economy." *Journal of International Affairs* 43, no. 2 (1990): 369–381.

Satã, Madame. *Memórias de Madame Satã*. Rio de Janeiro: Lidador, 1972.

Seigel, Micol. "The Point of Comparison: Transnational Racial Construction, Brazil and the United States." Ph.D. diss., New York University, 2001.

Severiano, Jairo, and Zuza Homem de Mello. *A canção no tempo: 85 anos de músicas brasileiras*. Vol. 1: *1901–1957*. São Paulo: Editora 34, 1997.

"Se você jurar." Sheet Music P5939. Sala Mozart Araújo, Library of the Bank of Brazil Cultural Center, Rio de Janiero.

Seward, Lori Ann. "Two Likeable Lads Loaded with Laughs: Olsen and Johnson and American Entertainment, 1914–1959." Ph.D. diss., New York University, 1992.

Shaw, Lisa. *The Social History of the Brazilian Samba*. Brookfield, Vt.: Ashgate, 1999.

Shohat, Ella. "Gender and the Culture of Empire: Towards a Feminist Ethnography of the Cinema." *Quarterly Review of Film and Video* 13 (1990): 45–84.

Silva Neto, Antonio Leão da. *Astros e estrelas do cinema brasileiro*. São Paulo: A.L. Silva Neto, 1998.

Skidmore, Thomas. *Black into White: Race and Nationality in Brazilian Thought*. 1974; Durham, N.C.: Duke University Press, 1993.

Soares, Maria Theresa Mello. *São Ismael do Estácio: O sambista que foi rei*. Rio de Janeiro: Funarte, 1985.

Soares Valença, Suetônio. *Tra-la-lá: Lamartine Babo*. Rio de Janeiro: Velha Lapa Gráfica, 1989.

Spengler, Osvald. *The Decline of the West*. New York: Alfred A. Knopf, 1926.

Stam, Robert. *Subversive Pleasures: Bakhtin, Cultural Criticism, and Film*. Baltimore: Johns Hopkins University Press, 1989.

———. *Tropical Multiculturalism: A Comparative History of Race in Brazilian Cinema and Culture*. Durham, N.C.: Duke University Press, 1977.

Sternbach, Nacny, et al. "Feminisms in Latin America: From Bogotá to San Bernardo." *Signs* 17, no. 2 (Winter 1992): 393–434.

Stevens, Wallace. "The Idea of Order at Key West." In *The Palm at the End of the Mind*. New York: Vintage Books, 1972.

Tannenbaum, Frank. *Slave and Citizen: The Negro in the Americas*. New York: Vintage Books, 1946.

Teixeira Alves, Walter. "A discogrfia de Aurora Miranda," unpublished catalog, 1976.

Terrace, Vincent. *Radio Programs, 1924–1984: A Catalog of Over 1800 Shows*. Jefferson, N.C.: McFarland, 1999.

Thorpe, Edward. *Black Dance*. Woodstock, N.Y.: Overlook Press, 1990.

Tinhorão, José Ramos. *Música popular: Do gramophone ao rádio e TV*. São Paulo: Editora Ática, 1981.

———. *Pequena história da música popular: Da modinha ao tropicália*. São Paulo: Art, 1986.

Ulanovsky, Carlos et al. *Dias de radio: Historia de la radio argentina*. Buenos Aires: Espasa Calpe, 2000.

Vargas, Alzira. *Getúlio Vargas, meu pai*. Odeon Records: Rio. Odeon no 11.450, recorded November 21, 1935, released January 1937.

Vasconcelos, Ary. *Panorama da música popular brasileira na belle epoque*. São Paulo: Livraria Sant'Anna, 1977.

———. *Raízes da MPB*. Brasília: Martins/MEC, 1977.

Vianna, Hermano. *O mistério do samba*. Rio de Janiero: José Zahar Editor/UFRJ, 2002.

———. *The Mystery of Samba: Popular Music and National Identity in Brazil*. Trans. John Charles Chasteen. Chapel Hill: University of North Carolina Press, 1998.

Viera, Jonas. *Orlando Silva: O cantor das multidões*. 2nd ed. Rio de Janeiro: Funarte, 1997.

Villa-Lobos, Heitor. *A música nacionalista no Governo Getúlio Vargas*. Rio de Janeiro: D.I.P., 1941.

Walker, Daniel E. *No More No More: Slavery and Cultural Resistance in Havana and New Orleans*. Minneapolis: University of Minnesota Press, 2004.

Werneck Lima, Evelyn Furquim. *Arquitetura do espetáculo*. Rio de Janeiro: UFRJ Editora, 2000.

Wicke, Peter. "Rock Music: A Musical Aesthetic Study." *Popular Music* 2 (1982): 219–243.

Williams, Daryle. *Culture Wars in Brazil: The First Vargas Regime, 1930–1945.* Durham, N.C.: Duke University Press, 2001.

Williams, Judith. "Uma Mulata, Sim!: Araci Cortes, 'the Mulatta' of the *Teatro de Revista.*" *Women & Performance: A Journal of Feminist Theory* 16, no. 1 (March 2006): 7–26.

Woll, Allen. *The Hollywood Musical Goes to War.* Chicago: Nelson Hall, 1983.

Wood, Bryce. *The Making of the Good Neighbor Policy.* New York: Columbia University Press, 1961.

Index

Beverly Hills, 156, 158, 178

Blocos (or *bandas*), 48

"Boeuf sur le toit, Le" (The ox on the roof), 25, 26

Borba, Emilinha, 126, 129, 142

Bossa nova, 14, 16, 45, 88, 102, 104, 110–111, 180, 189–190, 195

Botafogo, 113, 117

Braguinha (João de Barro), 67, 103, 104, 137

Brasilidade, 90, 131

Brazil: census of, viii, 43, 70, 227 (n. 24), 234 (n. 16); patriotism in, xvi, xxi, xxiv, 28, 32, 38, 41, 46, 61, 63, 78, 89, 91, 134, 137, 143, 148, 188–189; republic of (1889), 35

Brazilian Society of Theatric Authors (SBAT), 53, 171

Britto, Henrique, 175–176

Buenos Aires, 86, 135, 159–161

C

Cabral, Sérgio, 31, 74, 120

Café Nice, 139

Cafetinagem (café slumming), 138

"Cai cai balão," 136

Caldas, Sílvio, xvii, xxvii, 41, 50, 57, 80–82, 103, 112, 114, 188, 204 (n. 23)

Candomblé, 4

Capoeira, 5, 195

Cardoso, Elizete, 128, 141

Carioca, Joe, 38, 207 (n. 3)

Carmen Miranda: Bananas is My

Business, 148, 178

Carnival, xxx, 9, 18, 26, 32–33, 36–38, 42–49, 51–52, 91, 103, 127, 136–137, 208 (n. 24), 209 (n. 29); groups, 31, 37, 45–46; songs, 48

Cartola (Angenor de Oliveira), 4, 13–15, 83, 88, 96, 115

Carvalho, Joubert de, 132

Casa Edison, 27, 72, 104

Casino, xxiii, xxxv–xxxvii, 32, 37, 41–49, 55–60, 64, 82, 90, 100, 117, 158, 133, 150, 155, 175; da Urca, 23, 57–59, 129, 135, 141, 180

Caymmi, Dori, 195

Caymmi, Dorival, xvii, 55, 68, 74–77, 90, 106–109, 134, 148–152, 166, 168, 188, 225

Celestino, Vicente, 33, 97–98, 120

Cendrars, Blaise, 27

Césaire, Aimé, 17

Chagas, Nilo, 141

Charleston, 17

Chicago Defender, 169, 193

Choro, xxi, 4, 9, 18, 129

"Cidade maravilhosa" (The Marvelous City), 35, 137, 172

Cidade Negra, 195

Cinelândia, 52

Cinema, xx, xxvi–xxvii, 31, 36, 41, 53, 64, 84–88, 91, 100, 125, 142, 187

Commodification, 156

Companhia Negra de Revistas (Black Revue Company), 11

Composers, ix, xii, xix, xxii–xxiii,

Uruguay, 159, 226 (n. 6)

V

Vagrancy laws, 55, 138

Vai dar o que falar, 133

Valente, Assis, xvii, 52, 133, 136, 139–140, 149–151

Vargas, Darcy, 32, 66

Vargas, Getúlio: as president, xx, xxiv, xxix, 31, 48, 63, 91, 175, 185; dictatorship of, 60, 81, 119, 192

Vassourinha (Mário Ramos de Oliveira), 83, 90

Veloso, Caetano, xviii, 6, 107, 152, 181, 195

Victor Brasileira Orquestra, 146

Villa Lobos, Heitor, 20, 23, 25, 33, 142

Vocalists, xxviii, xxviii, 34, 37, 38, 41, 58, 79, 83, 86, 107, 108, 109, 111, 112, 114–116, 120, 133, 136, 137, 143, 190

W

Welles, Orson, 52, 177

Whiteness, 2, 3, 14, 78, 97, 127, 146, 157, 161, 183, 197

World War I, 19, 44, 69, 97

World War II, xxvii, 19–20, 60, 76, 145, 162, 164, 172

Z

Zona Norte, 37, 52, 55, 68

Zona Sul, 37, 57, 68, 72, 102, 108, 166, 189